WOMEN AND PUBLIC POLICY

Women and Public Policy

The shifting boundaries between the public
and private spheres

Edited by

SUSAN BAKER
Cardiff University

ANNEKE VAN DOORNE-HUISKES
Erasmus University Rotterdam

Ashgate

Aldershot • Brookfield USA • Singapore • Sydney

Published by
Ashgate Publishing Ltd
Gower House
Croft Road
Aldershot
Hants GU11 3HR
England

Ashgate Publishing Company
Old Post Road
Brookfield
Vermont 05036
USA

British Library Cataloguing in Publication Data
Women and public policy : the shifting boundaries between
    the public and private spheres
    1. Women - Social conditions 2. Public welfare 3. Feminism
    I. Baker, Susan, 1946- II. Doorne-Huiskes, Anneke van
    305.4'2

Library of Congress Catalog Card Number: 99-72664

ISBN 1 84014 936 1

Printed and bound by Athenaeum Press, Ltd.,
Gateshead, Tyne & Wear.

Contents

PART I: INTRODUCTION

Risking Difference: Reconceptualizing the Boundaries between the
Public and Private Spheres

PART II: GENDERED THOUGHT, PUBLIC ADMINISTRATION, AND POLICY NETWORKS

v

Figures

vii

Tables

Contributors

Susan Baker is Senior Lecturer in European Social Research at the Cardiff School of Social Sciences, Cardiff University. She was co-director of the 'Women and Public Policy' conference at Erasmus University Rotterdam and Leiden University in December 1994. Her research interests are both in Environmental Studies and Women's Studies.

Charlotte Bretherton is Senior Lecturer in International Politics at Liverpool John Moores University. She has researched and published in a number of areas, including human rights and the gender implications of global environmental change. She is currently working on a study of the European Union as a 'global actor'.

Evelyn Collins is Chief Equality Officer at the Equal Opportunities Commission for Northern Ireland. She is writing in a personal capacity.

Celia Davies is Professor of Health Care at the Open University. She previously held the founding chair in Women's Studies at the University of Ulster and established and directed the Centre for Research on Women. Her current research and writing is in the area of health professions, gender, and health policy.

Anneke van Doorne-Huiskes is Professor of Women's Studies at the Department of Sociology, Erasmus University Rotterdam. She was co-director of the 'Women and Public Policy' conference at Erasmus University Rotterdam and Leiden University in December 1994. Her most recent relevant publications include 'Equal Opportunities in the European Union: Theory and Practice', in G. Dijkstra and J. Plantenga (eds.), *Gender and Economics* (Routledge, 1997).

Jalna Hanmer is Professor at the Faculty of Social Studies and Director of the Research Centre on Violence, Abuse and Gender Relations, Leeds Metropolitan University. Her research interests are in abuse, criminal justice, Women's Studies related social-policy issues. Her most recent relevant publication is 'Women and Reproduction', in D. Richardson and V. Robinson (eds.), *Introducing Women's Studies* (Macmillan, 1997).

Therese Jennissen teaches social administration and policy at the School of Social Work, Carleton University. She has a Ph.D. from McGill University and worked as a Senior Researcher on the Canadian Royal Commission on New Reproductive Technologies. She has researched in the area of occupational health and safety and has published articles on the impact on women of recent changes in social security in Canada.

Ineke Klinge (formerly Van Wingerden) was trained as a biologist specializing in immunology. She has been working as a Research Fellow at the Dutch National Cancer Institute. Since the mid-1980s she has developed Women's Studies in Science at Utrecht University. Her current research, titled 'Bones and Gender', addresses the representation of the female body in biomedical practices concerning osteoporosis. She is Coordinator of the Dutch Research Network of Women's Studies in Science and Medicine and Chair of the Women's International Studies Europe (WISE) division 'Women, Science and Technology'. She has published on feminist science studies, the position of women in science and technology, medicalization of the female body, and women and gene technologies.

Elizabeth Meehan is Professor of Politics and Jean Monnet Professor of European Social Policy at the Queen's University Belfast.

Liesbeth Ottes has studied Human Geography and Political Science. At the Netherlands Institute for Physical Planning and Housing (NIROV) she has executed several projects concerning women's emancipation in relation to physical planning, housing, and mobility.

Janneke Plantenga is Lecturer at the Institute of Economics, Utrecht University. Her main fields of interest are welfare-state regimes, changing working-time patterns, and social policy. She is the Dutch member of the EU network on 'Gender and Employment'.

Vicky Randall is Graduate Director at the Department of Government, University of Essex. She currently works on the politics of childcare and media in Third World politics. She is the author of various articles on women and politics, as well as *Women and Politics* (The Macmillan Press, 2nd edn., 1987) and *Contemporary Feminist Politics* (co-author, Oxford University Press, 1993).

Marijke van Schendelen is a researcher at the Amsterdam study centre for the Metropolitan Enviroment, University of Amsterdam. She has published several advisory reports concerning the relationship of women's emancipation and urban planning commissioned by the Dutch Ministry of Housing, Urban Planning and Environment, the Dutch Ministry of Social Affairs, and the Dutch Ministry of Traffic and Transport.

Liz Sperling has been Lecturer in British Politics and Public Administration at Liverpool John Moores University since 1990. Her previous research has been on the Europeanization of local government in the UK, with Michael Goldsmith at the University of Salford, and she is currently researching issues of political representation and quangos.

Camilla Stivers is Albert A. Levin Professor in Urban Affairs and Public Service at Cleveland State University. She is the author of *Gender Images in Public Administration* (Sage Publications, 1993) and many articles and book chapters. From 1968 to 1987 she was an administrator in small non-profit organizations.

Acknowledgements

This book would not have been possible without the generous support of the following organizations: the *Ministerie van Sociale Zaken en Werkgelegenheid* (Dutch Ministry of Social Affairs and Employment); the Royal Netherlands Academy of Arts and Sciences (KNAW); *Vereniging Trustfonds Erasmus Universiteit Rotterdam* (Erasmus University Trustfund); *Vakgroep Bestuurskunde* (Department of Public Administration), International Program, and *Emancipatie Onderzoek* (Emancipation Research) of the Erasmus University Rotterdam; *Leids Universiteitsfonds* (Leiden University Fund); *Vakgroep Vrouwenstudies* (Department of Women's Studies), and *Emancipatiezaken* of Leiden University. Their generous funding of the international conference 'Woman and Public Policy: the Shifting Boundaries between the Public and Private Domains', at the Erasmus University Rotterdam and Leiden University, the Netherlands on 8–10 December 1994 helped to lay the foundation of this book. Thanks also go to the Cardiff School of Social Sciences, whose financial assistance made it possible to turn a collection of conference papers into a coherent book. Susan Baker would also like to thank her assistant, ir. Joek Roex, for his thoroughness in preparing this text for publication.

Susan Baker
Anneke van Doorne-Huiskes

Abbreviations

CMLR	*Common Market Law Reports*
DCLD	*Discrimination Case Law Digest*
DG V	EU Directorate General V Employment, Industrial Relations and Social Affairs
DG X	EU Directorate General X Information, Communication and Culture
DNA	Deoxyribose nucleic acid
ECJ	European Court of Justice
ECR	Court of Justice of the European Communities, Reports
ENOW	European Network of Women
EOC	Equal Opportunities Commission
ETUC	European Trades Union Congress
EU	European Union
EWL	European Women's Lobby
IRLR	*Industrial Relations Law Reports*
MEP	Member of European Parliament
MSF	Manufacturing, Science and Finance Union
NAWO	National Alliance of Women's Organizations
NI	Northern Ireland
OJ	*Official Journal of the European Communities*
PNA	Policy network analysis
QB	*Law Reports. Queen's Bench Division*

SEA	Single European Act
SI	Statutory Instruments
UK	United Kingdom
US	United States of America
WLAN	Women's Local Authority Network

PART I
INTRODUCTION

Risking Difference: Reconceptualizing the Boundaries between the Public and Private Spheres

SUSAN BAKER

Theoretical Considerations

Introduction

Western liberal thought has constructed a notion of rights based on an ideal type of citizen. This citizen is abstract, universal, non-gendered, and non-racial; a citizen who is entitled to what we may refer to as 'natural rights' (Benn, 1972). From the seventeenth and eighteenth centuries onwards, it has been commonly held that it is the task of the state and of the law to safeguard these rights, lists of which were drawn up in such documents as the American Bill of Rights and the *Declaration des droits de l'homme et du citoyen* (Declaration of the Rights of Man and the Citizen). However, political practice was such that the exercise of full citizenship continued to be confined to particular groups, for example, the fully literate, the sane, or the propertied, elite minority. Despite significant advances, both in political philosophy and democratic practice, especially since the development of the modern welfare state, the concept and practice of citizenship continues to be restricted. As second-wave feminism clearly exposed, women have been given only limited access to full citizens' rights, even in the modern welfare state. This led to activism on the part of liberal, or 'rights' feminists, aimed at ensuring that the rights traditionally ascribed to men were also made available to women and that barriers to women's participation as full citizens of the state were dismantled. Rights, it was argued, should be made available to the abstract, universal, non-gendered subject, that is gender should not be a valid basis upon which to exclude access to rights.

The aim of this book is to go beyond this debate and to explore the factors that have contributed to women's exclusion from rights and full citizenship. It begins by linking the construction of a dichotomous relationship between the public and private spheres to the theory and practice of women's exclusion. Its focus is primarily upon women's exclusion from the modern (welfare) state. However, the book attempts to move beyond the stage of critique and open up the way for an alternative and more positive project: the construction of a new understanding of the public–private worlds. This new understanding goes beyond the demands of liberal, rights feminism, because it seeks something more radical than women's inclusion into formal citizenship. It also wants to reconstruct the idea of citizenship, and to do so in a way that accepts the diversity and difference of both the female and the male. Rather than accepting the ideal that rights should accrue to the abstract, universal, and non-gendered citizen, this analysis argues instead for a concept of citizenship that is embodied, particular, and gendered. Only through this concept of citizenship can true equality be achieved, because it is only in this reconceptualization that the richness or full humanness of the other, their needs, aspirations, modes of thinking, and ways of acting can be fully realized. This project is of interest to more than feminist analysis: it is fundamental to the project of constructing a new understanding of politics and the political process. It is compatible with similar projects being undertaken by regional and ethnic minorities, by new social movements, and by social actors, who are all pushing the boundaries of what constitutes politics. These groups are moving society towards a model of governance that challenges the liberal conception of the abstract, universal, male citizen that is assumed to stand for all; there is increasing demand that social groups be allowed to stand for themsleves.

Background

The construction of a boundary between the public and the private can be found as far back as Greek philosophy, where a clear separation was made between the *polis* (the public sphere) and the *oikos* (the home or private sphere). The *polis* was the locus of freedom and equality, and was seen as superior, the sphere of rationality, moral choice, culture, and of intellectual endeavour. In contrast, the *oikos* was seen as the sphere of nature, nurture, and the non-rational, and was regarded as the subordinated realm of necessity. In Greek thought, the public was where human beings could fully realize their potential and express their rationality, while the private was seen as concerned with issues of mere survival. Women were confined to the world of the private sphere.

The idea of a separation between the public and private spheres has also been of major significance in the development of both Western political thought and political practice. It played a particularly important role in the development of liberal political theory. In Locke's work, for example, there is a strong belief in the separation of the two worlds, each of which ought to be governed by different rules. The family was seen as located within the private world. It was held that the state should not enter the arena of autonomy that existed around the (property-owning) individual and disrupt, for example, his pursuit of economic goals. As in Greek thought, liberal thought also tended to devalue the female: the ideal male citizen, who alone could also operate in the public world, was conceptualized as rational, independent, self-directed, autonomous, and cultural—in dramatic contrast to the dependent, emotional, natural, passive female confined to the private sphere (Naffine, 1995, p. 24). In liberal thought, this dichotomy was linked to a wider set of complementary dichotomies—such as between reason and desire. This latter separation continues to appear in modern political theory in the distinction between the universal, public realm of sovereignty and the state, on the one hand, and the particular, private realm of needs and desires, on the other hand (Young, 1998, p. 429). This, in turn, was linked to a gendered concept of citizenship, which will be discussed below.[1]

Rejecting the Analytical Usefulness of the Dichotomy

Since the 1980s, feminist scholars have been highly critical of the construction of a dichotomy between the public and private spheres.[2] Making such a sharp distinction does not provide us with a useful or insightful way of making sense of, and grouping patterns of, activity in the world. The private sphere is supposed to refer to the family, unsullied by state regulation, where women are confined and men absent. In contrast, the public sphere is supposed to refer to the world of rational discourse and political life, where men are engaged and women excluded. The reality of both men's and women's lives is more complex. Far from seeing the public and private as separated by a clear boundary, we need to recognize that they have always been connected. Furthermore, there is a wide variation in the rigidity of the distinction, and in the relative scope of, the two domains through time and between societies (Randall, 1991, p. 14). Even as far back as in Greek society, the interrelationship between the public and private spheres is revealed by the fact that the *oikos* provided the necessary support base to allow the master the freedom to participate in the *polis*. Similarly, in today's liberal democracies, there are both direct and indirect forms of state regulation of the family; men pass between the public and private spheres on a daily basis, and economic modernization and industrialization has brought increased numbers of women into the public through, for example, participation in the labour market. Furthermore, so-called private issues have a very public dimension. Reproduction provides a good example, as this has become a public-policy issue, particularly since the rise of second-wave feminism in the 1970s and 1980s. The private sphere is a site of sexual politics (as revealed, for example, by issues such as domestic violence and marital rape). Similarly, male violence against women is a public-policy issue, not least because it constrains women's freedom in the public spheres (*Van Schendelen and Ottes*).[3]

Rather than claiming a clear boundary between the public and private spheres, feminist analysis points to the complex interdependency between them. This interdependency provides scholars with a direct challenge: it renders inadequate the traditional liberal conception of the relationship between the state and the individual (Sassoon, 1987, p. 174). Feminist scholars are not alone in criticizing the usefulness of conceptualizing the relationship between the public and private realms as dichotomous. Habermas, for example, has argued that a simple dualism cannot adequately account for the individual's relationship with the modern welfare state (Habermas, 1981).

However, while the public–private dichotomy is analytically unhelpful—that is the distinction does not provide a conceptualization that adequately reflects the complexity of men and women's lives—the dichotomy has nonetheless been of major importance. Thus, even though the claim to a clear separation between the public and private spheres is not borne out by empirical study, this does not deny the fact that the claim can also serve other purposes—it can have an ideological function. From the viewpoint of feminist analysis, its significance is that it has formed part of the theoretical and practical support structures of patriarchy. The public–private split can be seen as a 'deeply gendered dichotomy' (Lester, 1997). In the modern welfare state, for example, the dichotomy has structured a political theory and practice of democracy and citizenship that has marginalized women.

Providing Ideological Support for Patriarchy

The argument that the construction of a dichotomy between the public and private spheres provided both theoretical and practical support structures of patriarchy can be illustrated by drawing from key examples: the process of cultural gendering, the conception of citizenship, and women's relationship to the (modern welfare) state.

Cultural gendering   In Western thought, the public–private dichotomy supports, and is supported by, a series of conceptual polarities, such as equality and difference, reason and emotion, independence and dependence (Okin, 1991, p. 77; James, 1992, p. 48). These polarities also separate men from nature and women from culture, a separation heavily criticized in ecofeminist analysis (Baker, 1995). This way of conceptualizing the world has had a profound impact on our cultural heritage—it sets in train a process termed 'cultural gendering' (*Davies*). Cultural gendering leads to masculinity and femininity being expressed through different developmental trajectories: the one towards separation and autonomy, the other towards connection and attachment. As a consequence, the route to masculinity comes to involve denial or repression of femininity (*Davies*). It makes masculinity hegemonic, not just in the sense of silencing non-masculine ways of thinking and acting, but also in the sense that actions in the public sphere become governed according to a masculine vision (Davies, 1995). The public world becomes conceptually associated with masculinity, the private world with femininity. The tragedy of 'cultural gendering' is that it acts to 'wrench apart the diversity and richness of human qualities' (*Davies*), impoverishing our culture as well as political practice.

Gendered concept of citizenship   The public–private dichotomy also helped in the development of an exclusionary, gendered concept of citizenship, although the actual expression of this may differ in different states. In classical liberal theory, the cloak of citizenship is supposed to sit on the shoulders of an abstract, 'disembodied' individual. Yet, this individual has visible and valued 'male' characteristics. Historically, for example, the value of citizenship has, at least partly, been derived from militarist norms of honour and camaraderie, which included only men (Young, 1989, p. 250). While these attributes have become less prominent for the modern state, the model of the citizen continues to be based on the rational actor who can transcend body and sentiment, engaging instead with the rational and the discursive. Conceptually, the feminine is excluded from the public realm of citizenship, because, in western cultural codes, the feminine is seen as the realm of desire and the body. In the modern state, the citizen is also the active individual who participates in the labour market and who votes. Until relatively recently, women were restricted in the exercise of citizenship through these channels. In short, both the functions and qualities deemed compatible with the exercise of citizenship are in fact those characteristics that are culturally associated with men (Lester, 1997, p. 69). As James has argued, the cluster of activities, values, ways of thinking, and of doing things, which have long been associated with women, are all conceived as outside the political world of citizenship and largely irrelevant to it construction (James, 1992).

However, because liberal political thought did not recognize that its concept of citizenship was based on male values and activities, this allowed the male subject to claim a universal validity, which transforms him into a paradigm of humankind as such. This undermines the claim that the liberal ideal of the citizen is impartial and universal (Young, 1998, p. 431). In other words, the concept of citizenship makes a false claim to universal validity (Lester, 1997, p. 69). Rather, it is exposed as gendered, as co-determinous with a Western ideal of masculinity. This idea lives on in the modern state, where the masculinist character of citizenship has been retained, despite, for example, feminist-inspired law reform (Cavarero, 1992, p. 38; Thornton, 1995b, p. 215). This is discussed below, when analysis is made of labour-market maternity legislation.

Relationship to the (modern welfare) state   As well as focusing attention on the theoretical weaknesses of the liberal concept of citizenship, attention also needs to be turned to the actual exercise of citizenship, in particular in modern liberal democracies. In liberal democracies, women have been granted restricted access to the complement of rights and privileges that is accorded to men. Women have been denied full rights, because their activities are deemed to be located within the private and thus outside the arena where public/citizen rights apply. There is, for example, a denial of the significance of care and services upon which the public sphere and citizenship depends. As such, neither were these activities considered the legitimate arena of legislative activity, nor was engagement within them considered as bestowing rights and privileges on women as citizens.

Despite the problematic nature of citizenship for women, this is not to claim that women have been denied access to citizenship in modern liberal democracies. Rather, women have been given formal admission to citizenship on different terms than men. By way of illustration we can turn to Lester's argument that, on entering the public sphere, women have not been able to shed the features that bound them in the private sphere: women enter public space as embodied individuals. As such, their citizenship can, and is, jeopardized by, for example, sexual violence, harassment, and pornography (Lester, 1997; *Van Schendelen and Ottes*). Sexual harassment, especially street harassment, reinforces the public–private divide by driving home the message that women belong only in the private sphere (Morgan, 1995, p. 98). These examples serve to illustrate that women experience only a precarious inclusion into substantive citizenship (Lester, 1997, p. 72). In other words, classical liberal theory and political practice did not completely exclude women from the political order, that is from civil society; rather, women were included as subordinated (Pateman, 1992, p. 19).

Thus, the theoretical and practical exclusion of women from the category of 'universal citizen' can no longer be seen as a mere accident. Rather, we now have an explanation for why, both historically and in the contemporary period, citizenship has come to be associated with actual men who monopolized the institutions of public power. Furthermore, in so far as public life is seen, culturally, as male and is defined in opposition to the private, domestic sphere of women, women will continue to lack full membership of the political world and be denied full citizenship. As is discussed below, the struggle to control the meaning and positioning of the public–private boundary becomes central to the project of what Lester calls 'engendering citizenship' (Lester, 1997, p. 125).

Nowhere is the paradoxical relationship between women and citizenship more evident than in the relationship between the individual, the citizen, and the state in the post-war welfare state. Despite the fact that the development of the welfare state significantly altered the liberal conception of the state, both theoretically and practically, there are still grounds to criticize the concept of citizenship upon which this kind of state has been built. We can point to Marshall (1950), in particular, who made a key contribution to the post-war understanding of citizenship. He examined the welfare state in terms of the development of citizen rights, by linking citizenship to membership of a community as well as to issues of rights, obligations, and equality. For Marshall, citizenship was not simply about a set of legal rules governing the relationship between individuals and the state in which they live, but also a set of social relationships between individuals and the state, and between individual citizens (Lester, 1997, p. 14). However, Marshall gave no explicit consideration to women, relegating women to an ascribed rather than an achieved status (Pascall, 1997, p. 13). Marshall's analysis of citizenship gave rise to a body of literature that takes citizenship as the core idea of the welfare state. However, most writings in this tradition have followed Marshall in ignoring the problematic nature of citizenship for women (Pascall, 1997, p. 14).

The picture of citizenship becomes both more complicated and paradoxical when the actual impact of the welfare state on women's lives is explored, particularly when that exploration takes account of different welfare state traditions. In the first place, the development of the welfare state has made it increasingly difficult to support the claim that there is a clear-cut distinction between the public and private spheres (*Sperling and Bretherton*). Under the welfare state, for example, new regulatory regimes emerged that were extended to the family and that resulted in an expansion of the public dimensions of policy. This resulted in a more explicit incorporation of the family into the public sphere. The development of the welfare state has also, for example, changed the location of specific issues, pushing some from the private to the public sphere. Reproduction, for example, 'has gone public', while at the same time retaining a private dimension. Consequently, a more complex mix of public–private relationships has developed, undermining the assumptions of classical liberal theory. With the development of the welfare state, new boundaries are drawn between the public and private spheres, and a new understanding emerges of what is public and what is private (*Sperling and Bretherton*).

Despite these developments, however, there is still the unresolved issue whether the expansion of the welfare state has been primarily an expression of patriarchal, male interest, or whether the enlargement of the public sphere under the welfare state has been a response to more general socio-economic changes, including changes fought for by the women's movement. This brings us to our second point: whether welfare state practices have helped to overcome the problematic nature of women's citizenship or continue the practice of including women as subordinated citizens.

On the one hand, we can point to the fact that the welfare state has worked to integrate women into the public sphere. As research on the Scandinavian countries has shown, the welfare state has, for example, helped women to become integrated as employees through labour-market policy initiatives and legislative changes. As a result, women have gained new powers as workers (by acquiring labour-market rights), as citizens (through active participation in trade unions), and as mothers (by acquiring childcare and maternity benefits). This has helped facilitate the development of a new form of 'social citizenship' (Siim, 1988). However, the impact of this on reducing structural inequality has been weakened by the fact that there is still a sharp sexual division of labour and still a distinct sexual power hierarchy, both within the institutions of the welfare state and within society (Siim, 1988, p. 161). In short, 'the structure of the welfare state embodies . . . sexual difference' (Pateman, 1992, p. 23). Thus, while the Scandinavian state has facilitated women's integration into the formal labour market, it has also, for example, institutionalized and legitimated women's double role as mothers and workers (Siim, 1991). Furthermore, the childcare, equality, labour-market, and welfare demands that form part of the liberal feminist agenda have made women more dependent upon the state as employee, client, and consumer of public services (Hernes, 1988; Siim, 1988, p. 173–4). Thus, the welfare state holds a double meaning for women: as well as facilitating the development of a new form of 'social citizenship', it has also resulted in the development of a form of 'social patriarchy' (Hernes, 1988).

Here it may be the case that women's dependency on the state (social patriarchy) can be more positive than their dependency within the family (private patriarchy). However, the evaluation of the relationship between women and the state needs to take account of the character of the state and the traditions embedded in different political cultures in different states (*Van Doorne-Huiskes*; *Randall*). This evaluation is of more than academic interest. The nature of the state has important implications for the strategies of the women's movement. Second-wave feminism has looked to the state for redress from a whole range of grievances. But, as Eisenstein has argued, if the state is a bastion of patriarchy, is it not then completely naive, not to say futile, for feminists to attempt to use the machinery of the state to transform the situation of women? (H. Eisenstein, 1985, p. 104). Here we are faced with the challenge of exposing the limitations of action: of identifying what can be achieved, through the promotion of equality of opportunity, in a world where structures are not gender-neutral, without changing the structures themselves.

Radical feminists, such as Pateman, have responded to this challenge by arguing that liberal theory has an inbuilt contradiction between the ideals of individual freedom and equality, in the public sphere, and the assumption that women are naturally subject to men, in the private sphere. This contradiction goes to the heart of democratic theory and practice, including in the welfare state (Pateman, 1992). The significance of this for Pateman is that it is not enough merely to extend the concepts of liberal democracy to women, as well as to men: the integration of women into full citizenship requires a rethinking of both our conceptualizations of citizenship and of the individual; in other words, a rethinking of the ideology upon which the public–private distinction is constructed. This structural critique allows us to see that efforts at extending political and civil rights to women as individuals are limited; they do not alter the structure or the ethos of the polity itself, although they do help to incorporate women into public life.

The Social Construction of the Public–Private Split

The examples discussed above show that the claim to a clear boundary between the public and private spheres is an ideological claim—that is it forms part of the theoretical and practical support structures of patriarchy. The distinction between the public and private spheres is best seen, therefore, as socially and politically constructed to serve an ideological function. Furthermore, the positioning of the boundaries is historically and culturally specific: 'a shifting political construction under constant renegotiation, which reflects both historical and cultural contexts as well as the relative power of different social groups' (Lester, 1997, p. 124). The difference between the gains of the women's movement in the later half of the twentieth century provides an example. The 1970s saw a number of issues move from being considered private issues to being seen as public-policy concerns. However, the public–private distinction took on a new significance in the 1980s, with privatization policies and attempts by the 'New Right' to push economic dependence from the public sphere back to the private sphere. As a consequence, the gains achieved by women proved vulnerable, particularly within the labour market (Forbes, 1996, p. 147). Similarly, efforts in the 1990s to develop a more communitarian relationship between the state and the citizen, as seen, for example, in the UK under the Blair Government, in the US, and in Germany, provide us with contemporary examples of the ways in which the relationship between the public and private spheres are subject to constant political and social negotiation (Loughlin, 1998).

The construction of the boundary between the public and private spheres, thus, becomes a political act (Landes, 1998, p. 3). Crucially, this involves the exercise of political power. In the context of modern, liberal, democratic society, the public–private boundary becomes part of the structural inequalities that are embedded in the state.

The Public-Policy Significance of the Public–Private Dualism

As we have indicated, the location of the boundary between the public and private spheres has had powerful material and experiential consequences for women. It has influenced formal state institutions, organizational forms, financial systems, familial and kinship patterns, as well as language. In short, the distinction has become 'a basic part of the way our whole social and psychic worlds are ordered, but an order that is constantly shifting, being made and remade' (Davidoff, 1998, p. 165). The political act of siting the location of the boundary between the public and private spheres has profound public-policy significance: '"private" being effectively invoked if the state espouses non-intervention; "public" to the contrary' (Thornton, 1995a, p. 11). Issues such as childcare, for example, have historically been treated as 'private' and less deserving of policy attention than the concerns of benchmark citizens (Thornton, 1995a, p. 3). Similarly, considering the home 'private' renders women's status a question of domestic relations to be analysed as a derivative of the public sphere (MacKinnon, 1989, p. 35). However, private concerns can become public-policy issues, but unless the public–private distinction is radically re-examined, they become public in a way that reinforced the construction of a public–private dichotomy. An example can be found in the public-hygiene legislation of the nineteenth century (*Van Schendelen and Ottes*). The distinction between the public and private spheres can also be used to legitimize practices that are oppressive to women (Randall, 1991, p. 18). Stivers, for example, argues that the public–private division keeps the private beyond public redress and depoliticizes women's subjection within it (*Stivers*).

However, it is the distinction between paid and unpaid work that goes to the heart of the issue—it clearly exposes the ideological nature of the construction of the public–private dichotomy.

The Distinction between Paid and Unpaid Work

It has long been recognized that women need to deepen their involvement with the public world, if they are to fully develop their human potential (Friedan, 1963; de Beauvoir, 1972 [1949]). While recognizing that women have a long history of participation in the labour market, feminist analysis points to the sexual division of labour, between unpaid work and time within the home, as a key factor moulding both men and women's access routes to the public spheres (Lester, 1997, p. 139). This is because the construction of a public–private dichotomy results in a sexual division of labour that naturalizes the assumption that women should take the responsibility for unpaid work (*Plantenga*). Yet, economic independence is one of the main criteria that help determine the status of the citizen (*Plantenga*). Paid work is, for example, a key route to both citizenship rights (through, for example, labour-market rights) and to active political citizenship (through, for example, participation in trade-union activities) (Lester, 1997, p. 139). So important is this issue, that some feminists argue that it is the sexual division of labour that is the key to the door that governs women's entry into the public sphere (Lester, 1997, p. 125).

Throughout feminist analysis, there is a close link between the social construction of gender and the political economy of gender (Game and

Pringle, 1984). The identification of the labour market as a critical site for facilitating emancipation led to the development of the liberal concept of equal opportunity, aimed at advancing women's rights in the workplace. Liberal feminists have argued that discriminatory laws and practices have acted as a barrier to women's entry into the workplace. The task of feminist activism is to force the state to remove these barriers and allow women to gain equality. As a result, more women have become enriched by experiences from both the public and the private spheres (Borchorst and Siim, 1987, p. 131). Here partnership between women and the state can be advantageous. But, as Randall argues, different national policy styles influence the capacity of women to shape the policy agendas, so that, without a strong 'philosophy of public intervention' and 'conducive framing policy concerns', the prospects are bleak for redistributive policies that help women transcend the confines of the public–private divide (*Randall*).

However, the equal opportunities approach has been criticized for not taking into account the reproductive capacity of women, the division of labour in the home, and care responsibilities of women. In other words, equality policies have failed to take account of the essential relationship between the public and the private spheres, and its significance for the lives of women. Despite women's greater participation in the paid-labour market, housework is still an important part of women's daily lives (*Van Doorne-Huiskes*). As a result, feminists are now increasingly aware that the continued inequality in the private sphere restricts women's attainment of equality in the public spheres. Thus, the scope and nature of state intervention in the market place—for example, the extent to which it helps provide childcare (*Randall*) or helps in the work–family relationship arrangements (*Van Doorne-Huiskes*)—becomes an important variable in shaping women's access to the public sphere of the paid-labour market. This allows us to understand why the integration of women into paid work has been most noticeable and permanent in countries where the shift from private to public responsibility for human reproduction has been more radical, such as in Denmark and Sweden (Borchorst and Siim, 1987, p. 128; *Van Doorne-Huiskes; Randall*). So too is the form and character of state intervention in reproduction (*Hanmer and Klinge*), because this also helps determine women's position in society, be it as worker, mother, or ultimately as citizen.

In short, the construction of a public–private dichotomy has allowed theorists and activists to ignore the interrelationship between the public and private spheres, as reflected in state (and European Union) labour-market equality policies. Highlighting the interrelationship between the public and private spheres forces a recognition that equal-pay legislation and other labour-market reforms are of only limited value. Women cannot achieve full economic independence, and equality in the paid workforce, if they are also expected to run the home, while this domestic work remains unpaid. Therefore, economic activity can neither be isolated as an autonomous arena of struggle, nor as the prime cause of women's oppression: struggles for economic independence may be important, but they cannot, on their own, bring an end to patriarchy (Bryson, 1992, p. 197).

The Difference Debate

More importantly, however, equality policies have been criticized for stressing the similarities between men and women, and for not acknowledging their differences. Radical feminists point out that the result has been that women were incorporated into the labour force, but were accepted according to male organization norms (Mahon, 1991, p. 158; *Davies*). The liberal-feminist promise of liberation from domesticity is criticized, for example, because it begs the question of who is to care for children and the home. Similarly, equal opportunities policy asks for equal access, but leaves the structure of the organization unexamined and intact (*Davies*).

The controversy surrounding fetal-protection policy goes to the heart of the debate over gender equality and gender difference (*Jennissen*). Fetal-protection policies present feminists with a paradox (Daniels, 1991–2, p. 64): on the one hand,

> to ignore difference is to risk placing women in a workplace designed by and for men, with all of its hazards and little of its concerns for the preservation of health and life; on the other hand, to design 'special' policies for women is to reinforce those assumptions and economic structures which form the foundation of women's inequality in the workplace.

Fetal-protection policies can result also in negative implications for women, leading, for example, to blanket bans on female employment without necessarily securing the objective of protecting reproduction or fetuses (*Meehan and Collins*; *Jennissen*). It also poses a danger to women, in so far as the ideological base of protective legislation can often lie in nineteenth-century, Victorian belief concerning the position of women in society. Thus, such legislation can be used to reinforce the dichotomy between the public and private worlds. Furthermore, many issues concerned with reproduction were shifted onto the public-policy agenda because this served the interest of the market economy and not necessarily those of women (*Jennissen*).

The debate on fetal-protection policy is linked to an intense and controversial debate in feminist theory, since the 1980s, between the issue of equality and difference. Bock and James have summarized the debate in the following terms (1992, p. 4):

> On the one hand, the issues concern whether or not a feminist politics based on a goal of equality—of equal treatment, equal rights, equal work and so on—aims to assimilate women to men, to erase gender differences and construct a gender-neutral society . . . On the other side lies the question of whether or not a feminist practice based on the ideal of difference—a world in which women are not subject to male-defined values and institutions which pretend to universal validity—plays into the hand of a tradition that has used the notion of female difference to justify inequality and aspires to a goal which is not, after all, desirable . . . On both sides, moreover, there are those who consider the conceptual couple 'equality and difference' as dichotomous and its terms as mutually exclusive, and those who aim to articulate other relationships between them.

There is a clear connection between the debate on equality and difference and the ideological construction of the two separate spheres of society: the public, political spheres of equal citizens; and the private, non-political realms in which difference, including gender differences, may be realized and expressed (Bock and James, 1992, p. 8; Cavarero, 1992, p. 45). The demand for full legal equality runs into immediate difficulties when it is extended to women, because it ignores the implications of basic biological differences. Here, the liberal idea of equality can be heavily criticized for leading to sex-blind legislation that ignores biological differences (Bryson, 1992, p. 168). This issue is returned to below, when we explore the construction of an alternative conception of the public–private, one that offers promising possibilities for going beyond the seeming impasse in the equality–difference debate.

Application in Law

Attention also needs to be paid to the ways in which legal systems, including modern legislation, make assumptions about a clear public–private divide. It has been argued, for example, that legislation in modern liberal democracies implicitly assumes that the male model of individual behaviour is the normal or natural one—a pattern to which women are expected to conform (Naffine, 1995, p. 20). Yet it treats as epiphenomenal, not as deep structural, the reality that women are seldom in similar circumstances to men because of their historical experience, reproductive capacity, or the domestic division of labour. As a consequence, liberal theory has been severely criticized for ignoring biological difference (*Meehan and Collins*).

There is also a disjuncture between the liberal ideal, which makes a distinction between the public person, who is legitimately a subject of legal regulations as well as a legal actor, and the private person, who is free from the law (Naffine, 1995, p. 20). Neither in traditional nor in modern law has this been true for either men or women. Throughout history, the very structure and form of private life was, and still is, determined by the law. But this does not make the distinction between the public and private spheres irrelevant. On the contrary, it remains important, because it has allowed a 'moral boundary' to be drawn between the family and the political spheres. This can, for example, be used to justify non-intervention by the state in the domestic sphere, for example in relation to domestic violence (Charlesworth, 1995, p. 246; Lester, 1997, p. 120). In short, the law can here be seen as having played a role in creating and policing the public–private dichotomy (Morgan, 1995). The public–private dichotomy in national legal systems also shapes the ways in which laws have been used to exclude women from the public spheres, such as the professions and the market place. At its more basic form, the dichotomy shapes what is considered the business of law and what is left unregulated. This can be seen, for example, in the distinction between the public character of the regulation of the paid-labour market and the private character of the obligations and relationships surrounding unpaid, non-market work (Cass, 1985, p. 70).

It can also be seen in the ways in which legislation and judicial interpretations that stem from European Union Treaty provisions on employment and rights relating to working status reinforce the public–

private divide (*Meehan and Collins*). Yet at the same time, EU labour-market policy is beginning to transcend the divide and influence the private spheres of women's lives (*Sperling and Bretherton*; *Meehan and Collins*; *Van Doorne-Huiskes*). Of late, the EU is, for example, giving increased recognition to the 'private' sources of women's public-sphere inequality (*Sperling and Bretherton*; *Van Doorne-Huiskes*). Indeed, it is claimed that the boundary between the public and private spheres may be seen to waver in the EU context, in areas where women's policy networking has extended the parameters of the public sphere to include issues that were previously a matter of individual or family redress (*Sperling and Bretherton*). These are problematic developments for the EU, because the Treaties of European Union leave virtually no room for fundamental issues stemming from a feminist understanding of the public–private divide (*Meehan and Collins*).

We argued above that the claims to universalism made for the liberal concept of the citizen has allowed the masculinist character of citizenship to be retained in the modern state, despite, for example, feminist-inspired law reform. An example of this is to be found in labour-market maternity legislation. For example, in modern legislation concerning maternity leave, pregnancy is treated as an illness that prevents female workers from working. According to Cavarero, this is because the male subject, for whom the law is designed, does not experience pregnancies, but only disabling psychological changes or illnesses. In this context (Cavarero, 1992, p. 37):

> the phenomenon of pregnancy comes to be 'adapted' to the language and the categories which sustain the law. Moreover, the protection of maternity, which might seem to be specific to the female subject, is usually orientated towards a concept of protecting the rights of the unborn or the new-born.

However, this may not be entirely the case in the European Union, as most European Court of Justice rulings on pregnancy can be construed not as reinforcing outdated claims about the private sphere, but as corroborating the 'difference feminist' position that situations specific to women should have a normal place in public policy (*Meehan and Collins*).

Daily Life: Planning and the Built Environment

Attention can also be turned to how urban planning reflects and reinforces a dichotomizing relationship between the private and public spheres. In many ways, the planning process reinforces the sexual division of labour and with it a domestic ideal, which emphasizes the importance of the home as a woman's place, and a man's haven (Wajcman, 1991, p. 110; *Van Schendelen and Ottes*). This helps to reinforce the separation between men and women, private and public, home and paid employment. While people do not leave according to these dichotomies, the widespread belief in them does influence decisions and has had an impact upon women's lives. For example, zoning policies that separate the home from the place of work, leisure, and shopping reduce women's mobility, intensify the privatized nature of women's lives, and are seen as contributing to their isolation from the public economy (Wajcman, 1991, chap. 5). Furthermore, here the city centre is seen as representing the public sphere, while outlying areas of the city and the suburbs, in their green settings, emphasizes the private world of the family (*Van Schendelen and Ottes*). Housing design has also been criticized, as has the use of space within the home.

Reproduction

While the issue of reproduction has been divisive for feminists, what they are united in is the belief that, particularly with the development of the modern welfare state, the bearing of children is not a purely private affair. As was seen above, for example, the issue of reproductive rights ultimately exposes the fundamental interconnectedness between the public and private spheres (*Jennissen*). Similarly, ongoing controversies over abortion and the new reproductive technology also reveal that there is a complex mixture of public and private issues involved, including issues relating to state power, privacy, the structure of family life, individual freedom, and social and ethical responsibility. These are also integrally related to issues of sexuality and the control of knowledge and values (*Hanmer and Klinge*).

This interrelationship can also be exposed through an examination of the differential impact of applied science in genetics on women (*Hanmer and Klinge*). In the late twentieth century, the new issues in relation to reproduction are coming to the fore as a result of new developments in genetics. These developments are giving rise to new dilemmas and contradictions clustering around social or public versus individual or private interests (*Hanmer and Klinge*). There are also ethical issues relating to consent and the use of genetic information held on individuals: who has access to and control of genetic information, how to balance individual rights and privacy with social and ethical responsibility, where to set the limits of scientific developments, and what weight is given to scientific as opposed to religious values. These issues undermine the claim that there is a dichotomous relationship between the public and private spheres (*Hanmer and Klinge*).

Organizational Culture and Practice

Images of public life and its organizational relations have also been influenced by the conception that there is a dichotomy between the public and private (*Davies*; *Stivers*). The process of cultural gendering, discussed above, has lead to the construction of an image of the public man who expresses only relations of masculinity. Only safely away from the world of the public can the qualities symbolically assigned to femininity be acknowledged (*Davies*). This leads to the image of a public world built on the principle of 'hostile strangers', which has resulted in a culture of competitive, distance, and hierarchical relations within public life and public administration (Davies, 1995, p. 26; Stivers, 1993). The masculine vision of the public world is incomplete, because it denies feminine qualities, and also rests upon an unacknowledged work of women in both the private and public spheres. In short, it denies the interrelationship between our public and private lives.

Feminists take particular issue with Weber's vision of the bureaucrat, involved in an isolated and lonely struggle to set standards that cannot often be met, which Stivers refers to as 'the struggle to get it right' (*Stivers*). However, Stivers exposes the false claims of public administration, the claim that it is merely engaged in the search for the right answers to questions of administrative technique. Far from seeing public administrators as engaged in routine work, their actions are essentially political: they govern and do so in a gendered-biased way (*Stivers*). Public administration is thus 'implicated', that is it is built upon a bifurcated process that divides activities according to whether they were thought to be appropriate for men or women, 'with men handling the task of making government operate in a business-like manner and women transferring their domestic benevolence to the enlargement of the state's role' (*Stivers*). This not only obscures the contribution of women to public life, but further legitimizes the belief that public administration is merely engaged with an objective concern for efficiency.

Seeing beyond Women as Victims

Despite the significant insights yielded by utilizing feminist analysis to investigate the public–private dichotomy, in particular the insights it helps to reveal into the theory and practice of liberal democracy, we need to remain cautious. First, while acknowledging the socially constructed nature of the public–private boundaries, care must be taken not to see women merely as the helpless victims of social processes. On the contrary, we need to acknowledge that throughout history, and in different cultural contexts, women have resisted the distinction, and negotiated and manipulated its boundaries (Randall, 1991, p. 65; Boneparth and Stoper, 1988, p. 1).

Care must also be taken, because our analysis may exaggerate the importance of the male-dominated 'public' space (Friedl, 1967). This may result in a denial of the fact that women have considerable, informal power, within the private spheres, for example in relation to decisions about the household's economy and their children's future. This links to the rejection of a concept of politics that locates politics within a specific public arena (Randall, 1991, p. 31). Rather than stress the importance of the public sphere, our analysis has also argued that we need to reconceptualize the household as an arena of non-market work and social caring. This requires a recognition that domestic activity represents work of value and that women who were presumed to be supported in the private sphere were also themselves supporters of the public. Here it becomes important to recognize that, throughout modern history, women have challenged the dichotomy that constructs women as dependent beings and men as independent citizens. This provides us with a starting point for the construction of a new understanding of the public and private spheres.

Towards a New Understanding of the Public and Private

Dealing with Private-Sphere Inequality

Recognition of the interrelationship between the public and private spheres points to the need for radical changes in personal and domestic life. This involves, for example, the reconciliation of employment and family responsibilities, through increased state-sponsored childcare provision (*Van Doorne-Huiskes*; *Randall*). However, our analysis also shows that new work–family arrangements are a necessary but not a sufficient response. Expanding the scope of public policies and making changes in the private sphere to free up women to participate in public life leaves the political terrain essentially unchanged. Neither does it address the increasing demand that women's work within the home be revalued. In other words, what this book argues is that there is need for a more encompassing set of changes and that this can only take place by reconceptualizing an understanding of both the public and private spheres of our lives. This reconceptualization needs to go beyond the dualistic way of thinking that underlies the public–private dichotomy (*Van Schendelen and Ottes*). We need to see the two spheres as 'dialectically interrelated and not dualistically counterpoised' (Pateman, 1989, p. 110).

Socially Negotiated Boundaries

However, in engaging in this reconceptualization, most feminists do not want to dissolve the categories of public and private altogether. Even the radical feminist slogan 'the personal is the political' does not deny the necessity of maintaining a distinction between the public and private spheres. Feminists have long since seen the danger in 'women going public', dangers associated with suppressing the traditional female social world at the expense of women's overidentification with the dominant values of the public world (see, for example, Elshtain, 1981; Thornton, 1995a, p. 16). Some feminists, for example, want to retain a private sphere around the body, especially in connection with sexual relations (Phillips, 1991, p. 119). What is required is to hold on to the distinction, but make women agents of its construction (Young, 1998, p. 441; *Van Schendelen and Ottes*). This means that the siting of the boundary between the public and private spheres has to be the outcome of a process of social dialogue.

This dialogue is opened up by deconstructing the gendered values that underlie liberal thought. This means transforming the distinction between the public and private spheres in a way that overcomes the opposition between, for example, reason and emotion (Young, 1998, p. 440). In short, the social dialogue must facilitate a process of social change whereby we move beyond the confines of traditional cultural gendering and engage in a reconceptualization of both femininity and masculinity (*Davies*). This will help us reconstruct a process of public policy-making that is less reliant on hierarchy and the isolated, self-referential, and commanding leader (*Davies*). In its place new forms of public life can be built, which rely less on rationality and more on dialogue. As we will see below, this also requires a reconceptualization of the individual as an 'embodied' citizen. Here full citizenship ceases to be equated with labour-market participation, and account can also be taken of the tasks and responsibilities traditionally associated with women's lives (*Plantenga*).

Understanding how the boundaries between the public and private spheres can be reconstructed through a process of social dialogue has involved feminists in a theoretical engagement with the works of Habermas, Arendt, and Dietz. Benhabib, for example, developed a modified, feminist version of Habermas's model of the public sphere, to take account of difference (Benhabib, 1998). Young is similarly optimistic about the potential of Habermas' theory of communicative action to ground a new understanding of how the boundary between the public and private sphere can be sited (Young, 1998, p. 425). This accords with Habermas' notion that the public space is not the sphere of rational debate, but of negotiation (Calhoun, 1992, p. 22). Here the boundaries between the public and private spheres are not given, but are decided through discursive contestation (Postone, 1992, p. 168).

Risking Difference

Social dialogue involves a process of discursive exchange that, at its most basic, requires recognition of the value of the other. Essential then to the new dialogue is the acceptance of diversity, through, for example, the encouragement of multiple voices in dialogue (Young, 1990; *Davies*; *Meehan and Collins*; *Stivers*). Through this we can break away from a constant comparison that renders the male normative and the female inferior, helping to facilitate the development of a distinctive 'women's world view' (*Davies*). This, however, brings our discussion back to the feminist debate on difference.

Some feminists hold that conceding any ground to a position that accepts sexual difference, such as a 'women's world view', risks the charge of 'biologism' or 'essentialism'—that is the reinstatement of gender characteristics as timeless and invariant attributes of persons (*Davies*). The dangers of essentialism are real, Davies argues, because of the purposes for which a difference argument may be used and the ways in which it is likely to be misunderstood. However, she is on the side of those who say that we must risk difference, despite these problems. We risk difference by acknowledging that, as in the masculine way of thinking, femininity is an equally coherent, yet equally partial, world view (*Davies*).

The Embodied Citizen

Risking difference facilitates the development of a new understanding of citizenship, one that moves away from the view of the citizen as the 'disembodied', but essentially male, individual, to one that builds upon an acceptance of the different characteristics of both male and female. The push to develop a new understanding of citizenship is coming not only from feminists. The limited understanding of politics found in liberal theory has also come under more general stress with the development of the modern state (Jones, 1988, p. 19). This makes the tasks called for by this book all the more urgent: reconceptualizing the relationship between public and private spheres, accepting difference, and creating a new kind of democratic citizenship wherein full citizenship is attained equally by all. The construction of a new understanding of the public–private becomes the fulcrum upon which a new understanding of citizenship is built (Lester, 1997, p. 200–202).

The construction of a new understanding of citizenship begins with the exposure of the false universalism embedded in the concept (Jones, 1988, p. 20). In the liberal model, to become a citizen one had to trade one's particular identity for an abstract public self. Instead of constructing citizenship in this way, the new model values feminine activities, such as caring. This helps to develop new norms and values that moves civic virtue beyond its traditional, one-sided, militaristic, or narrowly rationalistic codes (Jones, 1988, p. 19). Similarly, the incorporation of multiple identities into the concept of citizenship allows us to stop conceptualizing the citizen as abstract and degendered. Instead, we must focus on what is referred to as 'the embodied citizen' (Thornton, 1995, p. 216–218). A truly embodied polity is one that assumes responsibility for the allocation of housework and caring in the home.

As well as seeing the citizen as an embodied human being, there is also a call for developing a new model of politics, where participation is seen as a key to citizenship (*Stivers*). Here public identity is not given, but constructed in public practice. The active citizen not only embodies diversity, but also is built upon an inclusive, as opposed to exclusionary, understanding of the public sphere. As such, public administration ceases to be the arbiter of the public good, but instead the process of 'defining the good life or the public interest in particular policy situations is one in which there are no experts, only participants' (*Stivers*). These demands are very radical in that they require changes in social and political culture, a difficulty that feminists recognize. The tradition of liberalism in the US, for example, which placed a high value on individual freedom and which fails to see individuals as interrelated, makes it very hard to campaign for a reconstituted, more encompassing public sphere (Evans, 1995, p. 117–119). Difficulties in the way of change, however, do not deny the importance of the need for this change.

Politics as Participation

The liberal idea of citizenship is coming under stress from the new emphasis on citizenship as practice (Phillips, 1998). New ideas of participatory democracy are broadening the scope of 'the political' beyond that merely relating to the government of society. Instead, the political has increasingly become unrelated to any specific site or instigation. Furthermore, as the sharp distinction between the public and private spheres breaks down, the division between the overtly political institutions of society and the domestic sphere of home and family becomes harder to maintain. The traditional understanding of what constitutes political engagement is now seen as limited: it viewed the political spheres as a reified abstraction separated from the rest of social life (Pateman, 1989, p. 110). This ignored women's experiences of the political world and also a whole range of their activities in the private. Hence, it becomes clear that reconceptualizing citizenship does not simply mean extending women's access to the public sphere, because the problem of women's citizenship has never been a matter merely of women's exclusion from political life. It also involves a new understanding of the political, and of what it means to be a citizen.

The broadening of the understanding of the political to embrace participation yields a conception of public space that differs greatly from that presented in liberal thought: public space ceases to be a space for competition among a political elite, becoming instead the creation of procedures, whereby those affected by general social norms and by collective political decisions can have a say in their formation, stipulation, and adoption (Benhabib, 1998, p. 82). This new model of politics gives rise to less bureaucratic, more democratic, and more personalized forms of participation than those found in traditional modes of political practice. One such example can be found in the planning process in the Netherlands, where the government no longer disposes but negotiates, and it is these negotiations that, increasingly, determine the relations between the public and private spheres (*Van Schendelen and Ottes*).

The new conception that sees the private and the public spheres as the product of social dialogue may also help overcome the seeming impasse around the equality and difference debate, in particular as it relates to whether what is needed is a gender-neutral or gender-differentiated concept of citizenship. The gender-neutral concept focuses on equal citizen rights, while the gender-differentiated approach is based on recognition of women's particular concerns. In the patriarchal conception of citizenship, a choice has to be made between equality and difference: difference embraces the maternal and the belief that this should be valued and brought into the political arena, whereas equality focuses on citizenship not motherhood. In the contemporary variant of this dilemma, feminist are torn between wanting to validate and support, through some form of income maintenance provision, the caring work for which women still take the main responsibility in the private sphere and wanting to liberate women from this responsibility, so that they can achieve economic and political autonomy in the public sphere (Lester, 1997, p. 178). Pateman argues that these two routes to citizenship are incompatible, what she calls 'Wollstonecraft's dilemma': we can be equal (i.e. undifferentiated) or different, but not both (Pateman, 1992, p. 20).

However, as we see from this book, it is unhelpful to see equality and difference as dichotomies: the two are not incompatible but are essentially interrelated. Equal citizenship has to embrace difference, and difference cannot afford to be divorced from equality (Bock and James, 1992, p. 10; Lester, 1997, p. 115). In reconstructing a new understanding of the public and private spheres, it becomes clear that the notions of equality and difference turn out to be interdependent: we risk difference because it is only on the basis of acknowledging difference that true equality can be attained.

Notes

1   We need here to distinguish the Anglo-Saxon, Lockean concept of the individual, who ought to develop his economic interests free from state interference, from the continental European tradition. This latter tradition, albeit derived from Hobbes, was most clearly expressed in the writings of Rousseau and Hegel, who saw the state as having primacy over the individual. As discussed below, the idea of the citizen differed in these different state traditions.

2   See, amongst others: Z. Eisenstein (1979); Okin (1979); Elshtain (1981); Diamond (1983); Pateman (1983); Hernes (1984); Evans et al. (1986); Hernes (1988); Pateman (1989); Okin (1991); Phillips (1991); Bock and James (1992); Phillips (1993); Landes (1998).

3   References to contributions in this volume appear in italics in parentheses.

References

Baker, S. (1995), 'Ecofeminism and Its Contribution to Feminist Theory', in J. Lovenduski and J. Stanyer (eds.), *Contemporary Political Studies 1995, Vol. 2*, Political Studies Association of the United Kingdom, Belfast, pp. 651–9.

Beauvoir, S. de (1972 [1949]), *The Second Sex*, Penguin Books, Harmondsworth.

Benhabib, S. (1998), 'Models of Public Space: Hannah Arendt, the Liberal Tradition, and Jurgen Habermas', in J.B. Landes (ed.), *Feminism, the Public and the Private*, Oxford University Press, Oxford, pp. 65–99.

Benn, S.I. (1972), 'Rights', in *The Encyclopaedia of Philosophy*, vol. 7, Macmillan & Free Press, New York, pp. 195–9.

Bock, G. and James, S. (1992), 'Introduction: Contextualizing Equality and Difference', in G. Bock and S. James (eds.), *Beyond Equality and Difference: Citizenship, Female Politics and Female Subjectivity*, Routledge, London, pp. 1–13.

Boneparth, E. and Stoper, E. (1988), 'Introduction: a Framework for Policy Analysis', in E. Boneparth and E. Stoper (eds.), *Women, Power and Policy: Towards the Year 2000*, 2nd edn., Pergamon, New York, pp. 1–19.

Borchorst, A. and Siim, B. (1987), 'Women and the Advanced Welfare State—a New Kind of Patriarchal Power', in A. Sassoon (ed.), *Women and the State: the Shifting Boundaries of Public and Private*, Hutchinson, London, pp. 128–57.

Bryson, V. (1992), *Feminist Political Theory*, Macmillan, London.

Calhoun, C. (1992), 'Introduction: Habermas and the Public Sphere', in C. Calhoun (ed.), *Habermas and the Public Sphere*, MIT Press, Cambridge, Mass., pp. 1–50.

Cass, B. (1985), 'Rewards for Women's Work', in J. Goodnow and C. Pateman (eds.), *Women, Social Science and Public Policy*, Allen & Unwin, London, pp. 67–94.

Cavarero, A. (1992), 'Equality and Sexual Difference: Amnesia in Political Thought', in G. Bock and S. James (ed.), *Beyond Equality and Difference: Citizenship, Female Politics and Female Subjectivity*, Routledge, London, pp. 32–47.

Charlesworth, H. (1995), 'Worlds Apart: the Public/Private Distinction in International Law', in M. Thornton (ed.), *Public and Private: Feminist Legal Debates*, Oxford University Press, Oxford, pp. 243–61.

Daniels, C.R. (1991–2), 'Competing Gender Paradigms: Gender Differences, Fetal Rights and the Case of Johnson Controls, *Policy Studies Review*, vol. 10, no. 4, pp. 51-68.

Davidoff, L. (1998), 'Regarding Some "Old Husband" Tales: Public and Private in Feminist History', in J.B. Landes (ed.), *Feminism, the Public and the Private*, Oxford University Press, Oxford, pp. 164–94.

Davies, C. (1995), *Gender and the Professional Predicament in Nursing*, Open University Press, Buckingham.

Diamond, I. (ed.) (1983), *Families, Politics and Public Policy*, Longman, New York.

Eisenstein, H. (1985), 'The Gender of Bureaucracy: Reflections on Feminism and the State', in J. Goodnow and C. Pateman (eds.), *Women, Social Science and Public Policy*, Allen & Unwin, London, pp. 104–115.

Eisenstein, Z. (1979), *The Radical Future of Liberal Feminism*, Longman, New York.

Elshtain, J.B. (1981), *Public Man—Private Women: Women in Social and Political Thought*, Princeton University Press, Princeton, NJ.

Evans, J. (1995), *Feminist Theory Today: an Introduction to Second Wave Feminism*, Sage Publications, London.

Evans, J. et al. (eds.) (1986), *Feminism and Political Theory*, Sage Publications, London.

Forbes, I. (1996), 'The Privatisation of Sex Equality Policy', in J. Lovenduski and P. Norris (eds.), *Women in Politics*, Oxford University Press, Oxford, pp. 145–62.

Friedan, B. (1963), *The Feminine Mystique*, Penguin Books, Harmondsworth.

Friedl, E. (1967), 'The Position of Women: Appearance and Reality', *Anthropological Quarterly*, vol. 4, no. 3.

Game, A. and Pringle, R. (1984), *Gender at Work*, Pluto Press, London.

Habermas, J. (1981), *Theorie des kommunikativen Handelns*, Suhrkamp, Frankfurt.

Hernes, H. (1984), 'Women and the Welfare State: the Transition from Private to Public Dependency', in H. Holter (ed.), *Patriarch in a Welfare Society*, Oslo Universitetsforlaget, Oslo.

Hernes, H. (1988), 'The Welfare State Citizenship of Scandinavian Women', in K.B. Jones and A.G. Jónasdóttir (eds.), *The Political Interests of Gender: Developing*

Theory and Research with a Feminist Face, Sage Publications, London, pp. 187–213.

James, S. (1992), 'The Good Enough Citizen: Female Citizenship and Indifference', in G. Bock and S. James (ed.), *Beyond Equality and Difference: Citizenship, Female Politics and Female Subjectivity*, Routledge, London, pp. 48–65.

Jones, K.B. (1988), 'Towards a Revision of Politics', in K.B. Jones and A.G. Jónasdóttir (eds.), *The Political Interests of Gender: Developing Theory and Research with a Feminist Face*, Sage Publications, London, pp. 11–32.

Landes, J.B. (1998), 'Introduction', in J.B. Landes (ed.), *Feminism, the Public and the Private*, Oxford University Press, Oxford, pp. 1–17.

Lester, R. (1997), *Citizenship: Feminist Perspectives*, Macmillan, London.

Loughlin, J.P. (1998), 'Autonomy Is Strength', in R. Wilson (ed.), *Hard Choices: Policy Autonomy and Priority Setting in Public Enterprise*, Democratic Dialogue, NIEC, EHSSB, Belfast, pp. 13–36.

MacKinnon, C.A. (1989), *Towards a Feminist Theory of the State*, Harvard University Press, Cambridge, Mass.

Mahon, E. (1991), 'Women and Equality in the Irish Civil Service', in E. Meehan and S. Sevenhuijsen (eds.), *Equality Politics and Gender*, Sage Publications, London, pp. 154–74.

Marshall, T.E. (1950), *Citizenship and Social Class and Other Essays*, Cambridge University Press, Cambridge.

Morgan, J. (1995), 'Sexual Harassment and the Public/Private Dichotomy. Equality, Morality and Manners', in M. Thornton (ed.), *Public and Private: Feminist Legal Debates*, Oxford University Press, Oxford, pp. 89–111.

Naffine, N. (1995), 'Sexing the Subject (of Law)', in M. Thornton (ed.), *Public and Private: Feminist Legal Debates*, Oxford University Press, Oxford, pp. 18–39.

Okin, S.M. (1979), *Women in Western Political Thought*, Princeton University Press, Princeton, NJ.

Okin, S.M. (1991), 'Gender, the Public and the Private', in D. Held, *Political Theory Today*, Cambridge University Press, Cambridge, pp. 67–90.

Pascall, G. (1997), *Social Policy: a New Feminist Analysis*, Routledge, London.

Pateman, C. (1983), 'Feminist Critiques of the Public/Private Dichotomy', in S.I. Benn and G.F. Gaus (eds.), *Public and Private in Social Life*, St Martin's Press, New York, pp. 281–303.

Pateman, C. (1989), *The Disorder of Women: Democracy, Feminism and Political Theory*, Policy Press, Cambridge.

Pateman, C. (1992), 'Equality, Difference, Subordination: the Politics of Motherhood and Women's Citizenship', in G. Bock and S. James (ed.), *Beyond Equality and Difference: Citizenship, Female Politics and Female Subjectivity*, Routledge, London, pp. 17–32.

Phillips, A. (1991), *Engendering Democracy*, Polity Press, Cambridge.

Phillips, A. (1993), *Democracy and Difference*, Polity Press, Cambridge.

Phillips, A. (1998), 'Dealing with Difference', in J.B. Landes (ed.), *Feminism, the Public and the Private*, Oxford University Press, Oxford, pp. 475–95.

Postone, M. (1992), 'Political Theory and Historical Analysis' in Calhoun, C. (ed.), *Habermas and the Public Spheres*, MIT Press, Cambridge, Mass., pp. 164–80.

Randall, V. (1991), *Women and Politics: an International Perspective*, 2nd edn., Macmillan, London.

Sassoon, A. (1987), 'Women's New Social Role: Contradictions of the Welfare State', in A. Sassoon (ed.), *Women and the State: the Shifting Boundaries of Public and Private*, Hutchinson, London, pp. 158–90.

Siim, B. (1988), 'Towards a Feminist Rethinking of the Welfare State', in K.B. Jones and A.G. Jónasdóttir (eds.), *The Political Interests of Gender: Developing Theory and Research with a Feminist Face*, Sage Publications, London, pp. 160–86.

Siim, B. (1991), Welfare State, Gender Politics and Equality Policies: Women's Citizenship in the Scandinavian Welfare States', in E. Meehan and S. Sevenhuijsen (eds.), *Equality Politics and Gender*, Sage Publications, London, pp. 175–92.

Stivers, C. (1993), *Gender Images in Public Administration. Legitimacy and the Administrative State*, Sage Publications, Newbury Park, Calif.

Thornton, M. (1995a), 'The Cartography of Public and Private', in M. Thornton (ed.), *Public and Private: Feminist Legal Debates*, Oxford University Press, Oxford, pp. 2–17.

Thornton, M. (1995b), 'Embodying the Citizen', in M. Thornton (ed.), *Public and Private: Feminist Legal Debates*, Oxford University Press, Oxford, pp. 198–220.

Wajcman, J. (1991), *Feminism Confronts Technology*, Polity Press, Cambridge.

Young, I. (1989), 'Polity and Group Difference: a Critique of the Ideal of Universal Citizenship', *Ethics*, vol. 99, p. 250.

Young, I. (1990), *Justice and the Politics of Difference*, Princeton University Press, Princeton, NJ.

Young, I. (1998), 'Impartiality and the Civic Public: Some Implication of Feminist Critiques of Moral and Political Theory' in J. B. Landes (ed.), *Feminism, the Public and the Private*, Oxford University Press, Oxford, pp. 421–47.

PART II
GENDERED THOUGHT, PUBLIC ADMINISTRATION, AND POLICY NETWORKS

1 The Masculinity of Organizational Life

CELIA DAVIES

Introduction

Over the last few years, 'Gender and . . .' has begun to replace 'Women and . . .' in the titles of work by feminist writers. Yet, when people call for a gender analysis, when they remark that the gender dimensions of some phenomenon are interesting, or when they say that the gender issue needs to be considered, it is not at all obvious what they mean and whether they mean the same thing. On some occasions, what they intend is to draw attention to the absence of women and to call for immediate and practical measures through which women can be encouraged or enabled to participate. On other occasions, use of the term gender acknowledges the need to shift the focus away from the assumption that things need to be done by and for women, signalling a more critical attention to men and to the ways in which their practice might need to change and what the resistances to this might be. Rarely in all of this is the term gender given sustained scrutiny. It serves often as a synonym for women; it is individualized, trivialized, not used to carry any theoretical weight.

There is now, however, a growing consensus that the use of the term gender has to mean more than this, and that the project of theorizing gender needs to be brought more firmly into the arena of empirical work. In history (Scott, 1986), sociology (Acker, 1989), and in organizational analysis (Hearn et al., 1988; Acker, 1990; Mills and Tancred, 1992; Savage and Witz, 1992; Itzin and Newman, 1995; Collinson and Hearn, 1996;

Alvesson and Billing, 1997), as well as in political science, with the notable challenges to male theorizing of writers such as Pateman (1988; 1989) and Phillips (1991; 1993), the claim is being made good that gender is more than a matter of more or less stereotyped behaviour on the part of the members of the two sexes. There are a number of features, broadly stated, that the work of writers such as these have in common. There is an invitation to focus on the symbolic significance of gender and the way that the content of cultural codes of masculinity and femininity serves as a resource for understanding and shaping social relations. There is a demand that we consider in a systematic way the different *levels* at which gender enters structured social relations, as something that people bring to a social situation, something that is confirmed or challenged in interaction, and something also that in important ways is written into the very logic and design of the organizational relations of public life.[1]

This new turn to gender insists that, while cultural codes of masculinity and femininity have a relation to the beliefs and behaviours of actually existing women and men, the match will not always be a neat one. Cultural representations of gender pervade our earliest experiences and shape our sense of identity. They are then re-encountered in the frozen social relations of institutions; but masculinity and femininity are not 'attributes' that all men and all women enduringly possess, nor are they in any straightforward sense 'scripts', that we can simply learn and unlearn. All institutions are implicated—not only those relating to the family, sexuality, and reproduction, but also those which are apparently gender-free and which operate in the public domain of work and politics. Indeed, the public–private split is itself a fundamental part of this cultural heritage of gender. This kind of approach also insists that gender is relational and that masculinity and femininity can only be properly understood in constant reference to each other. They are neither separate nor in any simple sense complementary. Rather, they wrench apart the diversity and richness of human qualities, assigning the masculine set a privileged status and containing, denying, and repressing the feminine. I shall want to argue below that it is the failure to confront both the hegemonic character of masculinity and particularly its constant and uneasy relation to femininity, that has given much of the work in this vein a bad name.

Regarding gender as an active and continuing relational process in this way, and as being inscribed in identities, interactions, and institutions, is often signalled by a shift from using gender as a noun to using gender as a verb. Thus, it becomes possible to speak of the 'gendering' of organizations and the 'gendered' character of policies and organizational activities, and to mean by this that culturally constructed gender relations are called forth, overtly or otherwise, and in a diversity of ways, to enable the daily business of routinely organized relations to take place. To provide a gender-relations analysis in this way is not to ask where the women are, but to enquire how social organization in a particular area calls on understandings of masculinity and femininity to give it meaning and order, and how those meanings are challenged or reproduced. Gender is, hence, • regarded as a fundamental organizing principle of social life, deeply embedded both in the design and in the functioning of organizations (see especially Acker, 1990).

In this chapter, I seek to extend the relational understanding of gender that is implied in a focus on cultural codes of masculinity and femininity, and to argue for a deeper appreciation of the multiple ways in which binary forms of gendered thought saturate the public-policy process that is under discussion in this volume. I shall also attempt to set out some of the levers for change that such an analysis offers. In presenting the argument, I shall need to address quite an array of sceptics, not least those who see a danger in talking about masculinity and femininity of reinforcing the very stereotypes about 'women' that feminists have intended to subvert. My rejoinder is that, far from ignoring those stereotypes, we should make the understanding of them much more central to what we do. Only when we do this, we will see what kind of demand we are putting on women when we urge them to enter an already gendered terrain, and to work for change from within.[2]

Contrasting Pathways of Gendered Development

The first step in a gender-relations analysis involves giving specific content to the concepts of masculinity and femininity and to the nature of the relation between them. Writers from psychoanalysis provide the most detailed and coherent suggestions here, and the work of Nancy Chodorow (1978; 1989) offers a starting point and a continuing point of reference for many in this field. She locates the possibility of different developmental pathways in the sexual division of labour in parenting. Her argument, in essence, is that in a world where parenting is so overwhelmingly the responsibility of the mother, the psychosocial process of relinquishing infantile attachment and acquiring a sense of self apart from the parent, is a different task and takes on a different trajectory for the two sexes. Chodorow (1978, pp. 166–7) explains:

> Mothers tend to experience their daughters as more like, and continuous with, themselves. Correspondingly, girls tend to remain part of the dyadic primary mother–child relationship itself. This means that a girl continues to experience herself as involved in issues of merging and separation, and in an attachment characterized by primary identification and object choice. By contrast, mothers experience their sons as a male opposite. Boys are more likely to have been pushed out of the pre-oedipal relationship, and to have had to curtail their primary love and sense of empathic tie with their mother. A boy has engaged, and been required to engage, in a more emphatic individuation and a more defensive firming of experienced ego boundaries.

The girl and the boy, she continues, develop different inner worlds and different relational capacities. The girl comes to experience herself as less differentiated than the boy, as more continuous with the external world, more able to experience, or believe she can experience, another's needs and feelings. She retains a strong sense of connection with others and displays the empathy that goes with this. The boy, by contrast, has experienced an earlier and more complete 'pushing away' by the mother. For this reason, men are likely to find the expression of relations to others more threatening; they will stress autonomy rather than connection.

It was this notion of autonomy versus connection that Carol Gilligan (1982) utilized in exploring the moral development of children and in arguing that psychological theory had built on masculinity, and that there was 'another voice' to be heard in understanding this developmental process. There was an ethic of justice that was clearly exemplified by the reasoning of some of the boys in her study, and which proceeded from a sense of autonomous bounded selves developing a sense of coherent general rules to manage relations with others; there was also, however, an ethic of care, stemming from a recognition of interdependence and an acute awareness of the needs of the other, and the need to preserve an ongoing relationship. The essential idea of autonomy versus connection is also taken up in a number of popular texts where the 'difference writers' seek to illuminate the tensions between the sexes in styles of social interaction and patterns of communication (see, e.g., Tannen, 1991).

Gender difference expressed in this way has a paradoxical character.[3] On the positive side, there is no doubt that this thinking has an immense appeal. The books and articles of the popular difference theorists are much more widely known, bought, and discussed than are other writings in the feminist genre. By naming the feminine, they have given recognition where there was silence; by putting into words and indicating a coherence in the set of ideas labelled feminine, they have affirmed aspects of what women have hitherto been unable to express. The importance of this process of naming cannot be overstated. It does not mean, however, that we must accept uncritically that which they have named, or how they have named it, or assume that the process of naming is finished.

The difference writers, as critics have made clear, elide the distinction between gender as culture and gender as the characteristics of actually existing men and women. Frequently, and even if they disavow it at particular points, their arguments are presented as if all girls and boys, all women and men, differ in these ways. The crucial matter of the relation between the characteristics of masculinity and femininity and the characteristics of real people is nowhere fully explicated. Next, there is the matter of power and of the cultural and material dominance of men and the subordination of women. Power relations are only sketchily drawn, if they are alluded to at all. There are two important effects of this, which the critics are right to point out. The hegemony of the masculine—the way in which it pervades all institutional areas, appears as the norm that women as well as men must know, and to which all must respond—is not given weight. Also, the relation between masculinity and femininity, especially where an effort is being made to present the feminine in a positive light as having a coherence of its own rather than being simply the absence of the masculine, can easily appear as one of complementarity, rather than as the relation of 'othering'.[4]

Table 1.1 offers a summary and a reformulation of some of the themes proposed by the difference writers. This is not an exercise that seeks to celebrate difference. Naming of difference, as Sandra Harding has indicated, can be seen as part of a project, not just of reversal but of transcendence. As she puts it, we may 'often have to formulate a woman-centered hypothesis in order even to comprehend a gender-free one' (Harding, 1986, p. 138). It seeks to acknowledge the absent presence that is femininity and to give it a content that neither romanticizes it nor reflects the suppression and denial of masculinity, but instead regards it as an

equally partial and equally coherent world view. It regards the autonomy–
connection dichotomy not as a description of the complementary or
antagonistic ways that women and men behave, but as cultural codes of
gender.

Table 1.1   Cultural codes of gender

Theme	Masculine	Feminine
Development of self	separation boundedness responsibility to self self-esteem self-love	relation connectedness responsibility to others selflessness self-sacrifice

Cognitive orientation	abstract, rule-governed
	  thinking
	mastery/control
	emphasis on expertise
	skills/knowledge as
	  portable acquisitions
		concrete, contextual
		  thinking
		understanding/use
		emphasis on experience
		skills/knowledge as
		  confirmed in use

Relational style	decisive interrogative hierarchy oriented loyal to superordinates agentic/instrumental	reflective accommodative group oriented loyal to principles facilitative/expressive

The first heading, 'development of self', summarizes key features in
Chodorow's gendered image of child development. In the masculine way
of thinking, the project is separation, establishment of firm ego boundaries,
and the development of a sense of self and of responsibility for one's self;
in the feminine way of thinking the project is relation, a situation where the
girl remains connected to the mother, developing a sense through this of
responsibility to the other. And where for the boy learning masculinity
means striving for autonomous action and a growing confidence in himself

as an agent in the world, with an accompanying growth of self-esteem and perhaps we can say self-love, for the girl the relation to others means selflessness and even self-sacrifice in orienting to the needs of others.

The second heading, 'cognitive orientation', demonstrates that the two perspectives can also be seen as oriented differently in relation to a world of knowledge. On the one hand, there is a view of knowledge as abstract and rule governed. It is thus something to be taken hold of, 'mastered', and possessed. The concept of self as expert, of skills and knowledge as acquisitions, something that is displayed and can be put to use at will, flows from this. On the other hand, we can begin to discern another view, one which derives from a concrete and contextual cognitive orientation. Here, knowledge takes on a much more provisional character. Knowledge is an understanding that needs to be confirmed in context and in use; experience may need to accompany formal expertise, and, instead of a confident feeling of possession and mastery by the self, there is a need to have knowledge confirmed and validated by others.

Commentary on some of the items under the third heading, 'relational style', is reserved for the next section, where the extent to which the perspective of autonomous individuals is one that is centred on hostility to, and competition with, others is underlined. Once this is highlighted, the predictability of hierarchy and power relations demanding strong loyalty to those in superordinate positions can be seen as understandable, public-domain solutions to an environment seen always as a potential threat.

The next section brings us to the heart of the contribution of this chapter. I will propose that the value cluster just described under the heading of masculinity stems from, and further inscribes, a masculine vision of what it is to be and to act in public. I will further argue that the masculine view is seriously incomplete, that it rests on unacknowledged unconceptualized work of women, not just in the so-called private domain, but also in the public domain itself. I will then go on to emphasize the partial nature of relations in public that masculinist visions entail. The uneasy presence of diversity, innovation, and passionate commitment will be singled out. Though the argument is conducted in the main in relation to the specific case of the bureaucrat, it is no accident that these features are the very ones that are at the centre of the critiques that feminists have made of a wide range of figures in public life, including the professional and the public servant.

Masculine Blinkers of Bureaucracy

While important feminist insights into the nature and limits of bureaucracy have begun to emerge in a number of quarters (see, for example, Ferguson, 1984; Pringle, 1989; Savage and Witz, 1992; Morgan, 1996), it is the work of Roslyn Bologh (1990) that offers an approach that relates closely to the line of analysis developed here. Her scholarly reassessment of Max Weber, the theorist of bureaucracy whose thinking dominates our understanding of bureaucratic action to this day, teases out the interrelation between the man, his masculinity, and his world view in a particularly vivid and accessible way. A brief exposition of some of her arguments both serves to consolidate the argument and to offer a basis for its further development.

The route to masculinity—producing the strongly bounded, agentic individual who wishes to make a difference in the world, Bologh points out—involves certain assumptions about the possibilities for social and collective action. Since men, as bounded individuals, engage in autonomous action, each acting rationally in pursuit of their individual interests, their relation to each other is formulated as an aggressive and competitive one. On this model, the public world is devoid of any expectation of nurturance and support. It is comprised, in her memorable term, of 'hostile strangers'. And in a world of hostile strangers, collective action can only occur through the exercise of power and the dominance of some men over others. In this context, the pattern of rational, legal authority of a bureaucracy, with its emphasis on rules and on hierarchy, is to be preferred to the patronage and arbitrary rule of a traditional leader.

From this, Bologh teases out Weber's vision of the leader, the man whose vision inspires the bureaucracy. It is his behaviour that transcends ordinary, aggressive masculinity, for he is ennobled and achieves true manliness in pursuit of a cause. Such a man, her portrait reveals, is restrained. His belief in a cause disciplines him to self-control, and to a careful weighing of courses of action in pursuit of the cause. He must use his intellect and arrive at an independent judgement (remember that the world is full of hostile strangers). He must apply rational criteria to his decision-making. He must not allow his vision to be clouded by sentiment, and in this regard must welcome and foster the distance from others that this entails. This is not naked power. Manly behaviour can involve a chivalrous attitude to protection of the weak, and it always involves a careful consideration of the consequences of action in terms of achievement of the chosen end.

In imposing his will and taking personal responsibility, this truly manly man must endure the distrust of others. Given the importance of the cause, he will sometimes have to sacrifice ethics, ignore the welfare of others, and perhaps use violence. He must examine his conscience, maintain his dignity and his distance, sometimes keep silent, and always keep his own counsel. He is, if you will, cold, calculating, and ruthless in his relentless rationality. Yet he is more than this. He is not simply exercising his strength and power. These are mediated and redeemed by a commitment to an end, which requires him to relinquish the sympathy of others. Weber sees here a constant struggle for true heroic greatness, its tragedy being that it can only ever be achieved at the high points of life.

How are the rest of us—the men who do not reach or aspire to the manly ideal, and the women—to be seen within this masculine vision of the world? As far as men are concerned, we have already seen that Weber distinguishes between ordinary masculinity and ideal manliness. Pride in the exercise of restrained, independent judgement is accompanied by contempt for other men. They are to be controlled through loyalty and fear; they are cogs in the bureaucratic machine. The gulf between a leader and his followers is profound. Relations between men are distant, hierarchical, and based on fear; the potential violence of these relations between hostile strangers is nowhere far below the surface. The position of women in this construction of masculinity is very different, and Bologh's contribution is a particularly telling one.

Bologh has expressed masculinity and femininity in terms of two desires and two choices by the child: the masculine desire being for action in the world, the feminine desire being for love and protection. But Weber, in his masculinist world view, has concluded that love and protection are an illusion. They require trust in others, a belief that they will be sympathetic, will orient themselves to you, and will be concerned with your well-being. In a world of hostile strangers, the choice of femininity can only be achieved if the woman withdraws, becomes not a subject but an object in the world, remains in the private sphere dependent on the protection of a man. While masculinity requires strict self-control, femininity does not and, safely away from the world of public, can be acknowledged. On this model, women, she explains, 'like unrepressed children, are expected to express enthusiasm, liveliness, sympathy, delight'

(Bologh, 1990, p. 259). These qualities, from the standpoint of masculinity, are hopelessly undisciplined and emotional. Femininity, viewed from the masculine vision of the public world, is inferior, it is not part of the 'civilizing process', it lacks that discipline and constant struggle that allows the development of the intellect. It is concerned with the day-to-day, the practical, and the pleasurable. It is 'being', not 'doing'. Bologh (1990, p. 257) explains further that:

> because women's feelings for others obstruct 'rational' action, they are too 'soft'. They [*sic*] are unwilling or unable to make the hard decisions that are necessary for achieving the goal. They fall into the 'compassion trap'; they rely on intuitive judgement; they are concerned with 'the relationship' or others' feelings. Women, who by definition orient to the maintenance of relationships and the sustenance of human life 'do not know what the real world is like'; that hard decisions have to be made, that people have to get hurt, that if one is unwilling to hurt others, then others will take advantage.

She also insists that we understand the relation of the public and the private world as a relation of repression. Masculinity's version of rational action conceives itself as autonomous and independent of the other. In practice, as is already clear, while denying the other, it also needs and assumes it. In a highly insightful and crucially important passage, she observes (ibid., p. 242, emphasis added):

> Our very concept of what it is to be a man presupposes repression: a certain conception of and relation to women, a relation in which women are expected to fulfil men's personal and domestic needs, needs which are then not recognised as essential to being a man. If anything, they are viewed as weaknesses, needs that actors in the public world, men ought not to take seriously. *The very existence of the public world as we know it, presupposes, yet denies that it presupposes, the private world, and the kind of person, woman, who is defined in terms of that world.* This is not the same as saying the two are separate and complementary. Rather they are forcibly divided and the division is maintained by repression.

Femininity, repressed in this way, now appears not so much as something benign and childlike, but something that is to be feared as a temptation, something that, in other words, is seductive but contemptible.

Bologh's achievement here is threefold: she has provided a critical yet sympathetic account of masculinity, she has incorporated a strong sense of the 'devaluated other', and she has made the link between cultural ideas of gender and their embedding in organized social relations. There are two further steps that I wish to take with this analysis. First, there is the matter not only of the exclusion of women but of their attenuated and underconceptualized inclusion as vital to the functioning of bureaucracy. This, which will be examined briefly below, is important not only to complete the account but to critique the notion of the public domain and to understand the position of women and their potential place in a project of change. Second, we need to explore what it is that this limited vision, gendered masculine, omits from a public-policy decision process. In part, this will reiterate familiar criticisms of bureaucracy, but it will also put a new gloss on them.

Rosemary Pringle's pioneering study on secretaries has challenged the way bureaucracy, filtered through Weberian thought, understands itself. She points out that the boss–secretary relationship directly contravenes the Weberian model. The secretary, with direct access to the boss, at first glance is outside the hierarchy; her work is undefined, her relation with the boss can generate intense feelings of loyalty and 'a degree of intimacy, day-to-day familiarity and shared secrets unusual for any but lovers or close friends' (Pringle, 1989, p. 87). Pringle insists that this needs to be seen, not as some 'pre-bureaucratic relic', but as integral. We must understand 'ordered rationality' as an illusion; we must see that 'masculine rationality attempts to drive out the feminine but does not exist without it' (ibid., p. 89). It is because secretaries attend to needs that are personal, sexual, and emotional, and because they carry out work that is underconceptualized, devalued, and ignored, that their bosses can continue to act in a disembodied way and can continue to present their decision processes in terms of the abstract ideal that has been described. The ideal, therefore, cannot be sustained without the work of women inside as well as outside the public world (see also Davies, 1996).

Turning now to the limits of bureaucracy's masculinist vision, there are three apparently positive features that can be singled out, and regarded differently, once the character of the gendered thought that underlies them is made apparent. These are: the impartiality of the decision, the impersonality of the bureaucrat, and the unequivocally authoritative character of the hierarchy. We will need to dwell on each in turn to enable the project of transformation to come into fuller view. First, impartial decisions—these are decisions based on universal and delimited criteria;

particulars of the context or the case that are not covered by the criteria are ignored. There is no room, therefore, for the passionate personal plea or the elaboration of circumstances that would particularize.[5] Decisions that are abstract and acontextual in this way become susceptible to a formulaic solution, which owes nothing to novel information or argument. The decision process assumes a framework of broadly consensual social values, it involves predictable steps, and is conducive to clarity, orderliness, and confidence on the part of the bureaucrat. Second, there is impersonality— the facelessness of the bureaucrat. The official is detached/alienated from the decision, remaining 'outside of' or 'above' it. His is a routine decision process, and he can expect it to be reviewed by his superiors in a routine way. His private thoughts and judgements, if he has them, remain private; his history is irrelevant. He himself is replaceable, and indeed the physical moves of location are often part of the normal expectation of a bureaucratic career and is conducive to impersonality by militating against attachment and localism. Third, the hierarchy is a means of resolving any uncertainty or dispute. Since it expresses relations of command, the bureaucracy speaks with one voice. It expects loyalty and deference, not to individuals but to the offices that they occupy.

This is a resolution of the problem of organizing that attends to the cultural issues of masculinity as I discussed them in the last section in at least two senses. On the one hand, it creates a stable and predictable order in which the interests of men as hostile strangers are tightly controlled. A stable and known power replaces an arbitrary and unknown one. On the other hand, it also preserves the relations of strangers. Intimacy and the exercise of emotion are no part of the vision that is bureaucratic organization. The overwhelming, engulfing, and threatening character of a climate of nurturance and care is set aside. Formality and distance are not only valued, but are seen as the only route to a rational decision.

There are organizational costs, however, in what is suppressed. Stability comes at the price of losing both creativity and flexibility. The innovative solutions that might emerge from a decision process that mediated and negotiated between a diverse group of people with different histories and perspectives, are foregone. Indeed, any input that might come from valuing the diversity of personal experience of the office holders, and engaging with it, is denied. The process is necessarily inflexible; adaptability and change are a problem since the bureaucracy puts a premium on routine. Loyalty is to be had, but the kind of energy that comes from a passionate commitment to the goals, and the potential for questioning and renegotiating the mission in new contexts that this commitment often produces, is missing. No contributions are forthcoming, save those that are planned. The distinctions that were suggested in Table 1.1, between organizational loyalty and principled commitment, are now a little clearer. To sum up: bureaucracy's inflexibility, its tendency seemingly to forget its own mission, its lack of regard for persons, can all be understood in terms of the partial project of masculinity with which it is associated.[6]

Dislodging Public Man?

Are the qualities set out in the earlier section, and so vividly described by Roslyn Bologh for a nineteenth-century concept of bureaucracy, capable of broader application? Can we extend them to the entrepreneur and the businessman, the politician and the public servant? Elsewhere, I have been able to use them to provide a critical examination of professionalism, and the social relations of professionals. Both bureaucracy and professionalism, it can be argued, respond to the dilemmas of masculinity, and do so in the same way. The heroic training of the professional, for example, marks him [*sic*] off from ordinary men; the formulaic diagnostic process maintains impersonality and distance from the client; above all, the professional interview takes the form of the 'fleeting encounter', where mastered knowledge is applied and where others, almost always women, do the preparation, the follow-up, and the support (Davies, 1995; 1996).

Important steps in the translation of similar ideas to the realms of public policy have already been taken by Camilla Stivers. In her published work on the development of public administration in the US, she demonstrates that images of expertise 'contain dilemmas of gender' (Stivers, 1993, p. 4). The 'passion for anonymity' of the administrator that she describes, the notion that decisions based on sympathy are seen as 'sentimental', and the way in which this blocks dialogue and suppresses femininity (Stivers, 1993, chap. 4 and p. 49) find ready echoes in the themes of this chapter. In searching for further ways in which these arguments intersect with ideas in feminist theory, we can go in one direction here and draw links with feminist critiques of democracy: with Carole Pateman's argument about the unacknowledged sexual contract underlying and underpinning the notion of acting in public and engaging in political debate; and with the arguments Anne Phillips has expressed so eloquently against forms of political thought based on a male subject that routinely have pretensions to universalism.[7] We can go in a different direction and draw links with the burgeoning field of work on masculinity, at least with certain parts of it.[8]

Table 1.2   The gendering of social institutions and the place of women as change agents

1   Binary thinking associated with gender forms a fundamental basis for social relations.

2   This confirms men as active subjects in the public sphere, elaborates a language for reflecting on their experience, and separates and underplays sexuality, reproduction, and emotions.

3   It also devalues women—as objects—as the unbounded and unspecified 'other', as carriers of uncontrolled emotions.

BUT:

4   The jobs women hold often 'stand for' gendered characteristics. In this case, women are not excluded from social institutions but are included via a truncated and unacknowledged understanding of gender.

5   Women's contribution both in the public and private sectors, however, remains unacknowledged and misunderstood.

THUS:

6   Women are rendered marginal and will find it difficult to account for themselves.

7   Women will meet with failures of understanding and resistance to change.

HOWEVER:

8   Gendering is a social fiction, a defective vision that is not sustainable as a basis for daily practice.

9   Women as located on the 'fault line' are well placed to uncover the tacit gendering of institutions.

10   Men may also resist the existing forms of the masculine vision; in doing so they may create a clash of masculinities or ally with women in a bid for change.

With talk of gendering and gender relations, with reference to the gendered cultures of organizations, to gender imagery and masculinity, we probably have rather too many languages at present for expressing similar phenomena. This is not altogether surprising, given the way in which feminist thinking is developing both inside the more established disciplines and in women's studies. Rather than pursue this, however, I prefer to try to sketch how abstract notions of masculinity, and of cultural codes of gender, can be integrated into a more dynamic form of theorizing about change in the public domain. If bureaucratic man is one form of public man, there is more than one reason to think that public man—in principle at least— might be poised to fall from, or to be pushed from, his pedestal.

A key step in examining this possibility is to reconsider the status of the somewhat abstract masculinity discussed here and its links to specific historical masculinities. (Connell (1987) proposed the concept of hegemonic masculinity as a way of emphasizing both the shift away from individual attributes[9] and the possibility of multiple and competing masculinities at any one point. Hegemonic masculinity, he argued, is always constructed in relation to subordinated (and resistant) masculinities as well as in relation to femininity, and is always fragile and susceptible to alteration (Connell, 1987, pp. 183 ff.).[10] His own more recent work, as well as that of others, has shown how different masculinities can coexist and clash, as well as change, over time (Connell, 1993a; see also, for example, Roper and Tosh, 1991; Hearn, 1992; Morgan, 1992; Roper, 1994; Collinson and Hearn, 1996).)

The particular socio-economic situations that we have faced in recent years, the combination of financial crises, lengthy periods of strong right-wing governments and welfare retrenchment, have seen both bureaucracy and professionalism in retreat. New managerialism is not necessarily to be seen altogether as the 'ideological foreign body' that some have proposed (Pollitt, 1990). Whether in the big-business variant, applauding good financial control, speed in decision-making, and cost improvement, or the small-business variant, lauding price competition and entrepreneurial zeal (Cox, 1992), there are still recognizably masculine values, in some ways more blatant, in the stress on action and results, in the low-trust atmosphere, the performance related contracts, and the relentless comparisons and evaluations of results. It seems that there were signs in the early 1990s of a backlash against this new masculinism, in the NHS in Britain, for example, in alliances among the old bureaucrats, the professionals, and interestingly too among women who refer disparagingly not just to the 'balance sheet mentality' but in an unprecedented way are critical too of the 'grey men' and the cold calculations of the 'men in suits' (Davies, 1995).[11]

If there are new fragilities in contemporary reconstitutions of masculinity, what can be said about the potential for change? At the outset of this chapter I insisted that gender operates at many levels, including at the very least the level of subjective identity and of daily interaction, as well as at the level of being built into institutions. Each of these levels represent a site where gender is produced and reproduced; and a site, therefore, where there is scope for dissonance, disruption, and change, where, in other words, there are levers for dislodging the versions of public man that are enshrined in practice in the various institutional spheres. And it is in this context that I would like, finally, to return to the position of the increasing numbers of actually existing women who are finding places in organizations in the public world. What is their place in a project of change?

Table 1.2 suggests how we might think about the dilemmas of women's position within binary gendered thought and, despite its contradictions and constraints, explore the potentials for action that this contains. I have adopted Dorothy Smith's notion that women are 'on the fault line' (Smith, 1987). While women are not included, as women, in what she calls the relations of ruling, we move between, and mediate between, the abstract world of men and the more concrete, detailed, and immediate world of women that enables men's world to take the form that it does. Drawing from a Hegelian analysis of the master and the slave—where, though the master does not need to understand the world of the slave, the slave certainly needs to, and does, understand the world of the master in order to anticipate his needs and to serve him—she argues that women have a 'bifurcated consciousness' (Smith, 1987, pp. 78 ff.). This more complex subjectivity, whatever the problems of finding and giving expression to it, contains within itself an uneasy tension that can be conducive to change. This needs to be combined, on the one hand, with women's greater presence, the greater numbers of women entering male institutions, and, on the other hand, with the possibility for alliances with those experiencing the tensions of competing and subordinated masculinities. I am not suggesting that fundamental change is imminent or inevitable, but these lines of thinking may be helpful ones as we examine the present scope for forming new policy alliances and shifting the terms of the debates in ways that are more accommodating to women.[12]

Summary and Conclusion

This paper has argued that we operate in a world already deeply saturated with binary gendered thought, and that gendering calls on a notion of natural sexual difference that is replete with images of control and domination. The masculine is hegemonic; the feminine is masked, suppressed, and repressed. Understanding of this relation needs to be rescued from simplistic, essentializing, difference writing and brought much more to the fore. Gender also operates at different levels, near the surface as a resource for interaction and organizational culture, and buried beneath it in the logic of public forms of organization. Far from these latter being somehow gender-free, we have seen, taking the specific case of bureaucracy, how a partial and masculine vision of relations in public recurs, a vision whose limitations are obscured by the work that women do in accommodating and partially ameliorating some of its weaknesses.

These are not strictly, and certainly not solely, the familiar issues of the exclusion of women from areas of work and reward that men have kept for themselves. They are less understood and more complicated issues of inclusion—inclusion of women as 'other'—as carriers of qualities that are both feared and denied. We can be sure that whenever women have been able to construct for themselves a place in the public domain that is predicated on this denial, that place will be a contradictory and uneasy one. We can also be sure than when women seek to act in the same way as men, as colleagues, this too will generate unease. There is a very important sense in which women cannot be 'at home' in the public world—it is constructed in such a way that assumes home is somewhere far away and different. An important twist to the argument, however, is that masculinist vision is a fiction; it cannot be sustained without the work that women do.

The multiple and complex ways in which gender operates to constrain us—men and women alike—are difficult to pin down. Gender is both called forth and masked; it is particularly deeply covered at the level of the logic of organization relations, which has been the focus here. Current institutional arrangements are presented as the only rational and efficient way to proceed. The battle for an increased numerical presence of women in the places of the public world, the struggle against the physical exclusion of women, will go on. But it is by no means the only battle that is before us if the nature of the public domain, and the quality of the interactions and decisions that take place in it, are to become more inclusive and more expressive of divergent perspectives and interests. I believe that Joan Acker was right when she said, some years ago, that we are 'only at the beginning of working out what we mean, in concrete terms, when we say social relations and processes are gendered' (Acker, 1989, p. 77).

Acknowledgement

The ideas in this paper appear in an earlier form in Davies (1995). I am grateful to the University of Ulster for providing me with a period of study leave to work in this area.

Notes

1   There is as yet no very clear consensus as to what these levels are. Scott (1986, pp. 1067 ff.) proposes four ways in which gender is constitutive of social relations, involving culturally available symbols, normative interpretations, specific institutions, and subjective identities. Acker seems to vary in her formulations (see, e.g., 1989; 1990; 1992). See also Alvesson and Billing (1992) and various contributions in Mills and Tancred (1992).

2   Kathleen Jones has produced a strong argument that apparently essentializing claims can be read as 'classificatory fictions' and can be used 'against the grain' (Jones, 1993, pp. 12–13). She also points out that (1993, p. 176),

> bringing gender into focus is not the same thing as studying the actual behaviour of women and men. Noting gender and the difference it makes to the construction of knowledge should mean noting the ways in which the cultural codes of sexual difference structure social relations of human identity and signify relations of power and status.

3   The debates here are voluminous; for a helpful introduction, see Segal (1987). See also, on Gilligan's work, for example, Ferguson (1984); Kerber (1986); Benhabib (1987); Tong (1989, pp. 189 ff.). For some debates on Chodorow, see in particular, Lorber (1981); Eisenstein (1984); Tong (1989, pp. 153 ff.).

4   For a discussion containing a highly accessible account of the 'devalued "other"' and the binary thought that othering entails, see Hartsock (1990); and for a relevant application, see Hollway (1996). The classic discussion of the contradictions involved for women in renouncing autonomy and 'being-the-other' is given by Simone de Beauvoir (1969 [1949], p. 22).

5   For an excellent and accessible critique of the concept of impartiality by a feminist political philosopher, who is able to link it to the public–private dichotomy, to describe and question the implied notion of reason that 'stands apart from any interests and desires', and to argue for a new ideal in which diversity, difference, and emotion are recognized, see Young (1987).

6   Kathleen Jones (1993) has embarked on a project of teasing out an alternative concept of authority to that which involves bureaucratic command. She calls it 'compassionate authority'. Using a reading of the works of Hannah Arendt, and returning to the Greek root of the term, she proposes that authority could be better seen as linking to the notion of augmenting, of beginning something over which one does not have complete mastery, something that needs the help of others to complete (ibid., pp. 167–8). Camilla Stivers (1993, pp. 131–2) has worked with a similar idea with her image of the public servant as midwife, someone who attends, encourages, and facilitates a new and creative outcome.

7   See Pateman (1988) and Phillips (1993, chap. 3); see also note 6 for some of the discussion in Kathleen Jones (1993).

8   The sheer volume of literature on masculinity that has emerged in the last few years is daunting. For an indication of some of the authors whom I think are making contributions to an understanding of gendering, see the paragraphs below. Doubts about certain variants of the new men's studies enterprise have been cogently put by Hanmer (1990); see also Connell (1993b).

9   Connell, in a much quoted passage states that hegemonic masculinity is 'not necessarily what powerful men are, but what sustains their power and what large numbers of men are motivated to support' (1987, p. 185).

10   The relevant passage reads (Connell, 1987, p. 183):

   Hegemonic masculinity is always constructed in relation to various subordinated masculinities as well as in relation to women. The interplay between different forms of masculinity is an important part of how a patriarchal social order works.

11   It is still too soon yet to say what will come of the 1997 Labour Government's concept of a 'third way', as instanced, for example, in its proposals for the NHS, rejecting both what it sees as the command-and-control model of hierarchical bureaucracy and the unbridled competition of the market (Department of Health, 1997).

12   This approach might usefully be compared with that of Connell in his discussion of 'emphasised femininity' (Connell, 1987, pp. 185 ff.). It perhaps accords rather more space to the potential of women as agents of change. An initial attempt at

such an analysis in the context of mid-1990s managerialism in the NHS in Britain is contained in Davies (1995, chap. 8).

References

Acker, J. (1989), 'Making Gender Visible', in R.A. Wallace (ed.), *Feminism and Sociological Theory*, Sage Publications, Newbury Park, Calif., pp. 65–81.

Acker, J. (1990), 'Hierarchies, Jobs, Bodies: a Theory of Gendered Organizations', *Gender and Society*, vol. 4, pp. 139–58.

Acker, J. (1992), 'From Sex Roles to Gendered Institutions', *Contemporary Sociology*, vol. 21, pp. 565–9.

Alvesson, M. and Billing, Y.D. (1992), 'Gender and Organization: Towards a Differentiated Understanding', *Organization Studies*, vol. 13, pp. 73–103.

Alvesson, M. and Billing, Y.D. (1997), *Understanding Gender and Organizations*, Sage Publications, London.

Beauvoir, S. de (1969 [1949]), *The Second Sex*, New English Library, London.

Benhabib, S. (1987), 'The Generalized and the Concrete Other: the Kohlberg–Gilligan Controversy and Feminist Theory', in S. Benhabib and D. Cornell (eds.), *Feminism as Critique. Essays on the Politics of Gender in Late-capitalist Societies*, Polity Press, Cambridge, pp. 77–95.

Bologh, R.W. (1990), *Love or Greatness: Max Weber and Masculine Thinking—a Feminist Inquiry*, Unwin Hyman, London.

Chodorow, N. (1978), *The Reproduction of Mothering. Psychoanalysis and the Sociology of Gender*, University of California Press, Berkeley, Calif.

Chodorow, N. (1989), *Feminism and Psychoanalytic Theory*, Yale University Press, New Haven, Conn.

Collinson, D.L. and Hearn, J. (eds.) (1996), *Men as Managers, Managers as Men. Critical Perspectives on Men, Masculinities and Managements*, Sage Publications, London.

Connell, R. (1987), *Gender and Power. Society, the Person and Sexual Politics*, Polity Press, Cambridge.

Connell, R. (1993a), 'The Big Picture: Masculinities in Recent World History', *Theory and Society*, vol. 22, pp. 597–623.

Connell, R. (1993b), 'Editor's Introduction: Masculinities', *Theory and Society*, vol. 22, pp. 595–6.

Cox, D. (1992), 'Crisis and Opportunity in Health Service Management', in R. Loveridge and K. Starkey (eds.), *Continuity and Crisis in the NHS. The Politics of Design and Innovation in Health Care*, Open University Press, Buckingham, pp. 23–42.

Davies, C. (1995), *Gender and the Professional Predicament in Nursing*, Open University Press, Buckingham.

Davies, C. (1996), 'The Sociology of Professions and the Profession of Gender', *Sociology*, vol. 30, pp. 661–78.

Department of Health (1997), *The New NHS: Modern—Dependable*, Cm. 3807, The Stationery Office, London.

Eisenstein, H. (1984), *Contemporary Feminist Thought*, Unwin Paperbacks, London.

Ferguson, K.E. (1984), *The Feminist Case against Bureaucracy*, Temple University Press, Philadelphia, Penn.

Gallos, J.V. (1989), 'Exploring Women's Development: Implications for Career Theory, Practice and Research', in M.B. Arthur, D.T. Hall, and B.S. Lawrence (eds.), *Handbook of Career Theory*, Cambridge University Press, Cambridge, pp. 110–32.

Gilligan, C. (1982), *In a Different Voice. Psychological Theory and Women's Development*, Harvard University Press, Cambridge, Mass.

Hanmer, J. (1990), 'Men, Power and the Exploitation of Women', in J. Hearn and D. Morgan (eds.), *Men, Masculinities and Social Theory*, Unwin Hyman, London, pp. 21–42.

Harding, S. (1986), *The Science Question in Feminism*, Open University Press, Milton Keynes.

Hartsock, N. (1990), 'Foucault on Power: a Theory for Women?', in L.J. Nicholson (ed.), *Feminism/Postmodernism*, Routledge, New York, NY, pp. 157–75.

Hearn, J. (1992), *Men in the Public Eye. The Construction and Deconstruction of Public Men and Public Patriarchies*, Routledge, London.

Hearn, J., Sheppard, D.L., Tancred-Sheriff, P., and Burrell, G. (eds.) (1989), *The Sexuality of Organisation*, Sage Publications, London.

Hollway, W. (1996), 'Masters and Men in the Transition from Factory Hands to Sentimental Workers', in D.L. Collinson and J. Hearn (eds.), *Men as Managers, Managers as Men. Critical Perspectives on Men, Masculinities and Managements*, Sage Publications, London, pp. 25–42.

Itzin, C. and Newman, J. (1995), *Gender, Culture and Organizational Change. Putting Theory into Practice*, Routledge, London.

Jones, K.B. (1993), *Compassionate Authority. Democracy and the Representation of Women*, Routledge, London.

Kerber, L.K., Greeno, C.G., Maccoby, E.E., Luria, Z., Stack, C.B., and Gilligan, C. (1986), 'On *In a Different Voice*: an Interdisciplinary Forum', *Signs*, vol. 11, pp. 304–33.

Lorber, J., Laub Coser, R., Rossi, A.S., and Chodorow, N. (1981), 'On *The Reproduction of Mothering*: a Methodological Debate', *Signs*, vol. 6, pp. 482–514.

Mills, A.J. and Tancred, P. (1992), *Gendering Organizational Analysis*, Sage Publications, Newbury Park, Calif.

Morgan, D.H.J. (1992), *Discovering Men*, Routledge, London.

Morgan, D. (1996), 'The Gender of Bureaucracy', in D.L. Collinson and J. Hearn (eds.), *Men as Managers, Managers as Men. Critical Perspectives on Men, Masculinities and Managements*, Sage Publications, London, pp. 43–60.

Pateman, C. (1988), *The Sexual Contract*, Polity Press, Cambridge.

Pateman, C. (1989), *The Disorder of Women. Democracy, Feminism and Political Theory*, Polity Press, Cambridge.

Phillips, A. (1991), *Engendering Democracy*, Polity Press, Cambridge.

Phillips, A. (1993), *Democracy and Difference*, Polity Press, Cambridge.

Pollitt, C. (1990), *Managerialism and the Public Services. The Anglo-American Experience*, Basil Blackwell, Oxford.

Pringle, R. (1989), *Secretaries Talk: Sexuality, Power and Work*, Verso, London.

Roper, M. (1994), *Masculinity and the British Organization Man since 1945*, Oxford University Press, Oxford.

Roper, M. and Tosh, J. (1991), 'Introduction. Historians and the Politics of Masculinity', in M. Roper and J. Tosh (eds.), *Manful Assertions. Masculinities in Britain since 1800*, Routledge, London, pp. 1–24.

Savage, M. and Witz, A. (eds.) (1992), *Gender and Bureaucracy*, Blackwell, Oxford.

Scott, J.W. (1986), 'Gender: a Useful Category of Historical Analysis', *American Historical Review*, vol. 91, pp. 1052–75.

Segal, L. (1987), *Is the Future Female? Troubled Thoughts on Contemporary Feminism*, Virago Press, London.

Smith, D.E. (1987), *The Everyday World as Problematic. A Feminist Sociology*, Open University Press, Milton Keynes.

Stivers, C. (1993), *Gender Images in Public Administration. Legitimacy and the Administrative State*, Sage Publications, Newbury Park, Calif.

Tannen, D. (1991), *You Just Don't Understand. Women and Men in Conversation*, Virago Press, London.

Tong, R. (1989), *Feminist Thought. A Comprehensive Introduction*, Unwin Hyman, London.

Young, I.M. (1987), 'Impartiality and the Civic Public. Some Implications of Feminist Critiques of Moral and Political Theory', in S. Benhabib and D. Cornell (eds.), *Feminism as Critique. Essays on the Politics of Gender in Late-capitalist Societies*, Polity Press, Cambridge, pp. 56–76.

2   Reframing the 'Public' in Public Administration

CAMILLA STIVERS

Introduction

In recent years, feminist scholars have called into question the extent to which public-policy thinking is shaped by a gender-based split between public and private spheres, a dichotomy that has pervaded Western political thought since ancient Greece. Public-policy theorists typically understand the line between public and private as one that separates and protects private business enterprise, at least in certain of its activities, from the reach of government—a goal that classical liberal thinkers have held crucial in order to prevent tyranny and promote the liberty of individuals to pursue self-defined interests.

As Carole Pateman (1989) and other feminist scholars have pointed out, however, the conceptual divide that liberalism established between government and business has had the effect of diverting attention from the political implications of another sharp split: the one between the 'private' household and the 'public' activities of both government and business. By defining the line between public and private as having to do with the extent to which political considerations may encroach upon business prerogatives, liberal theory in effect depoliticizes the household.

Pateman argues that, as women have been granted the franchise and a number of other rights that approach formal equality with men, the contradiction between public equality and domestic inequality has become increasingly difficult to ignore or to rationalize: 'Liberal principles cannot simply be universalized to extend to women in the public sphere without raising an acute problem about the patriarchal structure of private life' — (1989, p. 129). (If women are free individuals, as both liberal philosophy and political practice must now either acknowledge or face unacceptable contradiction between principles and performance, then how can it be just to subordinate them in the household, as men seem able to do by refusing an equitable share of housework and childcare, if not by dominating in more overt ways? (Okin, 1989).)

The traditional liberal answer to this question of domestic oppression is that the household lies beyond justice: arrangements there are natural rather than rationally constructed. Liberals solve the dilemma of domestic injustice by defining it out of existence. The well-known feminist credo, 'the personal is political', calls into question precisely this idea that it is natural to consider one half of humanity equal in one sphere of life and unequal in another.

As a result of this feminist critique between public and private, many areas of public-policy theory are in the process of being rethought. No longer able to take the public–private split for granted, scholars are reworking their understanding of various aspects of public policy-making, including the process by which issues are framed and find their way onto the policy agenda, the dynamics of interest-group politics, and the content and outcome of the legislative process. Many scholars have been particular adept at reframing various policy questions by looking at them through a gender-analytic lens (Boneparth, 1982; Gelb and Palley, 1987; Turshen and Holcomb, 1993), at politicizing formerly non-political issues such as domestic violence (Gordon, 1988), or at calling into question the process by which certain factors are included and others excluded from policy considerations (Nelson, 1984).

Despite this ferment, one aspect of the policy process has, at least to date, received relatively little attention by feminist scholars: administrative action. Theorists have tended to see the workings of public administrative agencies as 'mere implementation' or the simple execution of legislative commands, and therefore as worthy of little attention. One might even draw a parallel between the neglect of administration, seen as the public sector's 'housework', and liberal theory's relegation of domestic life to the realm of the non-political. At any rate, the policy dimensions of administration have been overlooked, and with them the implications that gender analysis may have for understanding public administration's publicness.

Yet many, if not most, administrative actions have policy implications. Career civil servants commonly make decisions that amount to binding answers to public questions. Their interpretations of policy mandates put flesh on the bare bones of vague, and often internally contradictory, laws. Administrators exercise regulatory authority over the activities of private corporations and individuals. They decide whether certain individuals, organizations, or communities meet the guidelines that qualify them for the benefits of public programs. Administrators wield public power and, in fact, in doing so they govern. Their decisions have effects on the lives of members of the public, distinguishable from, as significant as, and frequently more direct than legislative action. In overlooking the administrative dimensions of public policy, feminist theorists have neglected a most important aspect of the overall policy process. I have argued elsewhere (Stivers, 1993) that public administration is shaped to its very core by gender in a manner that, like other better-studied parts of the process, works against the interests of women by obscuring its own gender bias and shoring up discriminatory and oppressive social arrangements.

If feminist policy theorists do, as I suggest, neglect public administration out of a sense that it has no important policy implications but simply consists of routine work (similar to women's work in the household), they are perpetuating long-standing practice. In the US, to take the case with which I am most familiar, the discipline of public administration initially organized itself in the early twentieth century around the notion that administration not only was but should be policy-neutral and politically non-partisan. The field's energizing impulse was a search for technically correct and efficient approaches to the execution of policy mandates, and early professional education in public administration took the same tack. Today, even though its conventional wisdom and rhetoric would lead one to conclude that the discipline has recognized the separation of policy and politics from administration as the naive dream of a simpler era, the search for correct solutions to administrative problems continues, with its attendant urge to brush aside the conflict-laden questions that inevitably surround any particular 'right' answer in the public sector.

My argument is that the US experience illustrates how public administration's continuing quest to 'get it right'—to identify and pursue technically expert solutions to public problems—diverts attention away from the policy dimensions of administrative action and blocks exploration of the publicness of public administration. In what follows, I explore the gendered historical roots of this development briefly, in order to make the point that, in the realm of administration, reframing the liberal public–private split must entail renouncing this urge to get public things right once and for all, in favour of another way of defining the administrative enterprise. Paradoxically, at least in the light of liberalism's covert reliance on gender to structure a coherent public space (with women constitutive of the non-public), reframing the public in public administration requires a deliberately gendered approach, one that renounces strict dichotomies along with right answers.

The Gendered Construction of Public Administration

In the US, public administration as a self-conscious enterprise was the product of the Progressive reform movement that dominated late nineteenth- and early twentieth-century politics. In an era of turbulent change marked by industrialization, corporatization, urbanization, influxes of immigrants from Ireland, Italy, and Central Europe, farmer and labour unrest, and the rise of city-based political machines, educated members of the middle and upper classes sought to destabilize and regain control of social processes. The Progressives shared visions of social harmony, of progress, that aimed to move beyond—and therefore underestimated—the class, race, and gender origins of intergroup conflict. An important focus of their work was the problems of rapidly growing cities (slums, unsafe water, overcrowding, inadequate schools, disease, and so on) and what they perceived as the failure of political machine-dominated municipal governments to deal with these conditions (Rogers, 1982; McCormick, 1986).

As American public administration currently constructs its history, we are told that the discipline emerged from the efforts of reformers to replace municipal-government fraud, corruption, and ineffectiveness with efficient public management practices. As the story goes, once reformers perceived that patronage and corruption lay at the heart of poor performance on the part of city governments, and that simply throwing the rascals out (as efforts to vote the machines out of office were styled) would not be enough to make permanent improvements in governmental capacity, they turned their efforts to documenting the factual dimensions of administrative ineffectiveness. This project was led by well-to-do businessmen, academics, and professional men. According to this historical narrative, the municipal research bureaux set up by these reformers documented the value of objective, meaning non-partisan and scientific, analysis and this led to training programs that emphasized the production of neutral, expert managers (Stone and Stone, 1975).

The reformers' stated hypothesis was that the root source of urban problems was the administrative shortcomings of machine-driven party governments, a diagnosis that justified replacing party loyalists with educated experts. Once the problem was defined as the need for better administrative skills, the importance of training for government service became paramount. Out of this priority the academic field of public administration emerged. American public administration, as it tells its own history, came out of a desire to understand and solve problems of administrative procedure. Thus the discipline defined its own role as helping the state become more efficient, more effective, at carrying out its tasks, rather than encouraging the examination of the proper ends of government and the extent to which administration is implicated in them. The genesis of the field can be traced to an urge to find the right answers to questions of administrative technique, a focus that obscured the policy dimensions of administrative action. The process by which the state took on increasing responsibilities, the reasons why it did so, and why it took on the particular functions it did—questions that address, in fact, the operational definition of 'the public'—are neglected issues in US public administration.

This neglect of substantive policy questions is rooted in Progressive-era gender typifications, which bifurcated reform activities in practice according to whether they were thought to be appropriate for men or women, with men handling the task of making government operate in a business-like manner and women transferring their domestic benevolence to the enlargement of the state's role (Stivers, 1995). This split eventually had the effect, in public administration's historical narrative, not only of foregrounding the reform activities of men and obscuring the contributions of women to public life, but perhaps more fundamentally of furthering the masculine reform project, which was to wrest control of administrative agencies from working-class immigrants and to legitimate this power as an objective concern for efficiency (Hays, 1964; Schiesl, 1977).

In contrast to male reformers, reform women frankly aimed to expand the range of government activity in order to help improve living conditions in cities. Residents of settlement houses and members of women's clubs not only delivered needed services to poor families and launched neighbourhood clean-up campaigns, but gradually extended their efforts to lobbying governments to take on responsibility for a wide range of social welfare and community betterment functions. Women defended their work as a natural extension of their appointed social role as nurturers, caretakers, and guardians of virtue. They referred to what they did as 'public motherhood' and 'municipal housekeeping' (Skocpol, 1992; Sklar, 1995). While men were involved in these efforts, women were in the majority and most of the leading figures were women, including such notables as Jane Addams, Julia Lathrop, Lillian Wald, Mary Simkhovitch, Florence Kelley, and Mary McDowell.

Despite the wide variety of government activities that can be traced to the work of reform women, including juvenile courts, public-health nursing, sanitary inspections, public employment bureaux, occupational-safety laws, and welfare payments to poor families, and despite the extent to which the women included sound administrative processes in their thinking and practice, American public administration has paid little, if any, attention to this aspect of the Progressive reform movement and its connection to the development of the field. By concerning itself almost exclusively with the work of reform men to grant scientific status to public management, the field has neglected substantive policy in favour of correct procedure. But pure proceduralism is ultimately an illusion. Administrative decisions serve certain interests and undermine others. Neglect of the political dimensions of administration makes it possible to write off administration as unimportant and thereby obscure the workings of bureaucratic power. Defined simply as matters of technical efficiency, questions of administration are depoliticized and, therefore, rendered impervious to public debate. In addition, premising the field on correct procedure assumes a taken-for-granted quality. Why, for example, did the new profession think of itself as 'public administration' and not as 'public service', which might have encompassed concern for the content and impact of government action as well as concern for efficient management of resources?

Refusing to Get Things Right

Having suggested the origins of the depoliticized view of administration and the impact that gender stereotypes can have on the construction of a disciplinary practice, I want now to explore what sort of reconceptualization might be involved in order to uncover the policy dimensions of administration and thus reframe the public in public administration. Such a task entails focusing on a tendency inherent in the quest to find right answers to technical-managerial questions: to, in effect, close down public dialogue and therefore 'displace' politics, to use Honig's (1993) terminology. My argument is that, in the tension between 'getting things right', which I take to be the fundamental administrative urge, and contesting existing societal arrangements, which is the essence of politics, politics has to have the edge over administration. Politics has to, in a sense, create the conditions under which public administration is possible, rather than vice versa. If the gender split that can be observed in the development of American public administration is neither coincidental nor totally idiosyncratic to the US, we might then characterize this tension between politics and administration, observable in modern states generally, as one between a political impulse towards diversity, in which considerations like gender and race open up the public space, and an administrative urge to obliterate differences under putatively universal-neutral, but historically and culturally, masculine standards. Contending with liberal theory, my argument is that the public—including public administration—is constitutively diverse.

The goal of legitimately politicizing administration—that is making it democratic without making it inappropriately partisan—is one that can only be achieved by exploring how taking gender and race seriously as bases for analysis changes the terms in which we think about public administration. There are a number of theoretical avenues one might pursue. My own approach has been to argue for a strong form of citizenship, in the Aristotelian tradition that defines citizens as those who rule and are ruled in turn (Stivers, 1990). Active citizens embody the urge to contestation; they enact it 'on the ground', so to speak, where administration happens. Active citizens also embody diversity, including diversity of ascriptive characteristics and of perspectives.

The problem with calling for active citizenship, however, is that existing models—both the weak liberal view that sees the citizen as simply a bearer of rights and the Aristotelian version—operate in a constrained public space from which differences have been excluded in order that the space might have coherent boundaries. Since ancient Greece, citizenship, and therefore the idea of the public, has been bounded by a process of exclusion through which citizens could know they were citizens because they were neither women nor slaves (Okin, 1979; Patterson, 1991). Despite this history of constitutive dependence on separation from excluded others, political theory has purged the identity of the citizen of gender and race or ethnic origin in order that it might be considered universal.

If, then, we are to have a politics strong enough to prevail in the face of the administrative urge to control public decision-making, we have to have a public space inhabited by a new kind of citizen. The public sphere has to be constituted in some other way than by excluding certain kinds of people or certain kinds of issues, that is by closing it off in some essential way. The distinction between public and private can no longer be thought of as a strict dichotomy that organizes all subsequent discussion and action.

What we need, I believe, is an understanding of public identity as constructed in public practices rather than essential (as in 'universal Man'). Such an understanding enables us to call into question gender and race as given dimensions of political identity; instead identity would be selected and debated in particular instances, rather than taken as a starting point. This sort of constructed identity is only possible if we understand the line between public and private not as hard and fast, as definitive, but as essentially contestable (Brown, 1988; McClure, 1992; Mouffe, 1992; Honig, 1993; Jones, 1993).

Honig, in particular, argues for politicizing the very question of the split between public and private. She sees this line not as defined, once and for all, regardless of the issue at hand but as debatable in particular situations. She argues that this posture is in fact more consistent with the idea that politics has an openness and a riskiness that make it unique—a view familiar to students of Hannah Arendt's work (e.g. Arendt, 1958), but one that avoids the firm line Arendt wanted to draw around politics. Honig asks: if, as Arendt believed, political action is by its nature boundless, then why should it respect this split that seeks to contain it? The public with a hard and fast boundary is a public that has shut itself in, and therefore depoliticized itself, in the process of trying to achieve coherence.

The question, then, of what is political is itself a political question. This assertion politicizes questions in public administration that otherwise have a way of submerging themselves in the administrative impulse to find correct answers. It renders clear the political dimensions of every administrative reform movement, even those, such as 'reinventing government' (Osbourne and Gaebler, 1992), that specifically attempt to purify their recommendations of political implications.

Following the lead of Honig and others, I argue that the only way in practice to maintain this kind of open, fundamentally political perspective on the nature of the administrative state is to have active citizens, with all their different identities and perspectives, contesting the administrative impulse to be definitive arbiter of the public good. Only by making room for the participation of diverse, active citizens in administrative affairs can we reach a legitimate, a justifiable, understanding of how 'public' administration is possible. The enterprise of defining the good life or the public interest in particular policy situations is one in which there are no experts, only participants.

Conclusion

Ever since the state assumed its administrative guise, the public power exercised by tenured, unelected bureaucrats has been defended or rationalized in a number of ways. One tactic has been to see the bureaucratic structure itself as a source of legitimacy, with its clear chain of command and a political officer at the top. The theory here is that a cabinet minister or politically appointed agency head spans the boundary between policy and administration, ensuring that legislative mandates are implemented and holding the agency accountable to legislative oversight (Wilson, 1887). Yet numerous observers have pointed out the inadequacy of this mechanism, given the power of administrative expertise and the countless opportunities for the exercise of administrative discretion (for example Friedrich, 1940). Relying solely on this structure, it is inevitable that in many instances, far more than we would want, managerial aims like 'results' end up smothering political questions like 'justice'.

Another tactic has been simply to acknowledge the inevitability of discretionary power in the hands of bureaucrats and justify it on the basis of the state's need for the expertise, continuity, and public spiritedness that only administrators can be counted on to have (Wamsley et al., 1990). This approach is not particularly reassuring either, because it seems to put too much faith in the goodwill of administrators and their ability to resist aggrandizing their own authority.

Instead, we need another way, in which, to the extent possible, bureaucrats construct their understanding of policy situations and, therefore, identify and justify the bases for their decisions in dialogue with active citizens. In my view, while tangible examples of such interaction between bureaucrats and citizens are relatively few, there are enough of them to suggest that many more such arrangements are possible (King and Stivers, 1998) if we are willing to reconstitute our understanding of the line between public and private as debatable in particular situations, so that we open up the public in public administration.

It seems to me that scholars in public administration and policy continue to ask the wrong question. Instead of asking, as we do, how administration can be legitimately political (that is, without losing a drop of efficiency and effectiveness), we ought to be exploring the extent to which politics can be legitimately administrative (that is, how much administration can democracy afford?). What is this hold that expertise and professionalism have on us, that we have been willing to accept the possibility that public questions have answers in the same sense that equations have solutions? A truly public administration must find a different way of thinking about itself. Perhaps it will be a way based not on the right answers but on giving good reasons, reasons that are constructed and redeemed in open debate. Such debate must occur in a space that does not depend for its coherence on excluding various others by definition but rather one that is compelling precisely because of its contingency, which gives us a basis for hope.

References

Arendt, H. (1958), *The Human Condition*, University of Chicago Press, Chicago, Ill.

Boneparth, E. (ed.) (1982), *Women, Power, and Policy*, Pergamon Press, New York.

Brown, W. (1988), *Manhood and Politics: a Feminist Reading in Political Theory*, Rowman & Littlefield, Totowa, NJ.

Friedrich, C. (1940), 'Public Policy and the Nature of Administrative Responsibility', *Public Policy*, vol. 1, pp. 3–24.

Gelb, J. and Palley, M.L. (1987), *Women and Public Policies*, Princeton University Press, Princeton, NJ.

Gordon, L. (1988), *Heroes of their Own Lives. The Politics and History of Family Violence: Boston 1880–1960*, Viking, New York.

Hays, S.P. (1964), 'The Politics of Reform in Municipal Government in the Progressive Era', *Pacific Northwest Quarterly*, vol. 55, pp. 157–69.

Honig, B. (1993), *Political Theory and the Displacement of Politics*, Cornell University Press, Ithaca, NY.

Jones, K.B. (1993), *Compassionate Authority. Democracy and the Representation of Women*, Routledge, New York.

King, C.S. and Stivers, C.M. (1998), *Government is Us. Strategies for an Anti-government Era*, Sage Publications, Thousand Oaks, Calif.

McClure, K. (1992), 'On the Subject of Rights: Pluralism, Plurality and Political Identity', in C. Mouffe (ed.), *Dimensions of Radical Democracy: Pluralism, Citizenship, Community*, Verso, London.

McCormick, R. (1986), *The Party Period and Public Policy. American Politics from the Age of Jackson to the Progressive Era*, Oxford University Press, New York.

Mouffe, C. (1992), 'Feminism, Citizenship and Radical Democratic Politics', in J. Butler and J.W. Scott (eds.), *Feminists Theorize the Political*, Routledge, New York, NY, pp. 369–84.

Nelson, B.J. (1984), *Making an Issue of Child Abuse: Political Agenda Setting for Social Problems*, University of Chicago Press, Chicago, Ill.

Okin, S.M. (1979), *Women in Western Political Thought*, Princeton University Press, Princeton, NJ.

Okin, S.M. (1989), *Justice, Gender and the Family*, Basic Books, New York.

Osbourne, D. and Gaebler, T. (1992), *Reinventing Government*, Addison-Wesley, Reading, Mass.

Pateman, C. (1989), *The Disorder of Women. Democracy, Feminism and Political Theory*, Stanford University Press, Stanford, Calif.

Patterson, O. (1991), *Freedom. Volume 1—Freedom in the Making of Western Culture*, Basic Books, New York.

Rogers, D. (1982), 'Progressivism: a Contemporary Reassessment, *Reviews in American History*, vol. 10, pp. 113–32.

Schiesl, M.J. (1977), *The Politics of Efficiency. Municipal Administration and Reform in America: 1880–1920*, University of California Press, Berkeley, Calif.

Sklar, K.K. (1995), 'Two Political Cultures in the Progressive Era: the National Consumer's League and the American Association for Labor Legislation', in L.K. Kerber, A. Kessler-Harris, and K.K. Sklar (eds.), *US History as Women's History. New Feminist Essays*, University of North Carolina Press, Chapel Hill, NC.

Skocpol, T. (1992), *Protecting Soldiers and Mothers: The Political Origins of Social Policy in the United States*, Belknap Press, Cambridge, Mass.

Stivers, C. (1990), 'The Public Agency as *Polis*: Active Citizenship in the Administrative State', *Administration and Society*, vol. 22, pp. 86–105.

Stivers, C. (1993), *Gender Images in Public Administration. Legitimacy and the Administrative State*, Sage Publications, Newbury Park, Calif.

Stivers, C. (1995), 'Settlement Women and Bureau Men: Constructing a Usable Past for Public Administration', *Public Administration Review*, vol. 55, pp. 522–9.

Stone D. and Stone, A. (1975), 'Early Development of Education in Public Administration', in F.C. Mosher (ed.), *American Public Administration: Past, Present, Future*, University of Alabama Press, University, Ala.

Turshen, M. and Holcomb, B. (eds.) (1993), *Women's Lives and Public Policy. The International Experience*, Greenwood Press, Westport, Conn.

Wamsley, G., Bacher, R., Goodsell, C., Kronenberg, P., Rohr, J., Stivers, C., White, O., and Wolf, J. (eds.) (1990), *Refounding Public Administration*, Sage Publications, Newbury Park, Calif.

Wilson, W. (1887), 'The Study of Administration', *Political Science Quarterly*, vol. 2, pp. 197–222.

3 Women and Policy: the European Union Dimension

LIZ SPERLING and CHARLOTTE BRETHERTON

Introduction

In considering the processes and mechanisms by which issues of significance to women are identified, prioritized, and placed on the public agenda, we have concentrated in particular on the European Union (EU) dimension and on women's networking activities.

We have focused our attention on the EU level for a number of reasons. Perhaps most significantly, the EU has produced a considerable volume of legislation, and accompanying action programmes, intended to further the interests of women. Moreover, policy in this area has evolved in such a way that it has sought to shift, and potentially transcend, the barriers between the public and private spheres. For example, while the emphasis of the EU equality legislation has been on women as waged workers, the medium-term action programmes have acknowledged and sought to address women's inferior social, economic, and political position in the private sphere as a means to redress imbalance in the public. This potential transcendence of the public–private divide is explicitly recognized in discussion of the Fourth Medium-Term Action Programme (1996–2000). Thus it is argued (Commission, 1996a, p. 5):

> The promotion of equality must not be confused with the simple objective of balancing the statistics: it is a question of promoting long-lasting changes in

parental roles, family structures, institutional practices, the organisation of work and time . . .

More broadly, much of the integration process of the EU impacts on women in the public and private spheres, perhaps more than is sometimes appreciated.[1] This may prove more stark as integration proceeds. For example, several commentators have highlighted the exacerbating effect on women's labour-market disadvantage of the labour-mobility provisions of the Single European Act (Commission, 1990; Pillinger, 1992).

Concentration on the EU has further significance, particularly for women in the UK, when considering the shifting barriers between the public and private spheres. Among social and Christian democrats there has been a concern that economic integration, and in particular the creation of the single market, should rest upon a foundation of social cohesion. This has been reflected in the transference of social policy competencies to the Union level, including allocation of resources to various 'structural funds' that target disadvantaged regions and social groups, including women. This, together with attempts to reinforce and implement equality legislation, stands in marked contrast to UK government policy since 1979, although since Labour's election victory in 1997 'social exclusion' has become a key policy issue. Commitment to market liberalization and reliance on market mechanisms for social-welfare provision have impacted particularly upon the poorest section of society, which disproportionately comprises woman-headed households. The UK Conservative Government's rejection of the EU Social Charter and subsequent opt-out from the Social Chapter of the Treaty on European Union, accentuated the EU's relatively sympathetic treatment of issues such as low pay and social exclusion.

The salience of EU policy competencies for women, together with the entrenchment of UK policy on social issues, prompted us to consider the level of UK women's awareness of, involvement with, and orientation towards the Union's policies and institutions. Mazey and Richardson (1992, p. 98) had already suggested that hostility in the UK to the Social Charter had caused women's groups to 'redouble their efforts at the Community level . . . and to link with equivalent groups in Europe'. We were concerned to elicit how this was done, and whether such activity was confined to 'elite' women or extended throughout organizations and to 'grass-roots' groups. Moreover, we wanted to know the extent to which women could influence the policy agenda and whether this was confined to 'adding women in' to existing policy or broadening the policy base.

As the concept of networking seemed to resonate with the preferred practices of both the EU and women's groups, we chose to apply this to our research.

Network Analysis

Networks are a form of social organization that provide an ability to coordinate dispersed expertise and resources, and to generate a capacity for collective action: that is, in relation to our study, to participate in or influence policy processes.

Based upon interdependence between participants, networks are relatively egalitarian in character when compared with traditional organizational forms. Importantly for our study, networks can link participants across spatial distance and at different levels, whether this be local, regional, or transnational. Most significantly perhaps, our utilization of the concepts of network, and networking, reflects two central premises: that these concepts, and the formation of networks, are explicitly promoted by the EU; and that networks are a form of organization which is particularly appropriate to the needs and preferences of women.

Policy Network Analysis and Women's Networks: a Disparity of Definition

The work of Rhodes (1990; Marsh and Rhodes, 1992) has set the agenda for policy network analysis (PNA) in political science in the UK, whether to improve, reprove, or approve his ideas. The 'Rhodes model' identifies five classifications of networks along a continuum: political community, professional network, intergovernmental network, producer network, and issue network. Each type of network is endowed with a number of characteristics that, it is argued, determine effectiveness in influencing policy. These include relative stability of membership, degree of openness to potential members, extent of value consensus, and access to material resources. The networks closer to policy-making elites tend to be those enjoying not only more attention from researchers, but also possessing 'favourable' characteristics. Thus, key networks are considered to be stable, elite and relatively closed, with access to resources, which enables a balance of power even if a dominant force exists within the network. Conversely, issue networks are regarded as inherently unstable with large and fluctuating memberships, low value consensus, and unequal distribution of resources, which creates an imbalance of power. Thus it becomes evident (and is confirmed by tabular representations) that the Rhodes model envisages not a continuum but a hierarchy of networks (Marsh and Rhodes, 1992, pp. 14, 251).

It is evident from research using PNA and the Rhodes model that women's networks fall into the lower-echelon categories. In conventional manner, such research tends to concentrate on traditional public-policy concerns, industry–government relations (Wilks and Wright, 1987; Grant et al., 1988; Saward, 1992), subnational government, and policy networks (Marsh and Rhodes, 1992; Bennett and Krebs, 1994; Gray, 1994). Very few critiques recognize the 'blindness' of the Rhodes model to issues such as race and gender, or the general exclusion of the majority of groups from PNA (Bennington and Harvey, 1994, p. 956; Gray, 1994, p. 127). However, together with issues of ethnic exclusion, the most obvious exclusions from traditional policy fields are those of women and the so-called 'soft' policy issues that affect, or are of specific interest to, them.

The concentration of most analysis on the upper echelons of the model may be due to the complexity of producer and issue networks, which, by Rhodes' admission, will be vast and mobile.[2] It is also likely that focus upon the upper-echelon networks is perceived as an honest reflection of how policy is influenced, with producer and issue networks contributing only a 'fringe' aspect. The problem with such seemingly reasonable conditions for exclusion is that they perpetuate the negation of women's political activities. Thus, 'feminist' concerns within the overarching objectives of any particular 'mainstream' policy area are marginalized. Moreover, by emphasizing criteria of networks, such as material resources, and using this as a basis for assessing ability to achieve positive aims, the model again denigrates women's groups, which are less well financed and more disparate. Where Rhodes can suggest that upper-echelon networks share basic values, are more organized and accepting of outcomes, issue networks are considered to be in a state of flux and conflict and, in consequence, less likely to achieve success. However, it is probable that even disparate issue networks share basic values and will accept compromise outcomes, whilst allowing for dissension on the means to achieve success, as also happens in the upper-echelon networks (Peterson, 1992, p. 238; Bennett and Krebs, 1994, p. 132).

Women's Networks and Networking: an Inclusive PNA Framework

Feminists have for some time considered the concept of the state to be problematic, both in terms of political activity generally and regarding political agendas specifically. Thus, they reject as illusory the idea of a coherent set of organizations addressing pre-existing interests, which groups can access and potentially influence (Watson, 1990; Pringle and Watson, 1992). Researchers and women active in bureaucracy (Eisenstein, 1990) are aware of the fragmented nature of policy activity and influence, which distorts or shifts demarcation between the public and private spheres. PNA supposes a similar notion, providing the potential to break down barriers between organizations and groups at different levels of decision-making. In practice, however, it reinforces the state by accepting the involvement only of well-organized and well-resourced groups closely aligned with accepted policy competencies. We believe that it is possible to develop an inclusive approach to network analysis by reconstructing the Rhodes model and redefining network criteria to include non-material resources, such as knowledge and support shared to the mutual benefit of members.

Figure 2.1 indicates that networks, as the term suggests, are not mutually exclusive clubs performing at different levels of a hierarchy. Rather, there can be considerable interaction between the levels. This accords with Dahlerup's (1986) thesis that for women to be effective they need to work cooperatively, from the grass roots, and throughout institutional hierarchies. Hence we can begin to see a transcendence of the barriers between the public and private spheres. Women at the grass-roots level, or involved in issue networks, give support to those in professional and institutional decision-making positions, both in influencing policy and preventing co-option. In this process, issues such as childcare and parental leave, as well as other 'women's issues', can be included in broader policy agendas across a range of issue areas. This is not to assume that women's policy interventions are automatically mainstreamed. Indeed, it is possible that women's networks, as the traditional PNA model suggests, will continue to be marginalized.[3] Moreover, the development of women's policy networks could create another barrier to women wishing to influence the policy agenda: if such networks become the accepted mechanism for accessing policy channels, 'outsider' groups, such as issue networks, could be increasingly disregarded, thus restricting more diverse input to the agenda. Despite these problems, networks seem set to remain a significant feature of the policy process; they provide the potential for a more inclusive approach to policy influence and decision-making.

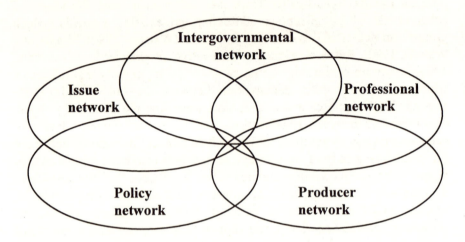

Figure 3.1   Integrated model of PNA

Women's Networking and Networks in the EU

The Research

The research was carried out between February and July 1994 and involved a UK-wide postal survey of national and local women's voluntary organizations aligned to the Women's National Commission, local-authority equality officers, and trade-union equality officers, at both the national and regional levels.[4] The questionnaire was concerned to elicit information on the extent of women's networking and whether women's groups perceived their cooperation as networking. It required respondents to define the issues on which their groups and organizations networked, and whether their network activity was utilizing EU resources.

The questionnaire was followed by a programme of thirty-five semi-structured interviews, balanced between the three types of organization and incorporating representatives at national, regional, and local organizations, across the UK.[5] We were concerned to follow up both negative and positive responses to our questionnaire. A further seven interviews also took place in Brussels with representatives of the European Commission and of four European-level organizations. The purpose of the interviews was to further elicit information on perceptions, and practice, of networking in the European Union.

What Networking Means to Women

The complexities of networks and networking does not lead to an easy analysis of the process of networking, or even a definition of what constitutes a network or networking. However, there was agreement between interviewees on a number of basic network functions. Networks were seen as an effective and efficient means of pooling information, expertise, and other resources. Most interviewees also regarded network involvement as an important source of mutual support and confidence building for participants.

Those organizations that engage in networking do so by a variety of means: sending regular newsletters, having either regular or occasional meetings, telephone contact, conferences, and seminars. For many groups, one or more such activities comprises networking, for others it is just organizational process. For example, a trade-union interviewee who was involved in what may be termed networking by these means explained: 'The term networking is not really used [here]. To me networking represents more informal ways of working together, whereas all our networking is very structured'. Indeed, trade-union respondents showed a distinct suspicion towards the concept of networking. Perhaps it implies behind-the-scenes deals, in preference to more 'upfront' and open decision-making. More significantly, this demonstrated the environmental aspects of networking. Women working in large, hierarchical organizations, where they are underrepresented in policy-making positions, are required to adhere to formal processes and may meet hostility when attempting to address 'women's issues'. In such circumstances, networking may set a dangerous precedent and be disavowed. Thus, it is not surprising to find that women's organizations in the voluntary sector are more likely to define their working with other women's groups as networking (49 per cent), compared to women in trade unions (16 per cent) and local government (18 per cent).

Despite the reticence of some interviewees and survey respondents to concede networking, at least in the formal structures of their organizations, the value of networking was widely acknowledged. In both local authorities and trade unions, networks were seen as a means to increase women's participation in the mainstream of the organization. On issues of policy, respondents in all three types of organization realized the potential of collective lobbying, even if this was limited by membership/constitutions (voluntary sector), the political climate of the organization, or the overwhelming responsibility of service delivery in cash- and staff-restricted times.

In contrast to political organizations in the UK, the European Union, particularly the Commission, has set up networks specifically to elicit information and attempt to reconcile the interests of governments and organizations from all Member States. Commission officials actively seek both to consult representatives of a range of interests and to promote transnational networking between groups with similar interests. This includes promoting networks and networking on equality issues. Indeed, DG V (Employment, Industrial Relations and Social Affairs) houses the Equal Opportunities Unit, while during the period of our research DG X (Information, Communication and Culture) was responsible for the Women's Information Service.[6] Moreover, the Commission, together with the European Parliament, instituted the European Women's Lobby in 1990, specifically to present a gender input to policy considerations. Thus, the EU can be seen to have a proactive view of networking, instituted from the top of the policy process, and women in EU organizations work hard to ensure wide participation from networks throughout the Union.

Women's Policy Networking and the European Union

Most survey respondents who were networking with EU organizations were interested in influencing policy (44 per cent) and trying to obtain funding for projects (33 per cent). Where UK women's organizations and networks were involved in attempting to provide input to EU policy, they were necessarily constrained by the remit of the Union itself. Thus, as Table 2.1 shows, employment and training issues were the most commonly cited by respondents as their targets for action, together with maternity rights and a variety of equal rights issues.

Table 3.1 Rank order of issues taken up in the EU and the UK

		UK			EU		
%	No.	Issue	Rank	Issue	No.	%
49.0	50	Employment/training	1	Employment/training	19	25.7
35.5	36	Violence/harassment	2	Maternity	11	14.9
26.5	27	Pay/pensions	3	Equal rights	10	13.5
26.4	27	Childcare	4	Pay/pensions	9	12.2
18.6	19	Maternity	5	Race/immigration	8	10.8
17.6	18	Women's health	6	Health and safety	5	6.8
9.8	10	Race/immigration	7	Childcare/parental leave	5	6.8
5.8	6	Health and safety	8	Violence/harassment	4	5.4

All the issues that women were pursuing at the EU level were those with which the Union was particularly concerned at the time of our research. Thus, women's networks may have been responding to, rather than influencing, the policy agenda. On the other hand, the broadening of policy to include, for example, maternity rights and parental leave, has occurred in response to women's political pressure, and to evidence that, despite a steady increase in women's involvement in waged work over the past twenty years, the labour market has remained segregated by gender whilst women's pay and working conditions continue to lag behind those of men (Maruani, 1992; Commission, 1993). Where policy issues, such as violence against women and women's health, are not on the EU agenda, groups obviously concentrate their efforts in the UK.

In addition to the limitations imposed by EU policy competencies, lack of resources inevitably prevented many women's groups from participating in transnational networks. Moreover, our survey data indicated either a lack of awareness of EU institutions and business, or a reluctance to use the EU even within its policy competencies. For example, there was a strongly expressed opinion amongst local-authority interviewees, also evident among interviewees from other groups, that the mobility provisions of the Single European Act (SEA) did not extend to black and Asian women, and that subsequent moves to harmonize EU immigration policy would prove seriously detrimental to these groups. However, these issues were of concern to EU policy-makers, and several studies had been funded by the Commission during the period when the SEA was under consideration (de Troy, 1987; Henriksen et al., 1987; Hecq et al., 1990). Nevertheless, despite some very positive feelings towards the EU and its processes, mainly from larger organizations like the trade unions and some national women's organizations, there tended to be an essentially negative attitude regarding EU institutions, their purpose, and how to access the resources available to support transnational networking by groups.

The pattern of networking in the EU was not uniform throughout the three sectors surveyed. Indeed, Figure 2.2 shows uneven pathways available to the sectors for linking into EU channels. In the voluntary sector most contact with the EU is through umbrella organizations dealing with specific issues or through the National Alliance of Women's Organisations (NAWO), an organization having direct links with the European Women's Lobby (EWL). While the NAWO interviewee considered that the four UK representatives on the EWL enjoyed 'quite a strong influence' in the Lobby, the representatives themselves complained that their work, and even their ability to attend regularly in Brussels, was impeded by lack of resources. Moreover, interviewees from NAWO member organizations felt that they were not being informed about issues or about the Lobby's activities.

Similarly, local-authority networking at the EU level was hindered by the dearth of pathways to the EU. For example, the Women's Local Authority Network (WLAN), the umbrella organization of local authority women's committees, is not a full member of NAWO and has no voting rights. Thus, although it is possible for individual organizations to contact EU networks directly, most local-authority women's networks tended to do so only to obtain funding, an experience that was judged to be depressing. As one local-authority officer explained:

> It is difficult for our officers, with very few resources, to see how we can tap into Europe . . . I'm unsure what we are supposed to be getting out of Europe . . . we are on the fringe of European networking due to lack of resources.

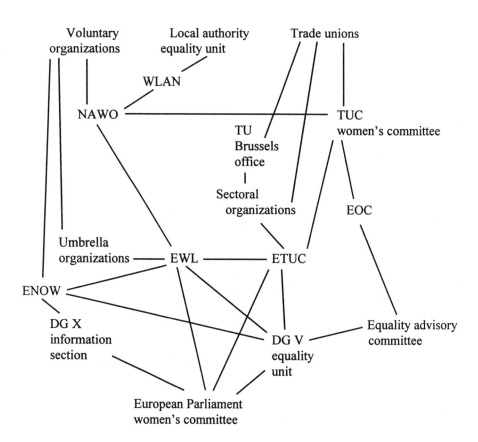

Figure 3.2 goes here — diagram with the following labels:

Voluntary organizations, Local authority equality unit, Trade unions, WLAN, NAWO, TU Brussels office, TUC women's committee, Sectoral organizations, EOC, Umbrella organizations, EWL, ETUC, ENOW, DG X information section, DG V equality unit, Equality advisory committee, European Parliament women's committee

Key: DG V   EU Directorate General V Employment, Industrial Relations and
             Social Affairs
     DG X   EU Directorate General X Information, Communication and Culture
     EOC   Equal Opportunities Commission
     ENOW   European Network of Women
     ETUC   European Trades Union Congress
     EWL   European Women's Lobby
     NAWO   National Alliance of Women's Organizations
     WLAN   Women's Local Authority Network

Figure 3.2 Pathways to the European Union: women's networking

In comparison, three local-authority interviewees had worked positively within EU networks: two being involved in successful, and innovative, transnational networks associated with the New Opportunities for Women programme; and a third emphasizing the quality of research funded by the Commission, in particular that produced by the European Network of Women.[7]

When local-authority and voluntary-sector groups demonstrated positive attitudes towards the EU, or transnational networking, it tended to be where they had joined with specific networks, such as the Migrants Forum or the Maternity Alliance. Generally though, in the instance of both local-authority and women's voluntary-sector networks, it appears that the initiation of national 'umbrella' networks may tend to inhibit direct access to the EU, creating a dependency that explains groups' lack of awareness of EU processes or participation in networking. In turn, this must impact on the issues that are considered at EU level. If lobbying activity is dominated by particularly proactive groups, the potential for widespread radical change to the agenda is limited. Moreover, the remit of the EWL is very much determined by the Commission's existing agenda, this in itself indicating the parameters for lobbying activity at national level.

While these concerns remain, our survey, by utilizing the inclusive model of PNA, elicited the influence of women's network activity on incorporating interests to mainstream policy. Even limited network access by grass-roots groups can effect influence, and our survey showed that 'elite' EU women's networks, for example, the EWL, the Women's Committee of the European Trades Union Congress (ETUC), and the Equal Opportunities Unit of DG V, worked hard to incorporate a variety of groups' work and views to their policy commitments.

In the case of trade-union equality officers, there has been a considerable shift in orientation towards the EU policy process. Perhaps much of this is due to the status of trade-union representatives in Europe as 'social partners', in marked contrast to their marginalization in the UK. It may reflect the fact that much EU policy is concerned with issues of direct concern to trade unions. For whatever reason, trade-union interviewees were far more aware of the growing significance of EU policy to their members, and of the potential for EU legislation to supersede domestic UK legislation. As one trade unionist commented: '[The EU] has been the only avenue for antidiscrimination activities, it has been the only course for British women . . . we have always been proactive in Europe. I feel that we have to be involved . . .'. In the majority of cases, EU-focused networks were associated with the formal channels indicated in Figure 2.2: the Trade

Union Congress Women's Committee, the ETUC, and various European sectoral organizations. Several interviewees also mentioned close links with MEPs sponsored by their union, whilst, in the case of the General and Municipal Boilermakers Union interviewee, the Union's office in Brussels was very highly valued as a source of up-to-date information on EU policy issues. The significance of EU orientation of trade-union interviewees should not be overestimated, however. Contact with EU networks is not necessarily indicative of the ability to influence policy; nor does it indicate the development of transnational networks between grass-roots members. Our evidence suggests that trade-union European networks are the domain of a small number of highly articulate and effective national officers, and that channels to the EU for smaller, grass-roots networks are as difficult to navigate from within trade unions as elsewhere.

While it is possible that the positive attitudes towards the EU shown by trades union interviewees reflect relative ease of access to the EU level, and the relevance of EU policy concerns to this sector, the EU is not only concerned with legislation on work. Indeed, the European Commission actively encourages and funds research into issues of, for example, women's poverty throughout the EU (ENOW, 1993), 'solo women' in Europe (Commission, 1992), black and migrant women in the EU (European Parliament, 1995). These broader concerns suggest the encouragement and inclusion of networks whose interests are not primarily work oriented. In these circumstances, the availability of access channels to the EU is unlikely to be the only factor influencing the pattern of EU networking demonstrated by UK women's groups.

Barriers to Effective EU Networking by Women's Networks

In addition to organizational, political, and economic obstacles to women's policy networking, it is perhaps the complex policy environment of the EU itself that provides many barriers to lobbying by women's networks. As Mazey and Richardson (1992, p. 105) suggest, successful lobbying on EU policy requires simultaneous efforts at national and EU level. This would involve coordinated actions with like-minded groups across several Member States. While we found examples of this, in relation to maternity rights and childcare, it occurs relatively rarely.

Geographical distance from the EU is a further factor that, combined with lack of finance and a consequent want of personnel, creates a physical barrier to greater EU networking. Ironically, this is the case even where such networking is initiated in an attempt to obtain funding. Such distance would limit not only direct contact with the EU but may result in an alienation from the processes that could otherwise work to benefit the groups concerned. Ultimately, therefore, many UK women's groups are concentrating their limited resources on lobbying their government.

The dearth of women at the senior levels of the EU has also been noted as a potential inhibitor of women's network activity ('EU promises to tackle sex bias', *The Guardian*, 4 September 1994; Hoskyns, 1994). Women's networks within EU organizations have been campaigning vigorously, with some success, for greater representation of women on the European Commission and in the Parliament.[8] However, the continuing deficit of women representatives is perhaps not as dangerous for women's political activity as is the lack of women at the senior levels of the bureaucracy. For example, under the Fourth Positive Action Programme, policy issues specific to such groups as women are intended to be mainstreamed throughout EU policies and programmes. This will be difficult to effect without sufficient women in senior positions to facilitate and monitor mainstreaming. In other words, it is possible for the EU to promote 'women's issues' and networking whilst perpetuating a situation that prevents full effectiveness. On the other hand, the relative disinterest in women in the EU can be beneficial to the small numbers of women working in the EU on equality issues. As one woman official told us: 'we've got freedom which is proportional to the disinterest of the structures in which we are working for women'. By admitting private sphere issues into the policy arena, even, as originally occurred, on a peripheral basis, the EU opened the door to a relatively small number of women to be influential.

The underrepresentation of women at the senior levels of the EU impinges not just on access to policy-making processes *per se*, but on the availability of relevant and accurate information about the EU, its work, future policy proposals, and methods of involvement. This may be a particular problem in the UK where public awareness about the EU appears to be low, and press and ministerial disinformation, or perhaps selective information release, contributes to a negative image of the EU. The European Commission has only one designated women's unit, the

Equal Opportunities Unit in DG V, and the General Public Unit in DG X is responsible for distributing the Women of Europe Newsletter. This means that relatively few women are responsible for gathering information of concern to women and disseminating it throughout the Member States. In consequence, the paucity, or patchwork pattern, of information about Europe, and its benefits to women, is likely to remain a problem.

Of course, the onus for distributing information does not fall singularly on the EU institutions. Much of this must necessarily fall to women within organizations in the Member States themselves. However, we have discussed above how groups can be marginalized within the European-focused networks. Thus, local-authority women's groups, through their affiliate status in NAWO, are not directly known within the EU and may miss information of relevance to them. Moreover, if European Officers within local authorities are unaware of the specific implications for women of their European policy and/or funding proposals, they will not necessarily pass on, or request, relevant information for women within the authority. Here it is interesting to note that, despite increased use of European Officers by UK local authorities, only 9.5 per cent of local-authority respondents reported using their services when dealing with the EU. In the voluntary sector, too, interviewees complained of poor access to information. One explained: 'I am dependent on NAWO giving us information but I don't really get a sense of what the Women's Lobby is actually doing'.

Even where groups may be aware of the potential benefits that the EU offers, the relationship between the UK government and the EU appears to inhibit EU-focused networking. The UK government has a record of 'opting out' of EU measures, such as the Social Charter, that would serve to benefit women in the workplace and on retirement. More generally, the government's actions on limiting the scope of EU decisions in Britain are well documented. For example, it is not unknown for ministers to drag their feet over provision of matched funding for projects won by organizations in the UK. It is not surprising, therefore, to find that many respondents perceived EU lobbying to be a waste of effort, due to the likelihood that the UK government would veto, or fail to implement, decisions, or refuse to provide the matched resources for implementation should their efforts prove successful.

Breaking through the Boundaries?

Clearly women's policy networks can be located in the mainstream of policy-network analysis, showing elite networks, or policy communities and professional networks, within the EU, and between the EU and national organizations in the UK. While it cannot be denied that the networks closest to, and those that include, the ranks of legislators will have more power of influence and more chance of affecting outcomes, the manner in which national organizations work with the more local groups to define, signify, and prioritize policy issues, and then organize to carry them through the policy process, negates the elitism inherent in PNA. Thus, the diverse and complex nature of issue networks is not excluded: unequal resource patterns are assimilated as each group contributes its own unique resources of contacts, expertise, enthusiasm, and commitment, as well as material resources; as the groups move in and out of the network, the exchanges and the lobbying/policy work continue.

There can be no doubt that women are networking in a range of policy areas. However, considering the extent of network activity within the UK, this activity is not necessarily being transferred to EU policy arenas. On the other hand, where women are networking in the EU, they are utilizing the institutions at all levels. Thus, while women's networks within the institutions of the EU are able to lobby MEPs and Commissioners, national and local groups within the UK are working together and with the 'upper-echelon' networks to achieve their policy and policy-related objectives.

Our understanding of the relative effectiveness of, and relationship between, women's networks in different contexts may be enhanced through examination of Atkinson and Coleman's assertion (1992, p. 165) that networks cannot be understood outside their political environment. Of particular relevance are the macro and meso-levels; that is the level of the EU, and the level of the organization in which the network operates.

Clearly of significance for women's networks is the meso-level wherein networks exist within larger organizations such as local authorities and trade unions. First, the differences between types of organization need to be adjusted if women are to fully exploit their potential for change through the range of their needs and interests, and the potential numbers on which they should be able to rely for a mass-support base. Thus Figure 2.2 indicates gaps in communication and activity not just between trade unions, who appear to occupy their own exclusive route to the EU, and others, but between local and national women's organizations. For example, an important linking role in the voluntary sector might have been played by the local-authority women's groups. However, this role has been diminished as a result of their precarious status within local authorities, themselves undergoing a continuous legislative and financial onslaught, and is exacerbated by their primarily negative attitude towards the EU.

The organizations within which women's groups exist may also fail to provide the environment in which their work can develop and prosper. For example, networking is a key concept in the EU, but the trade unions appear less than willing to condone, and therefore engage in, such activity. There is no doubt that they are highly involved in Europe, but they are also extremely hierarchical and inflexible. Despite the presence of many women's networks implemented to encourage the participation of women in individual trade unions, such as the Manufacturing, Science and Finance (MSF) Union's 'Women into Power', there is continued hostility to the idea of policy networks within the unions. Moreover, even with the changing pattern of work and the workforce, women's issues are still low on trade-union agendas and, therefore, unlikely to be represented in the EU. However, our research has found that the trade unions are a significant locus for women's political activism and will become more so as unions recognize women's presence in the workforce. Organizational context may also be significant in local authorities, where not only are women's policy networks dependent to some extent on the authority's attitude to the EU but to gender issues generally. Indeed, it is interesting to note that more trade unions are instituting internal women's support networks just as local authorities are terminating women's committees. Given the extent to which organizational structures, attitudes, and processes affect the role and efficacy of women's policy networks, it is perhaps not surprising that women's voluntary groups are the most willing of the sectors studied to overtly participate in and institute networks, and to define their activities as networking.

We remain convinced that women's networking accords with the inclusive model we have advocated and provides the potential both for influencing policy and for broadening the policy agenda. Nevertheless, there is a need to strengthen network links both with and between the three sectors we have investigated. Here it is of interest to note that implementation of the Fourth Medium-Term Action Programme will focus upon 'exchange, development and transfer of information and experience on good practice' (Commission, 1996b, Art. 4.1(a)). First priority for funding support will be accorded to projects at the local, regional, and national levels that (Commission, 1996c, p. 2):

> make provision for the participation of more than one partner, in particular the social partners, non-governmental organizations and especially women's organizations and local authorities.

At the macro level, as far as the EU is concerned, the environment for women's networks is a positive one. The Commission, in particular, actively encourages networking and is anxious to be seen to promote equality issues, especially gender. Moreover, the record of women MEPs in ensuring that EU equality Directives are implemented also encourages the development of women's networks. Hence, Mazey and Richardson's (1992, p. 100) assertion that issue networks will be more readily welcomed and successful in the EU.

A question remains concerning the extent to which women's networks influence the policy agenda, or whether their networking activities concur with existing policy parameters. Certainly, the EU policy remit is not exhaustive and tends to concentrate on traditional public-sphere legislative issues. Thus Hoskyns (1994, p. 227) contends that 'EC law itself therefore reinforces the public–private divide which has classically served to disadvantage women'. However, the EU gives explicit acknowledgement to the 'private' sources of women's public-sphere inequality. Unlike many other policy-making systems, the interests of women are not taken for granted, nor are their policy preferences taken as given. Rather the European Commission encourages research on a wide range of issues in specific relation to women throughout Europe, and is supportive of, and accommodating to, women's network activities. Indeed, the boundary between the public and private spheres may be seen to waver, in the EU context, in areas where women's policy networking has extended the parameters of the public sphere to include issues that were previously a matter of individual or family redress. Thus, childcare and parental leave are added to the agenda, as is the feminization of poverty, and the manner in which generic policy affects specific groups unequally. Indeed, women's networks within the EU have tended to illustrate that a real and sustainable divide between public and private is a political, rather than a natural, construct.

Notes

1   One of our interviewees demonstrated this when she highlighted the Common Agricultural Policy (CAP) as a key EU policy competence with no relevance to women in the UK, thus negating the relationship between the CAP and food price and availability.

2   Peterson (1992, p. 246) notes in his study of a European technology network that the multitude of actors contributing to research and development represent 'interests . . . far too diffuse to fit the policy community typology'. Indeed, Marsh and Rhodes (1992, p. 253) note that of the case studies included in their book on PNA, whilst authors recognize the existence of issue networks, none of the authors consider them to any further extent.

3   However, this issue is specifically addressed by the Fourth Medium-Term Action Programme (Commission, 1996b), which includes as its first principle 'integration of the equal opportunities for men and women dimension in all policies and activities (mainstreaming)'.

4   See Table 2.2.

Table 3.2 Questionnaire response rates by organizational type

Organization	No.	%
Local government	74	40.7
Women's voluntary	48	26.4
Trade union national	29	15.9
Trade union regional	31	17.0
Total	182	100.0

5   We would like to extend our thanks to Joe Cook, for her able undertaking of the interviews.

6   This has since become a General Public Unit.

7   ENOW is an independent network based in Brussels, comprising women's groups across the EU. It sometimes has its research on issues affecting women throughout the EU funded by the Commission.

8   The Equal Opportunities Unit of DG V, together with the EWL and the Committee on Women's Rights of the European Parliament, worked hard to ensure that women were represented within the Commission, and, since 1994, five women Commissioners have sat in that august place.

References

Atkinson, M.M. and Coleman, W.D. (1992), 'Political Networks, Policy Communities and the Problems of Governance', *Governance*, vol. 5, pp. 154–80.

Bennett, R.J. and Krebs, G. (1994), 'Local Economic Development Partnerships: an Analysis of Policy Networks in EC-LEDA Local Employment Development Strategies', *Regional Studies*, vol. 28, pp. 119–40.

Bennington, J. and Harvey, J. (1994), 'Spheres or Tiers? The Significance of Transnational Local Authority Networks', in P. Dunleavy and J. Stanyer (eds.), *Contemporary Political Studies 1994*, Political Studies Association of the United Kingdom, Belfast.

Commission of the European Communities (1990), *The Impact of the Completion of the Internal Market on Women in the European Community*, Commission for the European Communities, Brussels.

Commission of the European Communities (1992), 'The Socio-economic Situation of Solo Women in Europe', *Women of Europe Supplements*, no. 41.

Commission of the European Communities (1993), 'Occupational Segregation of Women and Men in the European Community', *Social Europe Supplement*, no. 3/93.

Commission of the European Communities (1996a), *Incorporating Equal Opportunities for Women and Men into All Community Policies and Activities. Communication from the Commission*, COM(96) 67 final (21.2.96), Office for Official Publications of the European Communities, Luxembourg.

Commission of the European Communities (1996b), *Fourth Medium-Term Community Action Programme on Equal Opportunities for Women and Men (1996–2000)*, V/231b/96, Commission of the European Communities, Brussels.

Commission of the European Communities (1996c), *Implementation of the Council Decision on 22 December 1995 on the Medium-Term Community Action Programme on Equal Opportunities for Men and Women (1996–2000)*, V/638/96, Commission of the European Communities, Brussels.

Dahlerup, D. (ed.) (1986), *The New Women's Movement. Feminism and Political Power in Europe and the USA*, Sage Publications, London.

Eisenstein, H. (1990), 'Femocrats, Official Feminism and the Uses of Power', in S. Watson (ed.), *Playing the State. Australian Feminist Interventions*, Verso, London.

ENOW [European Network of Women] (1993), *Effective Intervention into the Poverty and Exclusion of Women*, European Network of Women, Brussels.

European Parliament (1995), *Confronting the Fortress: Black and Migrant Women in the European Union*, European Parliament, European Women's Lobby, Brussels.

Grant, W., Paterson, W., and Whitson, C. (1988), *Government and the Chemical Industry. A Comparative Study of Britain and West Germany*, Clarendon Press, Oxford.

Gray, C. (1994), *Government beyond the Centre: Sub-national Politics in Britain*, Macmillan, London.

Hecq, C., Plasman, O., and Meulders, D. (1990), *La mobilité Européene de travailleurs feminins dans la Communauté*, Commission of the European Communities, Brussels.

Henriksen, I., Holt, H., and Knudsen, R. (1987), *Migrant Women in the European Community with Particular Reference to their Working Lives*, Commission of the European Communities, Brussels.

Hoskyns, C. (1994), 'Gender Issues in International Relations: the Case of the European Communities', *Review of International Studies*, vol. 20, pp. 225–39.

Marsh, D. and Rhodes, R.A.W. (eds.) (1992), *Policy Networks in British Government*, Clarendon Press, Oxford.

Maruani, M. (1992), *The Position of Women on the Labour Market of the European Community 1983–1990*, Commission of the European Communities, Brussels.

Mazey, S.P. and Richardson, J.J. (1992), 'British Pressure Groups in the European Community: the Challenge of Brussels', *Parliamentary Affairs*, vol. 45, pp. 92–107.

Peterson, J. (1992), 'The European Technology Community: Policy Networks in a Supranational Setting', in D. Marsh and R.A.W. Rhodes (eds.), *Policy Networks in British Government*, Clarendon Press, Oxford, pp. 226–48.

Pillinger, J. (1992), *Feminising the Market: Women's Pay and Employment in the European Community*, The Macmillan Press, Basingstoke.

Pringle, R. and Watson, S. (1992), '"Women's Interests" and the Post-structuralist State', in M. Barrett and A. Phillips (eds.), *Destablilizing Theory. Contemporary Feminist Debates*, Polity Press, Cambridge, pp. 53–73.

Rhodes, R.A.W. (1990), 'Policy Networks: a British Perspective', *Journal of Theoretical Politics*, vol. 2, pp. 293–317.

Saward, M. (1992), 'The Civil Nuclear Network in Britain', in D. Marsh and R.A.W. Rhodes (eds.), *Policy Networks in British Government*, Clarendon Press, Oxford, pp. 75–99.

Troy, C. de (1987), *Migrant Women and Employment*, Commission of the European Communities, Brussels.

Watson, S. (1990), 'The State of Play: an Introduction', in S. Watson (ed.), *Playing the State: Australian Feminist Interventions*, Verso, London.

Wilks, S. and Wright, M. (eds.) (1987), *Comparative Government–Industry Relations. Western Europe, the United States, and Japan*, Clarendon Press, Oxford.

PART III
WORK, WELFARE STATES, AND EQUAL OPPORTUNITIES

4 Work–Family Arrangements: the Role of the State versus the Role of the Private Sector

ANNEKE VAN DOORNE-HUISKES

Introduction

In their publications, the European Union and the Organisation for Economic Co-operation and Development (OECD) plead for structural changes in society in order to create more social equality between men and women. According to the OECD and the EU, the main issues for these alteration processes to deal with are the compatibility between family responsibility and labour-market participation and the sharing of roles between men and women. To achieve these shared roles, it is necessary for the so-called 'social contract' to be abolished. This social contract, which refers to a gendered division of tasks between men and women, seems to be present to a substantial degree in Europe. In households, some developments have taken place in the direction of more equality between men and women, although women have predominantly retained the primary responsibility for unpaid household work all over Europe. Persistent inequality between men and women still exists in the labour market. The latter manifests itself, for example, in the issue of occupational segregation and the resulting inequality in wages between the sexes.

Essentially, equality between men and women seems to be largest in those countries where minimum-wage regulations are strong and public facilities for the care of children and the elderly are highly developed. This raises the question whether, in terms of social status, women have attained better positions in countries where work–family arrangements are part of state policies, compared to countries where work–family arrangements are primarily seen as the responsibility of companies and firms; empirical evidence seems to support this (*Bulletin on Women and Employment in the EU*, 1994, no. 5; Den Dulk et al., 1996). According to the 1995 gender-related development index (UNDP, 1995), the socio-economic positions of women and men show the least inequality in the Scandinavian countries. These countries are characterized by an extended network of public-care facilities or work–family arrangements, which facilitate the combination of paid and unpaid work. Childcare and (paid-) leave provisions are part of these arrangements. Despite the evidence of a relationship between public-care facilities and the extent of (in)equality between women and men, it is unlikely that these facilities in all European countries will be expanded to the level that exists in, for example, the Scandinavian countries. This is due to different European welfare-state traditions. Further, the welfare state is under pressure from international economic developments and increasing competition. Does this signify that, in spite of the appeal from the OECD and the EU, public arrangements in relation to work–family issues gradually will disappear and that the social inequality between the sexes will increase rather than decrease?

In answering this question a simple yes or no will not suffice. Among other conditions, it depends on what will happen at the level of firms and companies. It is clear that, under the influence of economic and social shifts in the whole of the West, significant alterations are being established in the organization of labour. These alterations involve both opportunities and threats for women (and men). Such opportunities include the possibility that private enterprises in the near future will take more responsibilities for work–family arrangements than they generally have so far. Such arrangements could well be regarded as an increasingly important part of a more general personnel policy that aims to optimize the utilization of human resources for organizations and firms. The more companies are able to integrate work–family arrangements into their personnel policy, the greater the chances of more socio-economic equality between men and women. An important issue, however, is to which social class these facilities will be accessible. More equality between men and women with higher qualifications is likely to occur in conjunction with an increase in inequality between women themselves.

An Active and More Balanced Society: Messages from the OECD and the EU

In their report, *Shaping Cultural Change. The Role of Women* (1991), OECD experts plead for an active society that goes beyond attempts to achieve full employment or increased labour-force participation. The experts regard participation in the labour force as only one of the methods through which this active society can take shape. Besides, they point out, it is necessary to recognize and acknowledge the social and economic values of non-market forms of activity. Enhancing the compatibility between domestic and employment responsibilities in the lives of individuals constitutes, according to the OECD experts, one of the most important challenges in the process of structural change. To make these structural changes possible, the current 'social contract' must be abolished. This social contract consists of two components: the so-called gender contract and the employment contract. Both these 'contracts' define the current division of family and labour-market roles. The concept of contract refers to generally accepted social norms, according to which many men and women organize their lives. From the point of view of this book, these gender and employment contracts are social constructions that maintain the traditional division of tasks between men and women, as well as the split between the public, predominantly male, domain and the private, predominantly female, domain. In the gender contract, women are charged with the bulk of family care and domestic functions. In the employment contract, men are ascribed the primary responsibility for the family's economic and financial well-being. The persistence of this social contract leads to both underutilization of women in the world of paid labour and underutilization of men in the world of care. One of the most important current challenges, according to the OECD experts, is to change this traditional public–private split and to accomplish institutional changes that would abolish contradictions and tensions between the household and employment structures. The experts expect that the rewards of such changes will not accrue exclusively to women. Men's life choices will also be enhanced, and society as a whole can expect to benefit from such an integrated policy strategy.

Through which measures should this active society be achieved? The advice offered on this subject by the OECD report is formulated in a relatively open manner and has no, or no explicit, address. Keywords are:

flexibility in working time per day, per week, per year, per career; childcare facilities and other facilities for family care; amendment to the occupational chances of women through expansion of educational possibilities; upgrading female occupations and building career paths; the acknowledgement of the social and economic value of unpaid labour, including voluntary work; the abandonment of one standard form of employment (the full-time job) and promotion of equitable treatment for workers in non-standard employment; more scope for choice and mobility between non-standard and standard employment; and a social-security regime that increases opportunities and incentives for both social and economic participation. To make all this possible, women's direct representation in economic, social, and political decision-making forums ought to be improved. Finally, the progress of these alteration processes should be carefully monitored.

The Green Paper on social policy, presented by the European Commission at the end of 1993 (Commission of the European Communities, 1993a), points to a broad consensus that women will constitute an increasingly crucial component of the workforce at all levels. Despite this consensus, however, there still seem to be many obstacles to women's participation on equal terms with men, both in employment and society. Again, the gender-based division of family and employment responsibilities is seen as the most important cause of inequality in the labour-market participation of men and women. In order to nullify this gender-based division—the social contract, as exemplified by the OECD, or the public–private split in terms of this book—the Green Paper pleads for a better use of the talents of women and the development of a more balanced society. Three main issues are mentioned in relation to this concept of a more balanced society. First, the reconciliation of employment and family responsibilities. Second, the desegregation of the labour market in vertical and horizontal directions. And third, the increase in women's involvement in decision-making. One of the ten chapters in the White Paper on social policy of the European Union (Commission of the European Communities, 1994) is also devoted to the equal treatment of men and women. The analysis of the problem is identical to that of the Green Paper. In addition, the resolution to reconcile employment and family life has been adopted.

Men and Women in Europe: the Reality of the Social Contract

The Gender Contract

However refined and convincing the different appeals for reconciliation of employment and family life, the reality is that European countries appear to be at considerable distance from such an agreement. Based on international comparison, research conducted into changes in the way men and women spend their time in Denmark, Norway, the Netherlands, the UK, the US, and Canada between 1970 and 1990, reveals, as a consistent pattern, that domestic work has remained primarily a woman's responsibility (European Foundation for the Improvement of of Living and Working Conditions, 1991). During the specified time, men slightly increased their fraction of household work, while women slightly decreased theirs. This decrease is mainly due to a growth in women's participation in the labour market during those years. But in spite of this reduction, the woman's share of the 'real' household work is on average still nearly three times that of men.

At the household level, it seems that it is mainly the arrival of children that leads to a larger inequality in the division of unpaid and paid work between men and women. On par with economic theory, a process of specialization occurs in the division of tasks between partners after the birth of the first child. Women take on a larger share of the unpaid work inside the home, while men take on a larger share of the paid work outside the home. The measure in which such a specialization of tasks develops, however, depends on the institutional arrangements in the different countries. Accordingly, with ample public facilities for the care of children and the elderly, a smaller inequality exists regarding the division of paid and unpaid tasks between men and women in the Scandinavian welfare states than in all other Western countries. This fact gives rise to the hypothesis that, given the present qualitative potential of women in the paid-labour market, extensive public facilities are an indispensable factor in the reconciliation of family life and employment or in bringing about changes in the boundaries between the public and the private sphere, pleaded for by the OECD and the EU. Hence, a dilemma arises in the development of future welfare states: international economic developments, and the consequential increasing competition, result in greater inclination for welfare states to reduce their public domain rather than to enlarge it.

The Employment Contract

The fact that women do a (much) larger share of unpaid work than men is generally regarded as the most important cause of the persistent inequality between men and women in the labour market. This inequality expresses itself, for example, in the subject of wage-level proportions. Table 5.1 reveals that a gap still exists between the hourly earnings of men and women. Changes in these proportions are only achieved very slowly.

Table 4.1   Trends in the gender pay ratio for manual and non-manual workers in industry from 1980 to 1991

	Manual workers			Non-manual workers		
	1980	1985	1991	1980	1985	1991
Belgium	70.25	74.29	75.59	61.90	62.94	65.22
Denmark	86.05	85.83	84.47	n/a	n/a	n/a
Germany	72.37	72.84	73.39	65.98	65.96	67.09
Greece	67.46	78.79	79.18	n/a	64.31	68.54
Spain	n/a	n/a	72.22	n/a	n/a	60.93
France	78.28	80.76	80.25	61.13	62.92	67.16
Ireland	68.70	67.30	69.51	n/a	n/a	n/a
Italy	83.22	82.74	79.30	n/a	69.16	n/a
Luxembourg	64.71	65.92	67.95	49.74	54.16	55.18
Netherlands	73.05	73.56	76.17	59.11	63.64	64.78
Portugal	n/a	n/a	70.78	n/a	n/a	70.71
United Kingdom	69.77	67.09	67.15	54.48	56.25	58.27

Sources: Eurostat *Earnings: Industry and Services* (1992); *Bulletin on Women and Employment in the EU* (1994), no. 5

The differences in wage levels are, by and large, due to the occupational segregation of women and men in the European countries. It is striking that the rising female participation in the European labour market during the last decades has not resulted in a substantial decrease in occupational segregation. Although more women have made their entry into high-level jobs than in the past, they have increased their share in lower-level service and clerical jobs as well (Commission of the European Communities, 1993b). Even in the Nordic countries, which offer, relatively speaking, the best conditions for equality between men and women in terms of labour-market participation, occupational segregation persists. This is particularly due to the fact that many women are employed in the extensive public sector, a characteristic of the structure of the Scandinavian welfare states. What applies to all European countries is that the over-representation of women in the lower-level service and clerical jobs is connected to another characteristic of the female workforce: the high rate of part-time workers and/or a-typical work practices.

Work–Family Arrangements and their Impact on Labour-Force (In)equality between Men and Women

In the introduction to this chapter, it was suggested that in countries where the state takes more responsibility for work–family arrangements, there is less social inequality between the sexes. In recent research on the relation between statutory provisions in childcare and leave arrangements and the degree of inequality between women and men, Den Dulk et al. (1996) concluded that more statutory work–family arrangements are accompanied by less gender inequality in the labour market. It appears that in the EU Member States with more extensive government policy regarding work–family arrangements women have higher labour-participation rates and the wage differences between men and women are smaller. Occupational segregation, however, is less affected by work–family arrangements. The amount of statutory provisions that facilitate the combination of paid and unpaid work, and so contribute to a reconstruction of the traditional public–private split, is strongly connected to the kind of welfare-state model to which countries belong.

In his book, *The Three Worlds of Welfare Capitalism* (1990), Esping-Andersen explicitly elaborates the differences in institutional arrangements in Western welfare states. He perceives three welfare-state regimes, distinguished on the basis of the degree of social inequality in a country, the extent of employment prospects, and the measure in which people are (in)dependent of market forces (decommodification): the liberal, the conservative–corporatistic, and the social-democratic welfare-state regimes respectively. Sociological research practised with a more feminist bearing (Langan and Ostner, 1990; Borchorst, 1991; Plantenga and Van Doorne-Huiskes, 1992; Sainsbury, 1994 and 1996) revealed another important aspect of welfare states: the degree to which it is possible for women to have a livelihood away from or in parallel to the family. Most explicit in this aspect are the social-democratic welfare states, with their aim of complete employment, including for women. To make this possible, the care activities have been largely provided by the public sector. The Scandinavian countries, which predominantly belong to this type of welfare state, are—as mentioned earlier—characterized by an extensive network of childcare, care for the elderly, and care for sick dependants, financed by collective means. In addition, taxation laws underline the economic independence of men *and* women.

Despite egalitarian intentions, equal outcomes between men and women are difficult to achieve, even under these types of institutional arrangements. The Scandinavian labour market has remained highly segregated, as was revealed previously. Langan and Ostner (1991) put this in the context of a 'universalisation of a female social service economy'. It is women, paid women, who service other women to enable the latter to go out to work. The consequence of this female density in the service sector is that men experience relatively little competition from women in the private sector.

Within the so-called conservative–corporatistic welfare states, more importance is attached to family life than to the careers of women. If and when women are (temporarily) unable to work outside the home, compensation for foregone wages is provided via breadwinner facilities and other measures by way of taxation policy and social security. Men are primarily assigned to the role of breadwinner, while women are primarily responsible for the unpaid work in the home. Childcare facilities are available, but these are usually not adequate enough to sustain a full-time occupation of women. On the basis of role division between men and women, the Netherlands can be classified as this type of welfare state.

The UK and the US are liberal welfare states. Faith in the operation of the free market is substantial. Women and men are in principle treated as equals, without any attention being given to the current differences between the sexes with regard to their care duties. Accordingly, there are few public facilities to enhance the possibility of combining care and paid work. Even so, the number of women with an occupation is high, due to the fact that households often need a dual income. This demands a certain amount of organization in the private sphere, in which informal (family) networks play a substantial role. Of additional importance are the facilities offered by labour organizations.

Welfare States under Pressure

Research has shown that, given the current division between paid and unpaid work, on the economic front, women benefit greatly from a high degree of government intervention. Public-care facilities and systems of labour-market regulation seem to constitute a relatively favourable arena for equal pay (European Network of Experts on the Situation of Women on the Labour Market, 1994). This means the current public–private split, represented by a traditional division of the public, male, domain of paid work and the private, female, domain of unpaid work, is challenged most in those countries where the state has taken responsibility for organizing and financing work–family arrangements. But this is only part of the story. In general, it is true that gender inequality in the labour market is lower in countries where more public provisions are available to facilitate the combination of paid and unpaid work. The division of unpaid work, however, is still unequal, even in countries with an extended network of public care. Unpaid work in the household seems to be influenced far less by the nature of welfare-state regimes than are the patterns of paid work (e.g. Van Doorne-Huiskes, 1997). The reconstruction of the public–private split requires more than just publicly financed work–family arrangements. Public work–family arrangements seem to be a necessary, but not a sufficient, condition for the reconstruction of the boundaries between the private and the public spheres. In this respect, future developments in European countries, in which deregulation and reduction of public facilities are central issues, give reason for concern.

Changes in the Organization of Labour and the Possible Future of Work–Family Arrangements

Flexibility and Polarization

In the organization of labour, there are important developments that show a high degree of mutual resemblance and that will highly influence the lives of men and women. The distribution of know-how in the world, consequently, leads to an intensification of international competition and thus to an additional necessity to supply high-quality products. Even the products of organizations not directly connected to the market—state departments, hospitals, and law enforcement organizations—have to meet increasingly stringent demands. Intensification of competition leads to more economic use of materials. The gain in quality ought to be executed in a manner such that the amount of materials used in the process hardly increases. It thus stands to reason that corporations are focusing their attention on the execution of core activities. The remaining work is to a large extent covered by the supply industry and subcontractors, so that any fluctuations in the market can be relayed to this sector.

This has consequences for the workforce, which can be felt in the pressure to deregulate employment contracts and make them more flexible. These trends are not only occurring in the private sector. Similar developments are taking place in the public sector, which employs relatively more women in nearly all European countries. Trends towards flexibilization and deregulation have polarizing consequences. Apart from a circle of employees who belong to the core of the business and for whom a high degree of employment certainty, social security, and possible work–family facilities are available, the section of the population with only a low level of job security is steadily rising. For this part of the workforce it is highly unlikely that organizations will fund the provision of childcare facilities, (paid-) leave arrangements, and other sorts of work–family arrangements.

How Shifts in the Global Economy Affect Jobs and Careers

Moss Kanter (1993) reveals an interesting insight into the way fluctuations in the global economy will affect jobs and careers. Her attention is mainly focused on the higher-educated professionals. Recent 'downsizing' tendencies are rapidly reducing the 'overstaffing' factor, a striking characteristic of the large bureaucratic organizations in the 1970s and part of the 1980s. The demand for external suppliers for internal services will grow. This also applies to the demand for overtime from existing staff. Less job security is coupled with an increase in overload. Corporations will aim more and more towards a horizontal structure. The vertical chain of command, within which people need to be promoted in order to increase their status, compensation, and influence, has been diminishing. More work is being done in cross-functional or cross-departmental project teams. Employees will be strongly encouraged, more so than in the past, to concentrate on horizontal mobility and to acquire an attitude of including other branches and sections in their perspective. In addition to this move towards a horizontal structure, there is development towards greater diversity. Women and minorities have increasingly gained access to positions in which they were formerly rarely encountered. This applies in both the US and in European countries, although in varying degree. Diversity is regarded, at least in management literature, as a positive condition for the quality of corporations. Disregarding the possibility that managers may or may not experience this in a similar fashion in daily practice, a shift towards a more diversified workforce, given social and demographic developments in all Western countries, seems inevitable. Because hierarchies are being de-emphasized, formal authority will make way for an authority based on professional expertise. In addition, the rapport between the employees and their corporations will change. The identification with the company will diminish; the identification with their own profession or own project-team will increase. This will induce, according to Moss Kanter, a new career asset: from organizational to reputational capital. The 'new employee' does not primarily rely on the organization, but more so on his own set of portable skills.

The Necessity of Quality: Towards a New Type of Employer?

Schwartz (1989) establishes that in the case of the US, the careers of female managers have a more problematic character than those of males. Women interrupt their careers more often, or settle for a position on a lower level than their qualifications should render. This increases the costs and risks to employers of assigning women to managerial positions. This in turn gives a greater opportunity for men to occupy interesting functions and to be promoted. These facts cause a severe loss of talent. This reduction in talent is relayed to the corporations that do not fully utilize their human talent. This loss also shows in the individual lives of women who, in view of this, do not expand their talents to the full potential. Schwartz pleads for a differentiation in the approach to women and for a policy that acknowledges the entitlement of female employees to motherhood. Men are not emphatically mentioned in her argument.

The advice given by Schwartz to companies is to distinguish between what she calls 'career-primary' women and 'career-and-family' women. The first category of women give high priority to a career and are prepared to sacrifice much of their personal life for it. It is important, however, that companies are not guided by prejudices and that women do receive every chance to develop their talents. The majority of the women, however, those in the managerial positions included, will want to start a family and be actively involved in the upbringing of children. If these women are pressured, by means of exacting, inflexible, and rigid work schedules, to make a choice between work or family, and so between the public and the private sphere, then there is a question of loss. To avoid this loss, some form of flexibility is recommended. For example, the flexibility to work at home, to be able to take a, temporary, part-time job or to temporarily continue the career on a job-sharing basis. In addition, childcare needs to be established, either on the corporation level or with assistance from the local authorities. In a country where half the working population consists of women, the question whether companies should be involved in the private lives of their employees is, according to Schwartz, no longer a philosophical and abstract question, but simply a practical necessity. Employers can not afford to ignore social developments. A proactive approach demands an adaptation to developments and thus a reaping of the rewards.

Although Schwartz' argument mainly concerns women, her visions of making the careers of managers more flexible and of facilitating work–family arrangements can be extrapolated to a more general level. This general level is more explicitly elaborated in a study about the 'family-friendly employer', conducted under the auspices of the European Community (Hogg and Harker, 1992), in which the necessity of reconciliation of employment and family responsibilities is mentioned. Such reconciliation is not only a task for men and women in the domain of the households, but also one for governments and corporations.

Various European companies are acquainted with programmes which face the fact that a high percentage of the employees have other activities beside their careers. These programmes include many reoccurring themes. They can be distinguished by two facets: measures that specify the hours of work and the locations where this should be conducted, and those measures that offer assistance with the caring for children and/or (elderly) family members. Examples of family-friendly working practices are summarized in Table 5.2.

A publication that came out in 1994 mentions UK employer initiatives: working examples of family-friendly and equal opportunity policies (Parents at Work, 1994). This research involved forty-six organizations, from both the public and the private sector. The employers listed in the report cover roughly 600,000 employees. The report gives a positive and encouraging view of what steps these British corporations are undertaking in terms of equal-opportunity policies. However, it concerns only a specific selection of UK employers. A representative sample would reveal a substantially less hopeful image. This does not alter the fact that publications on this issue can serve as important examples for other labour organizations.

The *BMW Modell für Beruf und Familie* (BMW Model for Work and Family) is an example of a family-friendly policy in Germany. With the view that life has more dimensions than mere work alone and the fact that this concerns men in increasing measures, this model is presented by BMW in a glossy brochure. BMW organizes the possibility of a *Familienpause* (family break) that stretches across a number of years of a person's career. People who want to make use of this must have been employed by the company for at least three years. In addition, the employees are requested to stay in contact with the company during the period of leave and must be prepared to follow courses and undertake training to brush up on their qualifications, so that the return to work will pass off easily. The maximum period one can take as career break amounts to ten years. During this period there are a number of occasions when the person in question consults with the company whether a return to work is in order or if the career break will be extended. Apart from possibilities of leave, BMW assists in the search for adequate childcare facilities. Finally, the possibility of a temporary reduction of working hours is offered, to a minimum of nineteen hours per week.

Table 4.2   Family-friendly working practices

Flexibilization of time and location

- Possibilities for employees to vary the starting and finishing time of their working hours, within a certain timespan and with a block of compulsory hours (flexitime).
- Possibilities to work at home ('flexiplace' and teleworking).
- Possibilities to temporarily interrupt careers, with the entitlement to return to the company but with the obligation to follow courses during periods of leave in order to keep professional knowledge and skills at a required level.
- Possibilities to work part-time on a temporary or permanent basis, even in functions concerning coordinating and managerial responsibilities. A minimum of, for example, twenty-eight or thirty-two hours can be agreed on.
- Possibilities for job-sharing, even in management functions.
- Possibilities to take maternity and paternity leave.
- Possibilities to collect working hours and to take this at a later stage as long-service leave.

Assistance with the care for children and elderly

- Nursery/childcare facilities within the corporation or—mediated by the employer—in the immediate surroundings of the company or home.
- Out-of-school childcare provisions, organized by the company in conjunction with local authorities.
- A filing system—created by the company and kept up to date—of people who are able to work on short notice in case of illness of children or dependants.
- Referral services within the company, which assist employees to organize care for children and/or elderly dependants.

Of course, putting this model into practice will be more difficult than is stated on paper. The greatest obstacle will be the fact that at the conclusion of the parental leave (a maximum of nine months) income will cease.

However, the employee does receive extra benefits during the parental-leave period, like bonuses, profit shares, Christmas contributions, etc. Another obstacle is related to the career chances of people who make use of this career break. A short period of absence will have little influence on the career chances, but a prolonged break makes high demands on the company and the employee to maintain career prospects within the company. These prospects do not necessarily need to apply to vertical mobility alone. Horizontal transfers within a company offer employees ample scope. For the latter, good chances will be available if some employees leave the company for an extended period of time. The functions that subsequently become available could be included in so-called job-rotation programs and be filled by others. Much depends on the creativity and flexibility of managers and employees. More important than the question of how such arrangements are to be organized, however, is the problem of who they will target. It is this matter that will give rise to large differences between women and men in the near future.

Conclusion: Dilemmas and Challenges

Women seem to benefit from welfare-state regimes with extensive public facilities and a strong regulating capacity. Reconstruction of the traditional public–private split and the traditional division of tasks between women and men seems to be more likely in these welfare states than in welfare states where the market is given the highest priority. Concurrently, it is to be expected that, especially under pressure from international developments and their subsequent effects on national economies, governments will be more inclined to reduce their provision of public facilities. The legitimacy of collective facilities will come under pressure, the relative degree to which is influenced by the measure to which they are rooted in society. As such, a question voiced by the general public in the Netherlands is whether the recently established facilities regarding parental leave should be abolished, in view of the high costs involved. The same applies to the government expenditure on childcare facilities. The vision that the care of children under the age of 4 should be the sole responsibility of the parents is gathering strength. It is to be expected that such discussions will not develop quite as rapidly in the Nordic countries, where similar provisions have been under government responsibility for decades. But even there an austerity toward the welfare-state regime is more likely than a continuation of the status quo.

The call for efficiency, control on expenses, and austerity is even stronger within organizations. Arguments in favour of social protection and social justice, which are still valid in the political debate, have a lesser influence on the conduct of the most important actors within the corporations, the employers. One is confronted with the consequences in newspapers every day: loss of employment positions, deregulation and flexibilization of work contracts, a reduction in social security for employees, and a loss of lifetime employment. On the other hand, the emphasis on performance and achievement increases. All this will lead to a larger measure of inequality within the workforce, both between employees in general, and between male and female employees in particular.

Do these developments imply that work–family arrangements, as government facilities, will come under increasing amounts of pressure, and that within corporations they will not be substantiated? Are governments, in case of insufficient legitimacy, going to cut expenses in this domain and will employers abandon similar arrangements, because they are in conflict with the demand for efficiency and because of the inclination toward primary emphasis on the core of the business? Opposing these expectations, it can be stated that not only the demand for efficiency but also the demand for quality will remain of importance. If employers wish to keep their head above water in the future, they will have to satisfy both demands, that of efficiency and that of quality. The latter calls for a high innovative capacity and for careful management of the present human potential in the corporation. A good personnel policy is an important requirement to satisfy the quality demands. Whether or not quality is being produced not only depends on managers and on people situated in the internal market of companies. Irrespective of whether goods or services are concerned, the quality will be largely determined by those who perform the work. Quality will not be produced if employees do not consider themselves a part of the company. Nurturing their commitment is an eminent task of corporate managers. Partly influenced by demographic developments, attention to work–family arrangements will be of importance. This will not only be in the interest of women but, increasingly, to men as well. It does seem probable, however, that work–family arrangements will obtain a more individual character within corporations, rather than being arranged via general agreements. This could well mean that employers will become more willing to carry the costs of work–family arrangements for higher-educated women and men than for lower-skilled people. If this last expectation is valid, basic facilities at the government level regarding work–family policies ought to remain available, in order to facilitate the reconciliation of paid and unpaid work, which was the message of the OECD and the European Union.

References

Bochorst, A. (1991), 'The Scandinavian Welfare States, Patriarchal, Genderneutral or Woman-friendly?', paper presented at the European Research Conference 'Women in a Changing Europe' at the University of Aalborg in Denmark on 18–22 August.

Commission of the European Communities (1993a), *Green Paper. European Social Policy. Options for the Future*, COM(93) 551 final (17.11.93), Office for Official Publications of the European Communities, Luxembourg.

Commission of the European Communities (1993b), 'Occupational Segregation of Women and Men in the European Community', *Social Europe Supplement*, no. 3/93.

Commission of the European Communities (1994), *European Social Policy—a Way Forward for the Union. A White Paper*, COM(94) 333 final (27.7.94), Office for Official Publications of the European Communities, Luxembourg.

Doorne-Huiskes, J. van (1997), 'The Unpaid Work of Mothers and Housewives in the Different Types of Welfare States', in P. Koslowski and A. Føllesdal (eds.), *Restructuring the Welfare State. Theory and Reform of Social Policy*, Springer Verlag, Berlin, pp. 203–21.

Dulk, L. den, Doorne-Huiskes, A. van, and Schippers, J. (1996), 'Work–Family Arrangements and Gender Inequality in Europe', *Women in Management Review*, vol. 11, no. 5, pp. 25–35.

Esping-Andersen, G. (1990), *The Three Worlds of Welfare Capitalism*, Polity Press, Cambridge.

European Foundation for the Improvement of Living and Working Conditions (1991), *The Changing Use of Time: Report from an International Workshop*, Office for Official Publications of the European Communities, Luxembourg.

Hogg, C. and Harker, L. (1992), *The Family Friendly Employer. Examples from Europe*, Daycare Trust, London.

Langan, M. and Ostner, I. (1990), 'Gender and Welfare, Towards a Comparative Framework', paper presented at the Social Policy Association conference in Bath on 12–15 July.

Moss Kanter, R. (1993), *Men and Women of the Corporation*, Basic Books, New York.

OECD [Organisation for Economic Co-operation and Development] (1991), *Shaping Structural Changes. The Role of Women*, Organisation for Economic Co-operation and Development, Paris.

Parents at Work (1994), *UK Employer Initiatives. Working Examples of Family Friendly and Equal Opportunities Policies*, The Wainwright Trust.

Plantenga, J. and Doorne-Huiskes, J. van (1992), 'Gender, Citizenship and Welfare: a European Perspective', paper presented at the first European Conference of Sociology in Vienna on 26–9 August.

Sainsbury, D. (ed.) (1994), *Gendering Welfare States*, Sage Publications, London.

Sainsbury, D. (1996), *Gender, Equality, and Welfare States*, Cambridge University Press, Cambridge.

Schwartz, F.N. (1989), 'Management Women and the New Facts of Life', *Harvard Business Review*, vol. 67, no. 2, pp. 65–76.

UNDP [United Nations Development Programme] (1995), *Human Development Report 1995*, Oxford University Press, Oxford.

5 Comparative Childcare Policy and the Public–Private Divide

VICKY RANDALL

Introduction

Despite its implications for gender equality, the topic of child day care has been relatively neglected in feminist social science. One reason may be the undoubted complexity of the issues entailed. The subject of my own research has been more specific; it is an attempt to explain the striking contrast between the levels of public childcare provision in Britain and in a number of other European countries. Here, while the overall picture is still complicated, two connected considerations stand out and will be the focus of the following discussion: on the one hand, the character of childcare as an issue closely linked with the 'private' sphere of the family; and on the other hand, the existence of different state traditions or propensities for state intervention (these need to combine of course with specific national policy priorities). Thus, the making of childcare policy is crucially located along the public–private disjunction that is the central theme of this book.

The present paper builds upon my earlier analysis of the British case (Randall, 1995) and comparison of European cases (Randall, 1994) in order to show, first, how framing policy considerations, in particular state traditions and policy priorities, have varied cross-nationally; and, second, how such variations have both shaped and become institutionalized within the policy process itself. To this end it compares the making of childcare policy in Britain, France, and Sweden. Sweden and France both present a considerable contrast with Britain in respect of childcare policy, but also differ markedly from one another in the manner of arriving at it. A comparison of their respective policy processes will make possible a better understanding of how the shaping factors operate.

Table 5.1   Publicly funded childcare

Country	Year	% children under 3	% from 3 to school age	Age start school (years)
Belgium	1988	20	95+	6
Denmark	1989	48	85	7
Finland	1990	31	58	7
France	1988	20	95+	6
Germany	1987	3	65–70	6–7
Greece	1988	4	65–70	5.5
Iceland	1990	24	60	7
Ireland	1988	2	55	6
Italy	1986	5	85	6
Luxembourg	1989	2	55–60	5
Netherlands	1989	2	50–55	5
Norway	1990	11	57	7
Portugal	1988	6	35	6
Spain	1988	–	65–70	6
Sweden	1990	29	64	7
UK	1988	2	35–40	5

To reiterate, the focus of this paper is on the public provision of child day care, whether direct or through subsidy to suppliers or those seeking childcare. Furthermore, the paper assumes that not simply childcare but the public provision of childcare is an issue of tremendous current import for women, because of its bearing on the possibilities of meaningful equality between men and women. The extent of public, child day care provision varies significantly amongst European countries. The figures in Table 6.1, covering fourteen EU countries together with Iceland and Norway, are not quite complete, they are not all for the same year, and there are, moreover, variations in the age at which children in the different countries start formal schooling.* Even so, the remarkable divergences are apparent. Just taking the specific cases for our comparison: Britain was providing publicly funded care for 2 per cent of children under the age of 3 and for 35–40 per cent of children aged 3 to 5 in 1988; in France in the same year the figures were 20 per cent and over 95 per cent respectively; and in Sweden in 1990, 29 per cent and 64 per cent. Admittedly, the age for starting school is 6 in France and 7 in Sweden. On the other hand, the figure for Sweden of 29 per cent for children less than 3 years of age must be understood in the context of such generous, paid parental-leave provision that 'practically all Swedish children are at home with one of their parents until they are at least nine months old' (Broberg and Hwang, 1991, p. 76). How is this variation to be acounted for?

Childcare and the Policy Process in Britain, Sweden, and France: Some Framing Considerations

One possibility, which considerations of space prevent me from exploring here, is that the need, or at least the expressed need, for such provision differs between the three countries. But while there is evidence that both employment rates for mothers of young children and public approval for working mothers have been considerably greater in France and Sweden than in Britain (Rodgers, 1975; Moss, 1991; Gustafsson, 1994), what exactly does this mean? Are such employment patterns and attitudes best seen as a cause or a consequence of particular state policies?

At any rate, the focus of the present discussion will be on characteristics of childcare as a policy issue and on national policy-making traditions. As it has emerged in Western democracies, childcare is an issue that significantly straddles the boundary—however contested and conceptually muddled that boundary may be—between private and public spheres. First, and most crucially, it concerns the family, the division of labour within the family, and the well-being of children. As such it automatically invokes questions about the status of the family as a 'private' domain and the circumstances under which state or public intervention is appropriate.

Second, however, and using Theodore Lowi's classification, it is, potentially at least, a 'redistributory' issue; it involves the redistribution of resources between major social categories of 'haves' and 'have-nots' (Lowi, 1964). Specifically, public childcare provision entails not simply regulation but the expenditure of publicly gathered funds. Of course, this redistribution is not or not solely, as in Lowi's scenario, between social classes, capital and labour, but could be understood as taking place between families with children and other households, or even between men, in so far as they are the biggest earners and most heavily taxed, and women.

How have these characteristics interacted with national policy-making traditions? For a time at least, there was a trend in public-policy analysis that emphasized convergence, the tendency for economic growth to erode policy differences between nations (see Freeman, 1985). But childcare is one of the issue areas that has always run counter to this observation. National policy differences have not been linked in any simple way with different levels of economic development, but appear to reflect more specific traditions of political organization and culture.

In this context, it may be helpful to distinguish between different 'state' traditions on the one hand, and see how these combine with particular national policy agendas on the other. According to writers like David Marquand (1988), Britain, despite the flowering of the post-war welfare state, has been characterized by a 'liberal' state tradition, which has emphasized the boundary between public and private spheres, whether the latter are seen in economic or family terms, and mistrusted state intervention in either of these private domains. This could be contrasted with a much less rigid ideological conception of the private sphere and correspondingly more positive approach to state intervention in both France and Sweden.

These state traditions are closely linked to differences in 'national policy style' as discussed for instance by Richardson et al. (1982) and Freeman (1985). The suggestion is that in different national contexts, policy-makers 'develop characteristic and durable methods for dealing with public issues' (Freeman, 1985, p. 467). These styles reflect state traditions in that they incorporate long-standing assumptions about the appropriate scope of policy intervention, who should be involved in making policy, and so on. Of course, we need to be cautious about exactly how we understand these styles. Many commentators on this approach have stressed the variation in policy style that in practice can be discovered within a state, between policy sectors, and even within a single sector. Jack

Hayward has preferred to distinguish between a normative and an actual policy style. In the French case he contrasts a 'heroic' normative style, involving 'ambitious assertion of political will', with the more routine and reactive nature of much everyday decision-making. He concludes that although French policy-making may be characterized as having a predominantly reactive short-term and piecemeal approach to problem-solving, at the summit of the French state there is an informal network or nucleus of executive power capable of challenging the routine of norms and attempting to impose an active, longer-term comprehensive style of policy-making and implementation (1982, p. 116).

Again, in the case of Sweden, Ruin distinguishes between norms of policy-making and the actual 'standard operating procedures'. He argues that, in everyday decision-making, policy-makers seek agreement amongst participants, aim to build consensus, and avoid conflict, though the extent to which this is possible has varied between policy fields. But at the same time, there has been 'an emphasis on trying to direct events rather than letting events dictate policy, on being active and innovative rather than reactive' (1982, p. 141). In contrast, although in practice the British state has regularly intervened both in the family sphere and in the market, it is argued that this has often, though not always, been reactive rather than pre-emptive and that Britain, in Marquand's words, has lacked 'a philosophy of public intervention' (1988, p. 11).

Traditions or styles of policy-making will not of themselves explain variations in public childcare. But an interventionist style is a necessary, though not a sufficient, condition of more generous provision. The other crucial element is the nature of national policy priorities. A long time back I argued (1987) that precisely because states have been patriarchal, or male dominated, policies that affect women have often been framed not with women in mind but for other reasons. I suggested that three broad areas likely to be of concern were economic prosperity, political stability, and national security. More specifically, in the case of childcare, more extensive public provision has tended to coincide above all with some combination of concerns about population growth, labour shortages, social equality, and even cultural integration. It must be said that the interplay of these policy concerns can itself be quite intricate and take place over a protracted time period, as the sections on France and Sweden below will describe. Circumstances auspicious to a generous public childcare programme can be cumulative, with the story stretching back into the early decades of this century, if not before.

Britain: Fragmentation and Non-Decision-Making

In Britain, it has been established, public child day-care provision has been minimal. Nor is this simply attributable to the rigours of Thatcherite policies. In the 1970s also, when provision was growing in other countries, there was no significant increase in Britain. Though the reasons for this are complex (Randall, 1995) an important contributory role has been played by the 'liberal' state tradition—a certain reluctance, in theory at least, to intervene in the 'private' realm—which persisted even through the heroic days of the post-war welfare-state consensus and was fiercely reaffirmed in the 1980s. Childcare as an issue that straddles the perceived boundary between the public (the state) and the private (both in family and labour-market terms) thus tended to be marginalized.

Childcare is also potentially a redistribution issue. In the ultra-liberal Thatcher era this was a further potent reason for its neglect by government. But even in the earlier post-war decades, when certain kinds of redistributory politics prospered, childcare was neglected. Lowi has suggested that redistributory issues tend to be taken up by representatives of the major producer interests, or the parties closely associated with them. But reflecting, and perhaps exploiting, the liberal construction of the private sphere, trade unions and employers were very slow to acknowledge the childcare issue. Only really in the 1980s, especially towards the end of the decade following the brief 'demographic time-bomb' scare, when it was thought that young mothers would be needed back at work to make up for a shortage of new, skilled labour-force entrants, did they begin to campaign seriously.

It could of course be objected that Britain did not experience the same kind of policy imperatives that, over the longer term, more favourably disposed policy-makers to public childcare in Sweden and France. There were concerns in Britain about the birth rate, in the 1930s and for a brief spell after the Second World War, though lacking the urgency of population fears in the other two countries. Relevantly, Riley (1979, p. 102) notes 'the careful distancing' of English pronatalism in the late 1940s, not only from eugenic Nazi policies, but more generally from European family-allowance programmes. There was also a labour shortage in the 1950s, but the favoured solution was to turn to the former colonies for new supplies. The creation of the post-war welfare state itself implied a heightened commitment to social equality. But these policy concerns did not suffice at the time, or result in policy changes that later made it possible, to overturn liberal-inspired resistance to state intervention in the provision of childcare.

To draw a link between these observations and the childcare policy process, we can choose a moment—the mid- to late 1970s—when demands for a more systematic and extensive public childcare programme were beginning to be heard, however weakly. But these advocates of public childcare were faced with a situation in which the issue area, or potential issue area, of childcare was already institutionally embedded and discursively parcelled out in ways that embodied a surprisingly long history and provided distinct obstacles and few opportunities. That is, the determination of childcare policy remained largely a by-product of policy-making in two quite discrete fields: (nursery) education and (child) welfare. In an arrangement going back to at least the turn of the century, the Ministry of Education, under the 1944 Education Act, was responsible for ensuring that local education authorities 'have regard to the need for nursery education'. The Ministry of Health, on the other hand, under legislation going back to 1918, was responsible, again through local authorities, for state-provided child day care.

There had been occasions, earlier this century, when a different development seemed possible. By the 1900s, large numbers of children under five were already attending the new public elementary schools, but concerns were growing about the quality of the education received. There were at least two logical options: to withdraw the under-fives from school or to provide more suitable education. The first option was taken (Blackstone, 1971; Tizard et al., 1976). Likewise, it seemed as though provision of child day care might lose its residual welfare connotation, following its *de facto* expansion during the two world wars, especially the Second World War. But in retrospect it is clear that for most policy-makers, not only in the First but in the Second World War, such childcare provision was exceptional and a response to a particular emergency (Riley, 1983; Summerfield, 1984). Ruggie (1984) draws a perceptive analogy between this kind of emergency and the routine provision of child day care by local authorities for children perceived to be 'at risk', that is in a kind of private emergency. The Ministry of Health reaffirmed in 1948 that day-nursery places were intended only for children in 'special need'.

Though during the 1960s both the paid employment of young mothers and the use of private nurseries and childminders began to grow quite dramatically, this had little policy impact. By the end of the 1960s, however, the issue of childcare was being, tangentially, addressed by three government-appointed committees. The Plowden Committee, which reported on primary education, also advocated nursery education on demand, although this should be on a part-time basis. The background to this recommendation was the growing recognition that the welfare state had failed to eliminate poverty together with the perceived success of America's 'Headstart' pre-school education schemes (Banting, 1979). At much the same time the Seebohm Committee was reviewing the organization of the social services. One consideration behind the review was the commitment to a case-based approach to social work, aimed at preventing the breakdown of families 'at risk' and the desire to make this more effective. (This characteristically liberal approach to the family can be contrasted with the much more explicit and interventionist family policies of Sweden and France.) Though childcare was not a central concern of the Seebohm Committee, it called for expanded local authority provision for specified priority categories, that is children of lone parents, mothers who were ill, or 'incapable of giving young children the care they need' (cited in Tizard et al., 1976, pp. 86–7). It also called for better coordination of services for pre-school children. The Finer Committee on one-parent families, reporting a little later, echoed these demands.

While, therefore, by the early 1970s, a small head of steam was building behind the need to expand and to coordinate pre-school services, policy-making was still largely confined to distinct policy 'subsystems': education and welfare. Within these subsystems, moreover, much of the real initiative was left to individual local authorities.

Jordan and Richardson have noted 'a natural tendency for the political system in Britain to encourage the formation of stable policy communities' (1987, p. 181). They attribute this in part to the departmentalism of British government, which we might again want to link, albeit cautiously, to observations about Britain's non-interventionist, incremental, and pragmatic policy style. A policy community is a form of policy network consisting of a relatively stable and exclusive community of policy-makers, with few member groups, most of them based on shared economic or professional interests, a high degree of interaction and of consensus, and, although one group may dominate, without marked inequality of resources. It is certainly possible to identify education and social services/welfare in the 1970s as policy networks that tended in some respects towards the policy-community type, relatively integrated and stable. Local authority organizations and professional interests were incorporated in the policy process and their 'expertise' and role in implementation gave them something more than a merely consultative status, although central government was plainly the dominant actor. Within these policy networks, however, nursery education and child day care were always the poor relations and the professional groups associated with them had the lowest status.

It might be argued that what I have described is the policy-making process typically associated with routinized decision-making, that is where decisions taken long ago have been largely institutionalized. And indeed this is part of what I do want to suggest. But by the same token it might then be argued that one would not expect dramatic change from such a policy matrix. Rather, to quote Marsh and Rhodes' vivid phrase, it is the political party, as a vehicle for ideology, that can act as 'the blade for prizing apart the mollusc's shell of Whitehall and the policy networks' (1992, p. 257). But neither have parties, until very recently, taken the issue of childcare seriously.

I referred earlier to the emergence by the mid- to late 1970s of a lobby, in embryo at least, for more extensive public childcare provision. This included feminist groups, though British feminists were slow to take up the issue and campaign at national level (Randall, 1996). Its composition also reflected the growth of the child-oriented professions in promotional groups and those specifically representing implicated professional interests, local authorities, and academics. During the 1980s, individual trade unions increasingly addressed the issue of childcare and were more ready to relate it to the needs of working mothers. Nonetheless, this lobby was heterogenous and fragmentary, with constituent groups often at odds and even in competition with each other over what form expanded childcare should take. Such fragmentation itself partly reflected the institutional context within which the groups formed and operated. The lobby, or well-known figures within it, were increasingly incorporated into a process of consultation with the two departments concerned, and even in such formal interdepartmental consultation as occurred, but in so doing had largely to accept the compartmentalization of the institutional setting. But finally, of course, the implication of the preceding discussion is that the groups involved lacked an important kind of 'discursive resource', in the sense that Hobson has elaborated, that is 'ways of formulating public debate that allow for linkages to other policy concerns and hegemonic ideologies' (1993, p. 408).

France: State as Central Actor?

In France, by contrast, the possibility of a 'heroic' style of policy-making has been one element contributing to much higher levels of public childcare provision. State intervention clearly has a long history in France, going back to Napoleonic times and even earlier. Although liberal ideas were current in the nineteenth century, Ashford, amongst others, suggests that France never embraced them wholeheartedly: 'However slow the actual progress of the welfare state in France, reconciling the needs of state and society was a constant preoccupation of 19th century French political philosophers' (1986, p. 36). On the other hand, French national policy has been driven by certain overriding priorities, which have combined to create a relatively favourable context for the subsequent development of child day care. The most crucial of these has been a concern with population growth, but arguably this has been supplemented by an interest in what could be called the potential 'socialization' function of childcare.

Thus childcare has been debated and determined in the context, first, of an explicit and interventionist family policy whose roots go back to the turn of the century. Much of the inspiration for this policy has stemmed from recurring fears about population decline, but it has also constituted a point of consensus or common ground between political conservatives and traditional Catholics, on the one hand, and a more republican/technocratic and secular tendency, on the other. But second, the emergence specifically of the *maternelles* (discussed below) from the late nineteenth century onwards reflected not only concerns about the welfare of children but also a recognition of their potential role in children's 'moral education'. Although not providing education in the sense of instruction, they soon came to be seen as preparing children for more formal education and were taken under the wing of the Ministry of Education. Again to cite Ashford (1986, p. 56):

Perhaps more than any other democracy, France saw education as a central policy concern of the state, more accurately that education was such an important attribute of the state that it was conceptually inseparable.

Part of the reason for this was of course the struggle between republicanism and the Church, the urge to create a republican image of the state.

The existence of the *maternelles*, already catering for children aged 3 to 6, together with the legacy of institutions and funding created by earlier family policy meant that increasing numbers of married women were taking up paid employment and child day care. There was, therefore, a much more favourable environment than in Britain, both in terms of resources and in terms of the legitimacy of the redistributive and interventionist characteristics of the issue. Finally, it can also be suggested that although there was, as in Britain, institutional fragmentation, this tended to coincide with age groups. That is, the *maternelles* under the Ministry of Education have been responsible for the vast bulk of childcare for the three-to-six-year age range (as will be seen, however, the emphasis has been on integrating caring and educational aspects), while childcare provision for younger children has come under local *Caisse d'Allocations Familiales* (CAFs) and, at the national level, the *Caisse Nationale d'Allocations Familiale* (CNAF).

By the 1960s, the *maternelles* were already strongly established. Their origins lie in the nineteenth century (Norvez, 1990; Jenson, 1990). Industrial change in France was characterized by economic and political liberalism, though as already noticed this doctrine never achieved the authority it commanded in Britain. However, while Britain in the late nineteenth century remained largely confident in her imperial destiny, across the Channel was a growing preoccupation with the 'declin francais'. Disease, emigration, war, and especially defeat by Germany in 1870 and the accompanying loss of Alsace-Lorraine had contributed to stationary population levels, which were seen as leaving France economically and militarily vulnerable. As Jenson writes: 'within the concern about depopulation was an analytic link to the economic system, which people thought to be guaranteeing neither reproduction of the labour force nor a powerful nation state' (1990, p. 159).

In this context, there was growing official concern about the need to improve the health and welfare of the child and its mother, resulting eventually in a series of national policy initiatives. One of these was to build on the existing framework of *maternelles*, which developed from the 1820s as charitable bodies catering for children aged 2 to 6, but were increasingly brought under the auspices of the Ministry of Public Instruction. In the 1860s, standards of provision were severely criticized, but, in contrast to the British experience, the decision taken by policy-makers was to improve standards rather than dissolve the *maternelles* (Leprince, 1991). In the period 1880–1900, Norvez (1990) suggests, they were refashioned into an 'entirely original institution', combining both caring and educational perspectives. A subsidiary theme has been the education of parents via the children. For a long time, the intake of these refashioned *maternelles* were mainly working-class children. It was not until the 1960s, as growing numbers of middle-class women began entering professional jobs, that an unanticipated explosion in take-up rates occurred. By now, not only do over 90 per cent of French children aged 3 to 6 attend these schools but also one-third of two-year-olds (Leprince, 1991).

In addition to the *maternelles*, working parents have benefitted from France's distinctive family policy. We have seen how this policy originated in the circumstances of the late nineteenth century. Policy-makers were often inspired by humanitarian concerns themselves, but had to cite demographic and national power considerations as a justification for overriding the liberty of the individual (Norvez, 1990). In so doing, they were also able to exploit the consensus between the dominant and otherwise mutually antagonistic tendencies of social Catholicism and republican nationalism on the importance of the 'family'. The actual elaboration of family policy was left to the officials (Lenoir, 1991).

In the context of continuing population concern, in the interwar era and the aftermath of the Second World War, family policy became institutionally inscribed. First, there was a basic continuity in the ministerial setting within which it was coordinated and implemented, though its name might change from Ministry of the Family to Ministry of Population to Ministry of Health and Population. Second, there was the creation of a series of bodies, whether representative, research-oriented, or administrative, that, in Lenoir's words, gave the policy 'its specificity, its credibility and its effectiveness' (1991, p. 144). One of these was the National Union of Family Allowance Funds (referred to above as CNAF).

The system of family allowances established under the 1939 Family Code, was initially intended to stimulate population growth. It is also sometimes suggested that it was developed in a way designed to encourage mothers to stay at home, most specifically through the additional allowance for *la mère au foyer*. However, Rodgers maintains that following the Second World War, its rationale was increasingly to prevent families with children from being unduly disadvantaged in income terms. In any case, for a long time it provided a means of horizontal redistribution between families with children and those without (Rodgers, 1975). Moreover, while it is clear that provision of a family allowance was driven not by commitment to women's rights but by demographic concerns, Hantrais suggests that the motivation was basically gender-neutral. She points out that the allowance was actually introduced in the immediate post-war period when 'the shortage of skilled labour rather than of jobs was the main problem' (1993, p. 120).

The main point here is, however, that as women, including married women, entered the paid workforce in increasing numbers from the 1960s, and in the context of renewed fears about a falling birth rate, the institutional fabric and resources earmarked for family policy were potentially available to channel into increased childcare provision. How did this happen? Although French governments were conscious of a growing women's rights constituency—feminist groups were beginning to mobilize in the 1960s, during the 1965 presidential election, and especially after the student upheavals of 1968—this was only one influence on policy developments. By the 1960s, officials concerned with framing social/family policy were beginning to question the universalist basis of family benefits, that is giving identical benefits regardless of family income, in favour of a more selective or targeted approach. At the same time they recognized changing patterns of family life and in particular the increase in working mothers.

This recognition was spurred by information they themselves had helped to gather. As noted above, a feature of the institutionalization of French family policy was that it was underpinned by a series of research-oriented bodies. Rodgers contrasts in particular the scope of a CNAF/CREDOC study, whose findings were beginning to be reported by the early 1970s, with a contemporaneous Office of Population Censuses and Surveys (OPCS) report, the only British report for some time which could be said to have a bearing on the family policy. The French study 'was mounted with the express purpose of providing information that would enable family policy, and family benefits in particular, to be related more closely to the changing situation and expectations of families'. As such it documented, for example, the growth in numbers of women working, decline in ideal family size, and weakening of extended family ties. The OPCS survey, on the other hand, was devised mainly to improve demographic forecasting (Rodgers, 1975, pp. 122–5).

Much rethinking of French family policy in the late 1960s took place in the General Planning Commission, which emphasized professional training for women, childcare, and pre-school instruction. As part of a broader effort to target family assistance on groups that had hitherto been marginalized or excluded, a law was passed in January 1972 that simultaneously provided an increased allowance for mothers at home with young children and a childcare allowance for working mothers (Lenoir, 1991). The way that policy was formulated left the actual decision of whether to go out to work with the mothers, thus to an extent sidestepping the continuing differences between traditionalist and more 'liberal' views of the family.

This policy was actually implemented largely through the CAFs, in conjunction with local government. As Leprince (1991, p. 15) notes:

> Since 1970 CAFs have been increasingly involved in funding the capital and running costs of day care services, reducing the proportion of costs born by local authorities; day care provision for young children has become one of the main objectives of CNAF.

In more recent years there has been some disagreement amongst observers as to whether France still has a family policy in the sense it once had, so explicit and prioritized. Lenoir (1991) argues that it has been dissipated and fragmented since the 1960s, and seems to see the development of childcare policy as symptomatic of this. On the other hand, Hantrais (1993) argues that family policy has persisted, though in a changed form, but has become increasingly child-centered. Whichever of these views is most justified, it is clear that the legacy of family policy was important for the development of childcare.

Although moves to encourage expansion of public child day care, back in the early 1970s, did not then directly reflect feminist pressure, and women's representation in the National Assembly was and remains minimal, the role of such pressure in the continuing drive to expand cannot be entirely discounted. This was especially the case following the appointment of Yvette Roudy as Minister of Women's Rights in the

Socialist government of the early 1980s (see Duchen, 1986). In 1983, the CNAF initiated a new 'nursery agreement' with local authorities aimed at increasing nursery and organized childminding provision for under-three-year-olds. Between 1981 and 1986, 35,000 new nurseries were created. However, there was a further such initiative in 1988, under a Conservative government and in the context of renewed concerns about the falling birth rate.

To summarize, childcare policy in France has evolved against a background of population concerns and a degree of national consensus formed early on the need for a strong family policy and also on the broadly educational value of the *maternelles*. (Though family policy in this form may now be in decline, it has been replaced to an extent by a focus on the child, serving the same consensual function.) This helped, first, to give official policy-makers both the authority and the freedom from party/ideological interference to elaborate major policy initiatives absorbing sizeable public resources; and, second, to ensure considerable continuity in the development of these policies and their adaptation to changing patterns of employment and family life. Although, therefore, feminists may have had a limited impact in defining or redefining childcare as an issue of women's employment rights, such redefinition was made less necessary both by the greater availability of childcare and because, while the status of women was a polarizing issue between right and left in France, the terms in which policies involving childcare were couched were to an extent gender-neutral, in the sense of aiming to help families, whether or not the mother went out to work.

Sweden: the Social-Democratic State

We come finally to Sweden, where public child day care provision has in some ways, certainly for children aged under 3, been even more generous than in France. Sweden, like France, has a stronger tradition of state intervention than Britain. Some accounts want to take this right back to the national administration already developed in the era of absolute rule in the sixteenth and seventeenth centuries. Swedish state bureaucracy was further modernized on the Prussian model in the nineteenth century and has in turn 'played an enduring role in modernizing a nation that was at the beginning of this century still agrarian and pre-democratic' (Heidenheimer et al.,

1990, p. 21). As a consequence 'faith in the benevolence, capability and responsibility of the state is an old tradition in Sweden' (Edwards, cited in Haas, 1992, p. 51; see also Elman, 1995). At the same time, Sweden, like France, has been troubled by recurring population scares. More than France, it has also periodically faced severe labour shortages, which in the 1960s coincided with the new wave of female entrants into the paid workforce. But these two primary concerns have been resolved in the context of a strong commitment to social egalitarianism, as embodied above all in the Social Democratic Party's long-standing domination, from the 1930s to the 1970s, both of the party system and of the institutions of government.

These traits of Swedish policy-making have helped to legitimize state intervention in two important spheres—the family and the labour market—which in their separate ways could be construed as 'private', and which have given rise to strong national policies in each of these fields (each with significant consequences for childcare provision). Both these policies, or sets of policies, stem largely from the 1930s and specifically from the conjunction of economic depression, a major population scare, and the coming to power of the Social Democrats. From this time can be traced a continuous concern with child welfare, related both to natalist and equality considerations, but also a commitment to combatting unemployment through active intervention in the labour market. Child day-care policy has benefitted from both of these.

Given public commitment to these two major strands of policy, childcare policy in Sweden has also benefitted from the way in which national policy-making has typically proceeded, once government has identified an important issue area. Usually a commission is appointed by the cabinet or by a central government agency, with the job of investigating the issue and making policy recommendations. Commissions marshall and review evidence systematically, and their recommendations have tended to be largely accepted by parliament. Their membership has included senior 'experts' and more junior researchers from the state bureaucracy, as well as representatives of labour, business, other affected interest groups, and MPs (Ruin, 1982; Ruggie, 1984). Thus to an extent their composition lends support to interpretations of Swedish politics as tripartite or corporatist. The prevalence of this traditional mode of determining policy has meant that childcare needs and provision, once these were perceived to be an important dimension of both family and labour policy, have been carefully assessed and monitored.

As Ruggie writes: 'The story of modern daycare in Sweden begins in the 1960s' (1984, p. 255). It was only then that the numbers of young mothers in paid employment really began to grow and the inadequacy of existing childcare provision was highlighted. However, while there was no equivalent of the *maternelles* actually in place and indeed existing provision was not only meagre but quite traditional and fragmentary, as in France there were institutionalized policies and policy discourses that were relatively amenable to the recognition of childcare needs.

In order to show this, it is necessary to consider briefly the particular policy legacies that childcare could tap into. In the 1930s, Sweden had the lowest fertility rates in Europe. The famous social-democrat husband and wife, Alva and Gunnar Myrdal, were the first to address this issue systematically in *Kris i befolkningsfrågan* (Crisis in the Population Question), published in 1934. Initially their views were neglected, even mocked, but soon public concern was sufficiently mobilized to prompt the government to appoint a Royal Commission on the Population Problem. According to Adams and Winston (1980, p. 184), the Myrdals were able to demonstrate that lower-income families tended to have fewer children (not simply that there was a correlation between income and family size) and to use this evidence as a 'crowbar' for achieving social reform. They argued that young couples must be encouraged to have children by ensuring that their income did not suffer as a consequence. However, it required a certain kind of political climate for such an argument to be taken seriously. That is to say that pronatalism was not the only motive for Swedish family policy. Social egalitarianism, as represented particularly by the Social Democrats with their strong links with the trade-union movement but also, perhaps, reflecting more diffuse sources in Swedish culture and political history, contributed as well. Together these motives produced an emphasis on the well-being of the child, which 'has remained a driving force behind Swedish welfare and family policy' (Haas, 1992, p. 23).

The 1930s also saw the start of an active, interventionist labour-market policy. This originated in Social Democrat commitment to combatting unemployment through government expenditure. Though the various economic policies initiated at this stage were not directly concerned with women, they established a precedent for government intervention to remove obstacles to labour-force participation that later would prove very helpful to women. These policies also coincided with a signficant debate about women's employment, which resulted in the acceptance, in principle, of working women's right to have a family. Adams and Winston (1980) note that in generally defending married women's right to work, the Myrdals were able to cite figures that demonstrated that women working outside the home was not a reason for population decline; by 1930, after forty years of such decline, only 5 per cent of married women had paid employment. They even suggested that married women should have the opportunity to work to raise family incomes. These arguments certainly encountered opposition; Hobson (1993) describes how in 1934, at the height of the economic crisis, at least nine motions were presented in the *Riksdag* designed to prevent married women going out to work. But the Swedish parliament turned them down and instead set up a commission, in 1935, to report on the issue. Remarkably, four of the six commissioners appointed were women, and when the Population Commission reported in 1938 it argued against any discriminatory legislation against the employment of married women.

As Ruggie (1984) recounts, until the 1960s, day care was essentially a welfare issue in Sweden, as it was elsewhere. The 1935 Population Commission generally approved the existing division of pre-school services between day nurseries for children in special need and half-day nursery education, though it suggested that access to the latter should no longer be confined to the better-off. During the Second World War day-nursery provision expanded to enable women to take on jobs vacated by men who had been temporarily, and as a precaution, conscripted for military service, but then declined.

Only with the upsurge of women's employment, coinciding with a serious labour shortage, in the 1960s, did childcare policy really begin to be seriously questioned.

Representatives of industry, the trade unions, the press, child-centred groups, and women's groups began to draw public attention to the childcare issue and to demand reforms. In response, a series of commissions were established to review different aspects of the problem. Thus in 1962, a Family Commission put forward proposals for a new type of 'child centre'. In 1965, another Family Commission investigated childminding. The recommendations of these commissions formed the basis of legislation duly passed by parliament. Eventually in 1968 a Royal

Commission on Child Centres was established that served to integrate and systematize preceding policy changes.

The Royal Commission reported in 1972. Ruggie (1984) notes the matter-of-fact, non-judgemental way in which the Commission presented its findings about working mothers. Following its careful analysis, the Commission proposed completely reorganizing the system of childcare. Recognizing that while all children needed some form of pre-school provision, the need for day care was itself directly related to the needs of working parents, it demanded a public commitment to meet all these pre-school needs, both quantitatively and qualitatively. The Commission's proposals formed the basis for a Pre-school Act, passed in 1973, followed by further supplementary legislation in 1975 and 1976. As in Britain, and to a certain extent in France, policies were to be implemented by local authorities, but their active cooperation was to be facilitated by generous funding from the centre. Other political parties in the *Riksdag* did not oppose the Social Democrat government's legislation. There were, and have continued to be, differences of emphasis in the parties' approach to the question of childcare; the Conservatives questioned whether the country can afford the economic cost, while the Liberal Party expressed concern that individual children should not have to spend too many hours a day in non-parental care (Adams and Winston, 1980). Such differences of emphasis reflected more fundamental differences in attitudes to working mothers. As in France, these differences have persisted (Edwards, 1991), but have taken second place to a recognition that mothers, for one reason or another, may have to work outside the home and that the state needs to assist in the provision of child day care.

The Commission had addressed the issue of the harmful effects of the division of childcare services between caring and educational functions, but this was not immediately acted upon. Responsibility for child day care, at the national level, was entrusted to the National Board of Health and Welfare, coming under the Ministry of Health and Social Affairs. But subsequently the pedagogic aims of child day care were incorporated into a 'working plan for the pre-school' drawn up by the National Board of Health and Welfare in conjunction with the National Board of Education, thus permitting a significant degree of integration of the care and education aspects within national policy-making institutions (Ruggie, 1984). A report issued by the National Board of Health and Welfare in 1987, Pre-school

Educational Programme, went so far as to identify education as the primary task of child day care (cited in Broberg and Hwang, 1991).

The story of childcare policy-making in Sweden then offers some parallels to the French case, but is also significantly different. In both cases there has been a tradition and acceptance of state intervention and proactive policy-making, certainly in areas where some degree of wider political consensus prevails. But in Sweden, first, the nature of the consensus has been different, more egalitarian and focusing less simply on the 'family'. Second, it was less the case that political consensus left the state a free hand; rather the consensus worked through the state, in the form of Social Democratic control of government and a type of corporatist interest mediation, for instance in the succession of commissions. It is sometimes argued that this particular policy-making context has made it more difficult for feminists to organize autonomously and to effectively promote a radical feminist agenda (Elman, 1995). This is a complex issue that cannot be resolved here, although almost certainly this view understates the contribution of feminists within mainstream institutions. The point being made here, however, is that this policy context has been, in a comparative European context at least, unusually conducive to public childcare provision.

Conclusion

The preceding discussion makes no claims to an exhaustive account of the making of childcare policy. Many contributory elements, such as the impact of feminism, have remained largely unexplored. Nor have I followed up the story in any detail to the present day. What I have tried to show, first, is how the issue of childcare, sensitively situated on the contested boundary between the public and private spheres, has been differently defined and incorporated within different national policy styles and agendas. Second, I have suggested some of the ways in which these differences have been embodied more concretely in the institutional matrix within which policies have evolved and in other aspects of the policy process itself.

Contrasting the British case with experience in France and Sweden suggests a number of preliminary conclusions about, for instance, the relevance for childcare policy of population and family policies and of labour-market policies. However, to end this discussion I want to focus on one further implication, concerning the role of the state, an implication that is 'obvious' in a way if unfashionable, but that is insufficiently acknowledged, certainly by feminists. Feminism, especially radical feminism, has had, and continues to have, a highly ambivalent attitude towards the state. Is the state, as a dimension of patriarchal power, part of the problem for women, or can it be a woman-friendly instrument of reform? There is clearly no guarantee that a powerful state will be woman friendly, and here the fears of Elman (1995) and others are well founded. As Max Weber pointed out a long time ago, the 'state' itself has no goal but can be used for any end. What it may be possible to argue, however, is that *without* a strong 'philosophy of public intervention', and though there need to be conducive framing policy concerns, the prospects for public provision of child day care, and by extension for other redistributive policies that help women to transcend the confines of the public–private divide, are distinctly bleak.

Acknowledgement

I should especially like to thank Linda Hantrais for directing me to the work of Alain Norval, and also Maura Adshead and Claire Duchen for their helpful suggestions on source materials.

Note

*   Figures for this table are drawn from European Commission Childcare Network (1990) and Leira (1993).

References

Adams, C.T. and Winston, C.T. (1980), *Mothers at Work. Public Policies in the United States, Sweden, and China*, Longman, New York.
Ashford, D.E. (1986), *The Emergence of the Welfare States*, Basil Blackwell, Oxford.
Banting, K. (1979), *Poverty, Politics and Policy. Britain in the 1960s*, The Macmillan Press, London.
Blackstone, T. (1971), *A Fair Start: the Provision of Pre-school Education*, Allen Lane, London.

Broberg, A. and Hwang, C.P. (1991), 'Day Care for Young Children in Sweden', in E.C. Melhuish and P. Moss (eds.), *Day Care for Young Children. International Perspectives*, Routledge, London, pp. 75–101.

Duchen, C. (1986), *Feminism in France. From May '68 to Mitterrand*, Routledge & Kegan Paul, London.

Edwards, M. (1991), 'Towards a Third Way: Women's Politics and Welfare Policies in Sweden', *Social Research*, vol. 58, pp. 677–705.

Elman, R.A. (1995), 'The State's Equality for Women: Sweden's Equality Ombudsman', in D. McBride Stetson and A.G. Mazur (eds.), *Comparative State Feminism*, Sage, London.

European Commission Childcare Network (1990), 'Childcare in the European Communities 1985–1990', *Women of Europe, Supplement*, no. 31.

Freeman, G.P. (1985), 'National Styles and Policy Sectors: Explaining Structured Variation', *Journal of Public Policy*, vol. 5, pp. 467–96.

Gustafsson, S. (1994), 'Childcare and Types of Welfare State', in D. Sainsbury (ed.), *Gendering Welfare States*, Sage Publications, London, pp. 45–61.

Haas, L. (1992), *Equal Parenthood and Social Policy*, State University of New York Press, New York.

Hantrais, L. (1993), 'Women, Work and Welfare in France', in J. Lewis (ed.), *Women and Social Policy in Europe*, Edward Elgar, Aldershot, pp. 116–37.

Hayward, J. (1982), 'Mobilising Private Interests in the Service of Public Ambitions: the Salient Element in the Dual French Policy Style?', in J. Richardson (ed.), *Policy Styles in Western Europe*, George Allen & Unwin (Publishers), London, pp. 111–40.

Heidenheimer, A.J., Heclo, H., and Adams, C.T. (1990), *Comparative Public Policy. The Politics of Social Choice in America, Europe, and Japan*, 3rd edn., St. Martin's Press, New York, NY.

Hobson, B. (1993), 'Feminist Strategies and Gendered Discourses in Welfare States: Women's Right to Work in the United States and Sweden', in S. Koven and S. Michel (eds.), *Mothers of a New World*, Routledge, London.

Jenson, J. (1990), 'Representations of Gender: Policies to 'Protect' Women Workers in France and the United States before 1914', in L. Gordon (ed.), *Women, the State and Welfare*, University of Wisconsin Press, Madison, Wis.

Jordan, A.G. and Richardson, J.J. (1987), *Government and Pressure Groups in Britain*, Clarendon Press, Oxford.

Leira, A. (1993), 'Mothers, Markets and the State: a Scandinavian "Model"?', *Journal of Social Policy*, vol. 22, pp. 329–47.

Lenoir, R. (1991), 'Family Policy in France since 1938', in J.S. Ambler (ed.), *The French Welfare State*, New York University Press, New York.

Leprince, F. (1991), 'Day Care for Young Children in France', in E.C. Melhuish and P. Moss (eds.), *Day Care for Young Children. International Perspectives*, Routledge, London, pp. 10–26.

Lowi, T.J. (1964), 'American Business, Public Policy, Case Studies, and Political Theory', *World Politics*, vol. 16, pp. 677–715.

Marquand, D. (1988), *The Unprincipled Society. New Demand and Old Politics*, Jonathan Cape, London.

Marsh, D. and Rhodes, R.A.W. (1992), 'Policy Community and Issue Networks. Beyond Typology', in D. Marsh and R.A.W. Rhodes (eds.), *Policy Networks in British Government*, Clarendon Press, Oxford, pp. 249–68.

Moss, P. (1991), 'Day Care for Young Children in the United Kingdom', in E.C. Melhuish and P. Moss (eds.), *Day Care for Young Children. International Perspectives*, Routledge, London, pp. 121–41.

Mydal, A. and Myrdal, G. (1934), *Kris i befolkningsfrågan*, Bonnier, Stockholm.

Norvez, A. (1990), *De la naissance a l'ecole*, INED, Travaux et Documents, Cahier No. 126, PUF, Paris.

Randall, V. (1987), *Women and Politics*, 2nd edn., The Macmillan Press, London.

Randall, V. (1994), 'The Politics of Child Daycare: Some European Comparisons', in H. Kriesi (ed.), *Swiss Yearbook of Political Science 94*, Editions Paul Haupt, Bern.

Randall, V. (1995), 'The Irresponsible State? The Politics of Child Daycare', *British Journal of Political Science*, vol. 25, pp. 327–48.

Randall, V. (1996), 'Feminism and Child Daycare', *Journal of Social Policy*, vol. 25, pp. 485–505.

Richardson, J., Gustafsson, G., and Jordan, G. (1982), 'The Concept of Policy Style', in J. Richardson (ed.), *Policy Styles in Western Europe*, George Allen & Unwin (Publishers), London, pp. 1–16.

Riley, D. (1979), 'War in the Nursery', *Feminist Review*, no. 2, pp. 82–108.

Riley, D. (1983), *War in the Nursery*, Virago, London.

Rodgers, B.N. (1975), 'Family Policy in France', *Journal of Social Policy*, vol. 4, pp. 113–28.

Ruggie, M. (1984), *The State and Working Women. A Comparative Study of Britain and Sweden*, Princeton University Press, Princeton, NJ.

Ruin, O. (1982), 'Sweden in the 1970s: Policy-making Becomes More Difficult', in J. Richardson (ed.), *Policy Styles in Western Europe*, George Allen & Unwin (Publishers), London, pp. 141–67.

Summerfield, P. (1984), *Women Workers in the Second World War. Production and Patriarchy in Conflict*, Croom-Helm, London.

Tizard, J., Moss, P., and Perry, J. (1976), *All Our Children. Pre-school Services in a Changing Society*, Maurice Temple Smith, London.

6 European Policies and Women's Rights in the United Kingdom

ELIZABETH MEEHAN and EVELYN COLLINS

Introduction

It is argued in this chapter that the European Union (EU)[1] has had a positive impact upon the scope of British women's rights at work and in social-security schemes. This argument is made, however, in the context of the politics of European integration, a context which is ambivalent with respect to the totality of the interests of women. Though the founders of the original European communities intended economic objectives to be a means of social and political transformation, their successors have tended to allow the instruments to displace the long-term goals as the defining feature of European integration. Legislation and judicial interpretations necessarily stem from Treaty provisions on employment and rights related to working status, and, thus, 'reinforce the public/private divide' (Hoskyns, 1996a, p. 14; 1996b). Yet, at the same time, European policy 'is beginning to transcend the field of employment and influence the domestic and "private" spheres of women's lives' (Hoskyns, 1996a, p. 14).

The chapter begins by outlining the main legal developments and their underlying legal concepts. Since we have dealt in detail elsewhere with how the scope of rights has developed, through the interplay between United Kingdom (UK) courts and the European Court of Justice (ECJ) and with enforcement and remedies (Collins and Meehan, 1994; Meehan and Collins, 1996), the main section of this chapter focuses upon aspects of sex (in)equality that are significant for two reasons. On the one hand, they are issues where the public and private interconnect in real lives. And, on the other, they exemplify Hoskyns' (1996a, p. 14) point that 'artificial divisions' between them have not been able to be maintained in European policy. In conclusion, it is suggested that the existence of EU policies and institutions helped British women to circumvent a domestic political climate that was, until recently, inhospitable to intervention in respect of women's interests.

The Main Legal Developments and Underlying Concepts

The main legal developments in respect of British women's rights in employment since 1945 have been the Sex Discrimination Act 1975 (SDA) and its amendments,[2] and the Equal Pay Act 1970 (EqPA) and its amendments.[3] The former applies the principle of equal treatment to non-contractual employment matters, such as recruitment, promotion, training, and working conditions (and, in addition, to education and the provision of housing, goods, facilities, and services). Direct and indirect discrimination on grounds of sex are prohibited and, in the employment aspects only of the legislation, direct and indirect discrimination on grounds of marital status are also unlawful. Victimization, too, is prohibited. The Act applies equally to women and men, although it is aimed primarily at providing rights for women, who were considered 'more likely to be the victims of unfair treatment on grounds of sex' (Home Office, 1974, para. 1). The EqPA applies to contractual terms and conditions, including pay. As well as these laws, some positive changes have been made to the social-security and taxation systems, though they were excluded from the scope of antidiscrimination legislation.

The sex discrimination legislation established two Equal Opportunities Commissions—one in Great Britain (EOCGB), the other in Northern Ireland (EOCNI). These were given statutory duties to: work towards the elimination of discrimination; promote equality of opportunity generally between men and women; keep under review the working of the EqPA and SDA; and, when thought necessary by the Commissions themselves or the Secretary of State, to draw and submit to the Secretary of State proposals for amendment to the legislation.

In addition to domestic legislation, the EU has played a critical role in shaping the development of the nature and standards of rights available in the UK. It has done so through its substantive law and the jurisprudence of the ECJ. Article 119 of the Treaty of Rome 1957 required Member States to implement the principle of equal pay for equal work, and the Equal Pay Directive of 1975 (Council Directive 75/117/EEC, OJ no. L 45, 19 February 1975, p. 19) expanded this by obliging Member States to bring about equal pay for work of equal value; that is the standard of the International Labour Organization (ILO Convention 100 of 1951, entering into force on 23 May 1953). In 1976 the Equal Treatment Directive (Council Directive 76/207/EEC, OJ no. L 039, 14 February 1976, pp. 40–2) was adopted, guaranteeing the principle of equal treatment in access to employment, vocational training, promotion, and working conditions. In this Directive, equal treatment entails not only the absence of direct or indirect discrimination on grounds of sex but also in connection with marital or family status. Both these Directives have caused amendments to be made to British statutes and have enabled individuals to claim rights or standards that, prior to judgements in the ECJ, appeared to be outside the scope of domestic requirements (Collins and Meehan, 1994).

Prior to the UK's 'opt-out' from social policy in the Maastricht Treaty (agreed in 1991), British policy also had to comply with three other equality directives adopted by the EU's Council of Ministers: in 1979, one on the progressive implementation of the principle of equal treatment in statutory social-security schemes (Council Directive 79/7/EEC, OJ no. L 006, 10 January 1979, pp. 24–5); in 1986, one on the implementation of the principle of equal treatment in occupational social-security schemes (Council Directive 86/378/EEC, OJ no. L 225, 12 August 1986, pp. 40–2); and, again in 1986, one about equal treatment for women and men in self-employed occupations including agriculture (Council Directive 86/613/EEC, OJ no. L 359, 19 December 1986, pp. 56–8). In 1992, under the health and safety framework (procedures for which were agreed prior to Maastricht), the Council adopted a Directive on the protection of pregnant women from exposure to hazardous substances at work and about their rights of leave, and return to work, during and after pregnancy (Council Directive 92/85/EEC, OJ no. L 348, 28 November 1992, pp. 1–8). Throughout the period, the EU also adopted 'permissive' policies that aim to promote equality of opportunity; for example, recommendations and resolutions on sexual harassment, childcare, positive action, and funds for vocational training and retraining. The Amsterdam Treaty (agreed in 1997), which ended the British 'opt-out', now provides a legal basis for positive action and, since its agreement, the Council of Ministers extended a Directive on parental leave, previously agreed by other members, to the UK (to be implemented in two years) and has agreed upon Directives for part-time workers (to be implemented by 1999) and the burden of proof (to be implemented by 2001) (*Equal Opportunities Review*, 1998, no. 77, p. 1).

British developments took place in a context of legal and political controversy over the meanings of discrimination and the proper scope of action against it.[4] In one dominant approach, the proper aim of the law is to establish fair processes or the elimination of harmful consequences of decisions based on prejudice. Its proponents concentrate on fairness for individuals through the removal of arbitrary obstacles that lead to less favourable treatment of one person compared to another. Such an approach embodies the liberal presupposition that people start out as equals with the freedom to make rational choices about their destinies, or would do so if formal juridical barriers were removed. It gives rise to law that is expressed in universalistic terms and to the equal-treatment approach in sex-equality legislation.

A second approach moves away from ensuring that rules treat individuals equally to a concern with the impact of decisions and practices on groups. Here, the proper aim of antidiscrimination measures is to ensure an improvement in the social and economic position of disadvantaged groups, or to ensure a redistribution of benefits and opportunities from advantaged groups to disadvantaged ones. The presupposition of this approach is that the outcomes, even of processes that are individually fair, will be affected by differences between groups in terms of their social and historical circumstances. Specific measures are likely also to be necessary in order to ensure that members of disadvantaged groups can come to be in a position to enjoy the same chances under a regime of equal treatment.

Although the two approaches can clash in particular instances, the view that distributive justice is a legitimate reason for intervention also has liberal origins. And, like the first approach, the second entails comparisons between women and men as individuals, as well as members of groups.

The 1970s British legislation combines elements of both these liberal approaches within its scope. The individual approach may be seen in the provisions on direct discrimination and equal pay for like work, which are premised on comparing directly the treatment of similarly situated women and men. The distributive justice approach informs provisions relating to indirect discrimination, positive action (a voluntary provision), and, to an extent, equal pay for work of equal value, all of which allow for the possibility of taking into account the consequences of group membership. It has been argued that EU concepts of equality, compared to those of the UK, are more strongly rooted in the idea of distributive justice than on the principle of equal treatment (Edwards and McKie, 1993).

Feminist critiques of liberal legal and political theory, even the group-oriented version, are well known. In general, neither approach tackles head-on the origins and consequences of the public–private division. Pateman (1988; 1989), for example, argues that, even in the liberal revolution against patriarchy, men and women continued to be incorporated into civil and political society asymmetrically; men in their own rights, but women as the dependants, and under the control, of fathers and husbands. This structured inequality is disguised, but not eliminated, by extending the formal language of equal treatment to women. Different conceptions of the nature of men and women and their relations in the private sphere continue to affect their civil and public roles. For present purposes, there are two specific aspects to such critiques that need to be noted. All liberal legislation implicitly assumes that the male model of individual behaviour is the normal or 'natural' one—a pattern to which women are expected to conform or aspire. Yet it treats as epiphenomenal, not as 'deep structure', the reality that women are seldom in similar circumstances to men, because of their historical experience, reproductive capacity, the domestic division of labour, and comparable forms of occupational segregation. Particular criticism has been made of the thoughtlessness of liberal theory about biological differences (Bacchi, 1991; Sevenhuijsen, 1991). The limitations of liberal legal tools in dismantling institutionalized discrimination has been compounded by a sometimes unsympathetic judiciary, or, at least, one that adapts only slowly to new legal norms (Byrne and Lovenduski, 1978). Even though the UK government now seems more hospitable to intervention, a regulatory role for the EU, and is more accessible to the European Women's Lobby, the latter is somewhat sceptical of the former's commitment to tackling structural inequality (*European Women's Lobby Newsletter*, 1998, no. 2, pp. 17–18).

EU Influence upon Issues Where the Public and Private Interconnect

As all contributors to a recent book on sexual politics in the EU (Elman, 1996) point out, the original Treaty bases of European integration leave virtually no room for fundamental issues stemming from feminist understandings of the public–private divide; e.g. sexuality, pornography, sexual trafficking, reproductive technologies, and sexual violence. One essay (Smyth, 1996), however, points out that rules about service provision have impinged upon the prohibition of abortion in Ireland (and the Irish prohibition impinged upon the ratification of the Maastricht Treaty). Most of the essays refer to concerns in the European Parliament (EP) about the inability of the EU to tackle such issues—to which could be added the European Women's Lobby (*European Women's Lobby Newsletter*, 1998, no. 2, pp. 4–8). Since the publication of Elman's volume, the Amsterdam Treaty has introduced the possibility of legislating against discrimination on grounds of sexual orientation. Within the limits of scope for action so far, however, some measures and legal interpretations have dented prevailing national boundaries between the public and the private—at least where they most explicitly interconnect. For example, the ECJ held to be invalid the assumption of British policy that married women would not be in paid employment but at home to care for dependent relatives and, hence, ineligible for the invalid care allowance (*Jacqueline Drake* v. *Chief Adjudication Officer* [1987] QB 166; [1986] 3 CMLR 43; for other cases at this interface, see Collins and Meehan, 1994). In terms of EU equality legislation,[5] this impact upon the public–private divide can be seen in two areas of everyday life: first, matters relating to the economic circumstances of women; and, second, questions of reproduction, sexuality, and stereotypical assumptions about female labour.

Economic Circumstances

Here the effects of the EU are evident mainly in retirement, pay and pensions, and, to some extent, in income taxation.

Retirement In the SDA of 1975, there was an exception for provisions relating to retirement age, which differed for men and women because of the traditional assumption that women married, were usually about five years younger than their husbands, and that it was appropriate that spouses should retire at the same time as each other. Subsequent domestic case law confirmed that different normal retirement ages for men and women were excluded from the Act. The ECJ, however, ruled that the Equal Treatment Directive prohibited this exception (*Marshall* v. *Southampton and South West Hampshire Area Health Authority (Teaching)* [1986] QB 401; [1986] IRLR 140 (ECJ); and *Vera Mia Beets-Proper* v. *F. van Lanschot Bankiers NV* [1987] 2 CMLR 616). While different statutory pensionable ages could be maintained, the connection between these and different retirement ages was contingent, not necessary. Being made by an employer to retire was a form of dismissal, and dismissal was covered by the Directive.

Ms Marshall and, at the time, other women in satisfying occupations welcomed the ruling as an increase in opportunities. However, reflecting the fact that many people, both men and women, are not in fulfilling jobs, public opinion indicated a greater preference for both sexes to be able to retire when they wished between the ages of 60 and 65 than for equality at the upper age. The British government amended the law by permitting women to continue working until the age of 65 in the public and private sectors, and made consequential alterations to provisions for voluntary redundancy and early-retirement schemes.

Pay and pensions The related question of pensions has proved complicated. Part of the problem stems from whether an occupational pension is part of pay (thus covered by Article 119) or whether, in the case of a 'contracted out scheme', it is a substitute for the statutory pension (thus exempt, as allowed in the Directives, from equal-treatment requirements). And part of the problem stems from the practical effect on occupational pensions of hitherto different pensionable ages for men and women under the state scheme.

With regard to the first part of the problem, the ECJ ruled in 1990 that contracted-out pension schemes *are* part of pay and, like other occupational schemes, covered by Article 119 on equal pay (*Barber* v. *Guardian Royal Exchange Assurance Group* [1990] IRLR 240 (ECJ)). Such claims have often arisen when men have sought access to an occupational pension at the same (younger) age as women—a difference based on the convention of matching occupational pensionable ages with those of the statutory scheme, itself based upon different normal retirement ages. The 1990 decision raised a whole series of related questions—such as its retrospective effect, the use of actuarial assumptions, the raising of the female pensionable age to that of men, and access to pension schemes by part-time workers. These questions were addressed by the ECJ in a number of decisions in 1994 (Meehan and Collins, 1996) and, in 1997, it ruled, in a case arising from Northern Ireland, against certain limitations applied in the UK to part-time workers (*Magorrian and Cunningham* v. *Eastern Health and Social Services Board*, 11 December 1997, *Equal Opportunities Review*, 1998, no. 77, pp. 41–3).

Aspects of some of these rulings confirm the view adopted by the ECJ a decade earlier that part-time workers were entitled to rights comparable with those of full-time workers—a significant development in respect of inequality arising from the public–private division. But they have also resulted in new concerns. The fear that British women would be made worse off was confirmed by the Major Government's decision to equalize the state pensionable age at the age of 65, not 60, on the ground that 'the 60 option' would cost the country £7b. According to the EOCGB (1994) this will cost every woman now under the age of 30 £15,000. Contrary to the government's view, the Trade Union Congress calculates that equalizing upwards is *not* cheaper than equalizing downwards—because early retirements would make way for the unemployed, many of whom have children, and remove them from other, expensive benefit rolls.

Income taxation   Income taxation was also excluded from the scope of British legislation, though some changes to bring about more privacy for married women were introduced in 1990. In addition to being affected by vociferous domestic criticism of the previous rules, the government may have been influenced by the EU. Although Member States retain competence over taxation, the European Commission has taken an interest in how taxation systems affect women. In 1984, it presented a Memorandum on this subject to the Council of Ministers (1984). This recommended a system of totally independent taxation for all and at least the option of independent taxation for married couples. The British reforms fall short of completely independent taxation but the changes are partially positive. However, tax rules in general make it difficult to achieve compatibility between pensions provision and the goal of flexible, or 'gradual', retirement (*Equal Opportunities Review*, 1998, no. 77, pp. 10–11).

Reproduction, Sexuality, and Stereotypes

The three main areas of EU influence in this field are pregnancy and maternity rights, sexual harassment, and protective legislation.

Pregnancy discrimination and maternity rights   These issues form one of the most difficult areas in British law. Some statutory rights—such as protection against unfair dismissal, maternity leave and maternity pay, time off for antenatal care, and the right to return to work—are protected by an exception in the 1975 SDA. The Equal Treatment Directive also contains a derogation from the principle of equal treatment in respect of pregnancy and maternity.

However, the 'equal-treatment' basis of sex discrimination law has caused difficulties in the courts. At first, tribunals in Great Britain held that, since a man could not become pregnant and, therefore, that there was no possibility of comparison, the dismissal of a pregnant woman worker could not amount to direct discrimination. This approach was superseded by one which looked to the possibility of pregnancy being compared with 'analogous circumstances', such as sickness, experienced by men. While an improvement on earlier rulings, this approach was still inappropriate— since pregnancy is not an illness. Not only is it unhelpful, in terms of women's access to the labour market, for it to be considered as such but it reinforces the failure to see pregnancy as a normal, and valued, fact of life that needs to be accommodated routinely in public policy (Bacchi, 1991).

The Northern Irish tribunals adopted an approach similar to that which was to come in the ECJ. One NI tribunal held that the correct approach was to compare mothers-to-be with fathers-to-be, and another that discrimination against motherhood is the same as sex discrimination (*Donley* v. *Gallaher*, Case No. 66/86 SD. Decision 6 November 1987; *McQuade* v. *Dabering* [1989] DCLD 1, Case No. 427/89 SD. Decision 31 August 1989). The matter was clarified in 1990 in the ECJ in two cases that established that it is directly discriminatory for an employer to refuse to hire or to dismiss pregnant women, though not necessarily so to dismiss a woman because of extended sick leave (even if the illness is related to pregnancy) if men are dismissed in situations of comparable periods of sick leave (*Dekker* v. *Stichting Vormingscentrum voor Jonge Volwassenen (VJV-Centrum) Plus* [1991] IRLR 27 (ECJ); *Hertz* v. *Aldi Marked K/S* [1991] IRLR 31 (ECJ)). Since then, the Employment Appeals Tribunal in Edinburgh has ruled that when a contract of employment is still in existence, a woman should not be dismissed for being unable to return after maternity leave due to pregnancy-related illness (*Caledonia Bureau Investment & Property* v. *Caffrey*, 13 January 1998, *Equal Opportunities Review Discrimination Case Law Digest*, 1998, no. 35, p. 1).

In 1992, the Council of Ministers adopted Directive 92/85/EEC, referred to earlier, on the protection of pregnant women workers. The Directive provides for fourteen weeks continuous maternity leave and the maintenance of contractual rights, other than pay, during this period. Payment during this period must be at least equivalent to what would have been received by someone on sick leave, though it is permitted to make this dependent upon employment for the previous twelve months. Though the Directive is important because it explicitly protects women against dismissal, it received only a lukewarm welcome from national equality agencies—since its provisions were considerably weakened as a result of controversies during the politics of its adoption.[6] There were also criticisms of aspects of its implementation in the UK, such as the exclusion of low-paid women and anomalies between the period of leave allowed and the period of pay entitlement (EOCGB, 1993; EOCNI, 1993). Further criticism concerning the confusing plethora of statutes governing maternity rights has been reduced recently with their consolidation in the Employment Rights Act 1996.

Sexual harassment   As the problem of unwanted sexual attention at work began to be recognized, some efforts were made to deal with it through general employment law. In the 1980s, it began to be addressed as an issue of sex discrimination. In 1983, the Trade Union Congress (1991 [1983]) defined it in terms of unequal power relations between men and women in the workplace, and a number of cases began to surface. National courts accepted that a degrading, and uncomfortable, work environment caused by sexual harassment could constitute a detriment under the SDA.

The growing number of sexual harassment cases has been accompanied by significant action at the level of the EU (Collins, 1996). A European-wide study and extensive lobbying for a Directive led to statements by the Commission and Council that the Equal Treatment Directive may already outlaw sexual harassment. A Council Resolution stated that conduct of a sexual nature was 'an intolerable violation of the dignity of workers' (Council Resolution 90/C 157/02, OJ, no. C 157, 27 June 1990, pp. 3–4). Such conduct was to be regarded as unacceptable if it was unwanted or offensive and adversely affected a person's access to employment, training, or dismissal, and/or if it created a hostile, intimidating, or uncomfortable working environment. This was followed up with a Commission Recommendation and code of practice (Commission Recommendation 92/131/EEC, OJ, no. L 049, 24 February 1992, pp. 1–8) about the appropriate steps to be taken. There appears to be growing reliance on the Recommendation in national tribunals, including the UK, though there, as elsewhere, the status of the code of practice *vis-à-vis* legislation has still to be clarified. In 1997, one industrial tribunal accepted that an employer defence under the SDA was incompatible with the code, while another allowed the legislative provision to stand (*Equal Opportunities Review Discrimination Case Law Digest*, 1998, no. 35, p. 11–12).

As Collins (1996) points out, the Women's Rights Committee of the European Parliament fully intends to keep this issue in the public eye. Doubtless, this has helped to keep the attention of the European Commission on the issue. In July 1996, it produced a consultation document seeking views on the need for a binding Community measure on sexual harassment (Commission of the European Communities, 1996).

Protective legislation   In 1975, the SDA left intact, as an exception to the principle of equal treatment, laws that excluded women from certain types or patterns of work. This was controversial at the time, some people believing their repeal would lead to exploitation and others that outdated laws gave employers an alibi for excluding women from work that commanded higher salaries or wages. The Equal Treatment Directive of 1976 obliged Member States to review all protective measures and make changes in situations where 'the concern for protection which originally inspired them is no longer well founded'.

In carrying out the review on behalf of the government, the EOCGB accepted the argument that legislation barring women from working at night was being used as a pretext for denying sex equality and higher earnings (EOCGB, 1979). Its recommendation that these regulations be abolished was criticized (Jarman, 1991), but its view was corroborated in a European Commission report of 1987 that many provisions still in place across the EU had a negative influence on women's employment prospects. Since then, some British restrictions have been abolished outright; for example, the ban on the employment of women in mines and on cleaning machinery. Second, other protective measures have to give way to the principle of equal treatment, except where protection relates to pregnancy, maternity, and risks specially affecting women, or where the Secretary of State uses his or her power to modify the scope of the override.

The override is most likely to be used where there is a reproductive or fetal risk. Yet such risks do not affect only women, and men ought to be protected against them too, as the European Commission pointed out in its 1987 Communication. Focusing on the risks transmitted through women could lead to a continuation of 'blanket bans' on female employment, without necessarily securing the objective of protecting reproduction and fetuses.

Impact of the Legislation

EU influence on enforcement and remedies has brought about very considerable relief in particular cases (Collins and Meehan, 1994; Meehan and Collins, 1996). In terms of general outcomes, however, it is difficult to establish causal connections between legal reform and material change. There is a perennial debate about whether the law promotes or follows change that has taken place because of wider socio-economic factors. Perhaps it is possible, at most, only to establish correlations, or their absence, between the existence of legal rights and the scope of opportunities in the labour market.

In the UK, women's pay as a ratio of men's has remained at about 75 per cent since the late 1970s (having risen initially from 50 per cent, weekly figures, or 60 per cent, hourly figures); the number of applications to equal-pay tribunals has dropped, reflecting the likelihood that 'like work' provisions had outlived their usefulness; various factors have caused a low take-up of the alternative—'equal value'; and, even if 'equal value' steps are taken, differentials continue to exist because of differences in productivity systems and the like—or because, perhaps, of defective job-evaluation schemes.

One test of the effectiveness of the SDA would have been a decrease in occupational segregation; that is, if it had become normal to find a more equal proportion of both sexes working in occupations, or at levels of seniority where one sex had predominated previously, it could have been inferred that employers had made their recruitment or promotion practices more open. But the statistics show only a few signs that the labour market may be becoming more undifferentiated by sex. At the same time, the legal tool of indirect discrimination—a potentially powerful lever against systemic patterns of inequality because of its focus on the proportions of men and women who may or may not be able to comply with conditions of employment—has not been used purposively by the courts. Instead, it has become bogged down in technicalities and procedural issues (Collins and Meehan, 1994).

Moreover, as already indicated, UK governments have been ungenerous in their compliance with new requirements stemming from the EU. For example, ignoring, or responding slowly, to some key rulings; making it more difficult to claim disability allowances; challenging the content of the Directive for pregnant women workers; and equalizing retirement and pensionable ages upwards instead of downwards.

The evidence of the EU's impact is more positive or, at least, ambiguous. The positive interpretation by Edwards and MacKie (1993) of the EU conception of equality could be reinforced by reference to the ECJ's definitions of key aspects of the issue; for example, its narrowing of exceptions and its broadening of the concept of pay and retirement construed as dismissal. Other support could be found in European

Commission views about sexual harassment, income taxation, positive action, and so on.

On the other hand, others could argue that European policies embody a 'fiction' of sex equality—along the lines of Pateman's (1988; 1989) accounts of domestic polities. They could cite the watering-down of policies to meet the willingness of the slowest partners or the thoughtless adoption of concepts such as 'breadwinner', which, while eliminating direct discrimination, may reinforce indirect discrimination. Another illustration might be found in the statements of the ECJ that the two Directives on social security were intended to address only the situations of men and women as workers and not the general question of sex equality; and that, even so, this objective might be subordinated to others such as the relief of poverty (Nielsen and Szyszczak, 1993).

Also ambiguous is the special significance the Court initially attached to the bonding between mother and child in cases where it permitted the continuation of sex differences in rules about leave for adopting parents (*Commission of the European Communities* v. *Italian Republic* [1983] ECR 3273) and allowances for single mothers (*Ulrich Hofmann* v. *Barmer Ersatzkasse* [1984] ECR 3047). Yet, in a further twist to possible analyses, most ECJ rulings on pregnancy could be construed, not as reinforcing outdated values about the private sphere, but as corroborating the 'difference feminist' position that situations specific to women should have a normal place in public policy. Hoskyns (1996a, p. 17), for example, explains other positive rulings by reference to the judges' political awareness of the agenda set by feminist politics.

The fact that it is possible to have competing views argued out in more arenas than have been available in the past contributes to our conclusion, which sees some hope in the capacity of the EU to put a brake on the marginalization of equality issues in the UK.

Conclusion—the Promise of Pluralism

The UK was not a Member State of the EU when it introduced its EqPA, and the possibility of the SDA existed before membership was confirmed. Thus it could be said that the UK was a pioneer in this field. On the other hand, there had been warnings during earlier applications that the UK would fail the test of Article 119 (equal pay for equal work) and that this would matter. Also, by the time of discussion of a potential sex discrimination law, EU membership was certain and it was known that the EU was contemplating something like the eventual Equal Treatment Directive. So, conversely, it could be argued that it was EU membership that forced the UK to be a pioneer. Moreover, as noted, the government has experienced infringement proceedings in the ECJ, and many of the path-breaking individual cases in the Court have arisen from allegations by British women and men that domestic policy did not conform with European requirements.

It has, perhaps, not been a British tradition to use litigation to enforce either individual rights or collective public policies. At a general level, many advocates of constitutional reform in the UK, while concerned about 'democratic deficits', also appreciate that EU membership gives British citizens aspects of a kind of written constitution.

The introduction of equal-pay and antidiscrimination legislation was almost immediately followed by the advent of a series of Conservative Governments noted for their deregulatory philosophy. The sea change away from mixed economies and welfare states has occurred all over Europe, but in more muted forms than in the UK. In an era in which British governments tried to minimize rights and the roles of regulatory and collective bodies, resort to European law has provided virtually the only enforceable way of securing improvements to and filling lacunae in domestic equality legislation. It remains to be seen whether the coexistence of UK acceptance of a common European social dimension, which would facilitate progress on the Commission's Green and White Papers on social policy (1993; 1994), and the bases in the Amsterdam Treaty for human rights and anti-discrimination policies will be of more than cosmetic significance.

It can be argued that politics is not only about competition over the distribution of material resources, but is also a conflict over definitions in policies and about the distribution of opportunities for people and groups to be able to voice their interests and for their voices to be taken seriously. Siim (1991) and Hart (1993) have shown that women can succeed in inscribing their meanings into policy and practice in Scandinavia and the US. The cases referred to in this chapter exemplify what can be done as the result of a judicial channel in addition to those in the UK.

Breaking down the discriminatory consequences of thoughtless conceptions of the public–private division also needs vigilance in ensuring that the political system is pluralist enough for marginalized voices to be heard and an acceptance that this may entail special steps (Phillips, 1991; Mouffe, 1992). For reasons that are not always motivated by the idea of sexual justice, European institutions are hospitable to women lobbying for their definitions of what they think they need. The Commission is more open than the British civil service and is also accessible through its numerous advisory and monitoring groups and its support for networks and groups. The extensive consultation of 1993–4 initiated by the Green Paper on social policy is an example of the pluralistic opportunities it provides. Sponsored transnational networks in vocational training and childcare (Moss, 1990) raised awareness of differing standards and helped to inform calls for improvements. The EP is also more serious about women's rights at the European level than many national parliaments.

This is not to say that the political arrangements in the EU are ideal; as Bretherton and Sperling (1994), for example, point out, only some women's networks in Great Britain have become aware of, and able to use, such additional institutions and opportunities. On the other hand, Cockburn (1991) shows that these can be made accessible and exciting for women not normally at the centre of trade unionism and politics in Britain and other countries. It is also noteworthy that remoteness from mainstream UK politics appears to have been both an incentive and opportunity, not a barrier, to extensive participation by Northern Irish community associations—which are often women's groups—in European programmes of regeneration. In Northern Ireland, the EU notion of 'partnership' has been particularly important in a twofold way. It enables women to exploit what they are good at—for the sake of immediate concerns about, for example, training, the infrastructure, economic development, etc. And 'partnership' provides society at large with a pretext for new kinds of organization and behaviour that have helped to ameliorate the local political climate within which 'picking up the pieces' has fallen largely upon women (Women and Citizenship, 1995).

Thus, without wishing to overstate the significance of a European impact upon the adverse consequences of traditional conceptions of the public and private spheres, and the roles of men and women within them, it can be said that the existence of EU policies and practices has hindered the marginalization of sex equality in the UK. And the existence of EU institutions and transnational networks means that women have allies elsewhere and other arenas in which to stake political claims that may be thwarted at home.

Acknowledgement

The authors would like to acknowledge that this chapter draws upon Collins and Meehan (1994). Much of the original conference paper was used for an article in *Parliamentary Affairs* (Meehan and Collins, 1996). This chapter, therefore, now also draws extensively upon the latter article.

Notes

1   The chapter uses the term European Union (EU) throughout because of its now regular usage. Strictly speaking, the matters discussed here should be designated as emanating from the European Community (EC), since they are common policies arising under the first 'pillar' of the Maastricht Treaty, initiated in the Commission, considered by the European Parliament, decided upon by the Council of Ministers, and subject to the jurisdiction of the European Court of Justice. The EU also includes the two intergovernmental 'pillars' of the Maastricht Treaty covering Justice and Home Affairs, and the Common Foreign and Security Policy.

2   Amendments to legislation in Great Britain include the Sex Discrimination Act 1986, the Sex Discrimination (Amendment) Order 1988 (SI 1988, no. 249), and the Employment Act 1989. In Northern Ireland the comparable legislation is the Sex Discrimination (Northern Ireland) Order 1976 (SI 1976, no. 1042 (NI 15)), the Sex Discrimination (Training Designation) Order 1987 (SI 1987, no. 319), the Sex Discrimination (Amendment) (Northern Ireland) Order 1988 (SI 1988, no. 1303 (NI 13)), and the Employment Act 1989. This chapter refers to legislation applying in Great Britain, except where necessary in relation to cases in Northern Ireland.

3   Amended in Great Britain by the Equal Pay (Amendment) Regulations 1983 (SI 1983, no. 1794). Amended in Northern Ireland by the Equal Pay (Amendment) Regulations (Northern Ireland) 1984 (SI 1984, no. 16).

4   Word limits rule out full jurisprudence references to these debates. See, instead, Collins and Meehan (1994).

5   There are also examples of the relevance of the EU to disadvantaged women—especially those affected by deregulatory policies—arising from regulation in

spheres other than sex equality. One is the success of a reference to the ECJ aimed at ensuring that the 'Acquired Rights Directive' (for workers in general) was applied in the UK, not only to private sector employment but also in the public sector. This led to an amendment to the Transfer of Undertakings (Protection of Employment) Regulation 1981 (SI 1984, no. 1794) (TUPE), which now protects jobs, pay, and conditions when public sector is contracted out. Consequently, since 1993, workers (often female) who are the victims of competitive tendering and contracting out are able to rely on TUPE rules about the safeguarding of rights in the event of the transfer of business (EOCNI, 1996).

6   The British government opposed the legal basis on which the Directive was brought forward—that is on the basis of health and safety (where majority decisions could be taken) instead of workers' rights (requiring unanimity). While it was accepted that part of the Directive, on exposure to dangerous hazards, etc., was a legitimate health and safety concern, it was thought that bringing all aspects together was a means of circumventing the British 'veto'.

References

Bacchi, C. (1991), 'Pregnancy, the Law and the Meaning of Equality', in E. Meehan and S. Sevenhuijsen (eds.), *Equality Politics and Gender*, Sage Publications, London, pp. 71–87.

Bretherton, C. and Sperling, L. (1994), 'Gender and Policy: The European Union Dimension', paper presented at a conference on 'Women and Public Policy: the Shifting Boundaries between the Public and Private Domains' at the Erasmus University, Rotterdam, and Leiden University, Leiden on 8–10 December 1994.

Byrne, P. and Lovenduski, J. (1978), 'Sex Equality and the Law in Britain', *British Journal of Law and Society*, vol. 5, pp. 148–65.

Cockburn, C. (1991), *Getting Involved in Europe: the Experience of Three Innovatory Workshops for Women Trade Unionists*, European Trade Union Confederation, Brussels.

Collins, E. (1996), 'European Union Sexual Harassment Policy', in R.A. Elman (ed.), *Sexual Politics and the European Union. The New Feminist Challenge*, Berghahn Books, Providence, RI, pp. 23–33.

Collins, E. and Meehan, E. (1994), 'Women's Rights in Employment and Related Areas', in C. McCrudden and G. Chambers (eds.), *Individual Rights and the Law in Britain*, Clarendon Press, Oxford, pp. 363–407.

Commission of the European Communities (1984), *Memorandum on Income Taxation and Equal Treatment of Men and Women*, COM(84) 695 final (14.12.84), Office for Official Publications of the European Communities, Luxembourg.

Commission of the European Communities (1987), *Protective Legislation for Women in the Member States of the European Community. Communication by the*

Commission, COM(87) 105 final (20.3.87), Office for Official Publications of the European Communities, Luxembourg.

Commission of the European Communities (1990), *Equal Opportunities for Women and Men. The Third Medium-term Action Programme 1991–1995*, COM(90) 449 final (6.11.90), Office for Official Publications of the European Communities, Luxembourg.

Commission of the European Communities (1993), *Green Paper. European Social Policy. Options for the Future*, COM(93) 551 final (17.11.93), Office for Official Publications of the European Communities, Luxembourg.

Commission of the European Communities (1994) *European Social Policy—a Way Forward for the Union. A White Paper*, COM(94) 333 final (27.7.94), Office for Official Publications of the European Communities, Luxembourg.

Commission of the European Communities (1996), *Consultation of Management and Labour on the Prevention of Sexual Harassment at Work. Sexual Harassment*, COM(96) 373 (24.7.96), Office for Official Publications of the European Communities, Luxembourg.

Edwards, J. and McKie, L. (1993), 'Equal Opportunities and Public Policy: an Agenda for Change', *Public Policy and Administration*, vol. 8, no. 2, pp. 54–67.

Elman, R.A. (ed.) (1996), *Sexual Politics and the European Union. The New Feminist Challenge*, Berghahn Books, Providence, RI.

EOCGB [Equal Opportunities Commission GB] (1979), *Health and Safety Legislation: Should We Distinguish between Men and Women?*, Equal Opportunities Commission, Manchester.

EOCGB [Equal Opportunities Commission GB] (1993), *Formal Response to the Trade Union Reform and England Rights Bill*, January 1993, Equal Opportunities Commission, Manchester.

EOCGB [Equal Opportunities Commission GB] (1994), *What Price Equality?*, Equal Opportunities Commission, Manchester.

EOCNI [Equal Opportunities Commission NI] (1993), *EOC NI Comments on the Trade Union Reform and England Rights Bill*, January 1993, Equal Opportunities Commission, Belfast.

EOCNI [Equal Opportunities Commission NI] (1996), *Report on Formal Investigation into Competitive Tendering in Health and Education Services in Northern Ireland*, Equal Opportunities Commission, Belfast.

Hart, V. (1993), 'The Right to a Fair Wage: American Experience and the European Social Charter', in V. Hart and S.C. Stimson (eds.), *Writing a National Identity: Political, Economic, and Cultural Perspectives on the Written Constitution*, Manchester University Press, Manchester, pp. 106–24.

Home Office (1974), *Equality for Women*, Cmnd. 5724, HMSO, London.

Hoskyns, C. (1996a), 'The European Union and the Women Within: an Overview of Women's Rights Policy', in R.A. Elman (ed.), *Sexual Politics and the European Union. The New Feminist Challenge*, Berghahn Books, Providence, RI, pp. 13–22.

Hoskyns, C. (1996b), *Integrating Gender. Women, Law and Politics in the European Union*, Verso, London.

Jarman, J. (1991), 'Equality or Marginalization: the Repeal of Protective Legislation', in E. Meehan and S. Sevenhuijsen (eds.), *Equality Politics and Gender*, Sage Publications, London, pp. 142–53.

Meehan, E. and Collins, E. (1996), 'Women, the European Union and Britain', *Parliamentary Affairs*, vol. 49, pp. 221–34.

Moss, P. (1990), 'Childcare and Equality of Opportunity', in L. Hantrais, S. Mangen, and M. O'Brien (eds.), *2. Caring and the Welfare State in the 1990s*, Cross-National Research Papers NS 'The Implications of 1992 for Social Policy', Cross-National Research Group, Aston University.

Mouffe, C. (ed.) (1992), *Dimensions of Radical Democracy. Pluralism, Citizenship, Community*, Verso, London.

Nielsen, R. and Szyszczak, E. (1993), *The Social Dimension of the European Community*, 2nd edn., Handelshøjskolens Forlag, Copenhagen.

Pateman, C. (1988), *The Sexual Contract*, Polity Press, Cambridge.

Pateman, C. (1989), *The Disorder of Women. Democracy, Feminism and Political Theory*, Polity Press, Cambridge.

Phillips, A. (1991), *Engendering Democracy*, Polity Press, Cambridge.

Sevenhuijsen, S. (1991), 'Justice and Moral Reasoning and the Politics of Child Custody', in E. Meehan and S. Sevenhuijsen (eds.), *Equality Politics and Gender*, Sage Publications, London, pp. 88–103.

Siim, B. (1991), 'Welfare State, Gender Politics and Equality Policies: Women's Citizenship in the Scandinavian States', in E. Meehan and S. Sevenhuijsen (eds.), *Equality Politics and Gender*, Sage Publications, London, pp. 175–92.

Smyth, A. (1996), '"And Nobody Was Any the Wiser": Irish Abortion Rights and the European Union', in R.A. Elman (ed.), *Sexual Politics and the European Union. The New Feminist Challenge*, Berghahn Books, Providence, RI, pp. 109–30.

Trade Union Congress (1991 [1983]), *TUC Guide; Sexual Harassment at Work*, Trade Union Congress, London.

Women and Citizenship Research Group (1995), *Women and Citizenship: Power, Participation and Choice*, Equal Opportunities Commission/Women's Resource and Development Agency, Belfast.

7 Welfare-State Reform and Equal Opportunities: the Case of the Netherlands

JANNEKE PLANTENGA

Introduction

The Dutch welfare-state regime is under pressure. Established and expanded in the 1950s and 1960s, the first cracks were already visible in the 1970s, and in the 1990s few people believe simple repairs will suffice: the structure is in urgent need of complete renovation. Measures and proposals are aimed primarily at improving the Netherlands' competitive position and at stimulation of market forces—privatization and deregulation are the keywords here. The primary aim is economic growth and the prime tool is flexibilization. An extensive collective sector does not mesh with this image. Indeed, the search for a new economic and social order is also a search for a new distribution of responsibilities between the individual, the social partners, and the government.

Obviously, this reorientation also affects the position of women. Under the old regime, women were defined primarily as wives, housewives, and mothers. Women were held responsible for the domain of informal, unpaid care, while men were allocated the domain of formal, paid labour. This division of labour would be abolished to a major extent in the proposed new order. Influenced by urgent economic circumstances, but underpinned by ideas on the importance of paid work, everyone is supposed to capture a niche on the paid-labour market; however, without considering the implications for the organization of unpaid labour. In practice, it will mean that the differences between some men and some women will decrease, but the differences between women (and between men) are likely to increase.

This chapter focuses on the present debate about restructuring the Dutch welfare state. First, we will examine the historical points of departure of the Dutch regime and the current problems. Subsequently, we will look at the proposals designed to solve present problems and what they will mean for women. Then, the search for a new division of labour and care is documented by an overview of some recent measures and proposals in the field of social policy, working hours, and social security. In the next section the focus shifts towards socio-economic reality. The still persisting problems are examined, and the following question is asked: what can be expected from the new policy initiatives with respect to the unequal socio-economic positions of men and women? The chapter ends with some discussion of future developments.

The Dutch Welfare-State Regime: Points of Departure and Problems

When defining the historical keystones in the Dutch welfare-state regime, we can discern at least three major politico-ideological points of departure (Plantenga and Van Doorne-Huiskes, 1993). To start with, it can be concluded that the Dutch regime emerged from the realization that government could be used as an instrument to achieve certain goals. An important aim here was a striving for a legitimate division of income. The general feeling was that market mechanisms had to be corrected so that people who found themselves without paid employment were still able to lead a dignified life. A second important factor was the perception of the family as the anchorage of social stability and individual well-being. The family, and not the individual, was taken as point of departure for policy and regulatory measures. In practice this meant that the aim of full employment was translated into one paid job per family and that the wage structure was based on a breadwinner with a dependent spouse. This touches on the third aspect, i.e. the conviction that men and women were different. Man is active, rational, and goal-oriented and as such is ideally suited to work outside the home. In contrast, woman is passive, emotional, and dependent, meaning she is primarily suited to live inside the home.

The combination of these three starting points led to a labour structure with a very narrow base, in the sense that the aim was not maximum labour-market participation but rather the labour-market participation of the male breadwinner. At the same time, the care system was relatively broadly defined. Through a large-scale operation designed to redistribute income, attempts were made not only to ensure everyone had a reasonable income but it also left about half of the Dutch labour force free to provide the required household work and care. By an all-pervading system of breadwinner facilities, women were defined as mothers, destined for the private sphere, whereas men were responsible for the public sphere, the world of paid employment. In this division of work and care, the market plays a very modest role. In contrast, government has a large part to play, partly because it takes on certain care activities, but also and primarily because it creates a socio-economic environment in which care can be carried out informally, within the family unit.

The economic and social consequences of this specific welfare-state regime are extensive and—as has become apparent—untenable. Low labour-market participation implies a high fiscal and social-security premium burden on those who are in employment, because all of the 'inactives' have to be maintained. As a result, labour costs are high, which means productivity has to be equally high. Low-productivity employees— in practice people with little training and older employees—do not fit into this structure. They are then nudged out of the labour market and into the care system, via all kinds of unemployment, early retirement, and disability measures. The threat here is that an already narrow labour base becomes even narrower and the care system increasingly broader. This negative-feedback mechanism—more people with social security entitlements means more fiscal and premium pressure, which means higher wage costs, which means higher productivity requirements, which means even more people on benefit, which means even higher wage costs, and so on— emerged especially during the recessionary periods of the 1980s and forced government into action. The new slogan became 'A Working System of Social Security'. Central to this policy is that a solid system can only be brought about if calls on it are controllable.

The specific Dutch welfare-state regime is also under pressure for other reasons. Various social developments are at odds with the system's politico-ideological points of departure and compel adjustment. A welfare state based on the principle of the family as the smallest unit, with women prevented from participating fully in the labour market, no longer meshes with the reality of a society in which individualization is becoming increasingly the norm. Nor does it mesh with a world in which women and men are increasingly better educated and trained, and in which the right to self-determination is hardly questioned any longer. The Dutch welfare-state regime thus scores badly on two exceptionally important points: not only is a gender-specific division of labour between paid and unpaid work morally untenable today, the costs of such a structure threaten to become too high.

Reorientation

Problems surrounding the Dutch welfare-state regime led to the publication in 1990 of a classic of Dutch policy literature. *Een werkend perspectief* (A Working Perspective) is a report by the *Wetenschappelijke Raad voor het Regeringsbeleid* (WRR, Scientific Council for Government Policy), one of the country's most important advisory bodies on government policy. The Report points out the need to increase labour-market participation levels in the Netherlands, and introduces both cultural and economic arguments to support its recommendations. Paid employment, according to the WRR, is an important form of social integration. At a time when other integrative ties are withering (Church, family), participation in the labour process is especially important for social cohesion. The welfare state, in their view, only creates collective dependency rather than independent citizens. In contrast, formal employment is considered a major dimension in participatory citizenship. The economic argument refers primarily to the social waste generated by low participation, given the fact that human capital is not used productively. A further aspect is the negative consequences of low labour-market participation on the Dutch competitive position, because this generates an environment of high fiscal and premium pressure. Agreements made within the framework of European economic and monetary union may not prohibit breadwinner facilities, but the continual advance of economic entwinement forces EU countries to reach a certain level of conformity on socio-economic organization (WRR, 1990, pp. 7–8).

However, it has proved extraordinarily difficult to restructure a society whose organization is based on the traditional division of labour into a society facilitating more individualized lifestyles. There are several practical and principle objections. A practical objection is that the transitory stage is extremely complex and painful, because government policy is caught in the middle ground between attempts to protect existing facilities and the need to develop new initiatives. For example, the striving to dissolve breadwinner facilities on order to stimulate labour-market participation of the dependent spouse can lead to a situation in which one income is no longer sufficient to support a family. In reality this means a family is punished for the choices it made earlier, influenced by the selfsame government policy.

A principle objection has been picked up especially by the women's movement and refers to the fact that this new policy orientation overemphasizes the importance of paid work. The WRR proposals are criticized for its equation of full citizenship with labour-market participation, without taking into account or creating a place for the tasks and responsibilities traditionally associated with women's lives. Care has suddenly become ballast, to cite an influential article by Zwinkels (1990): deadweight that impedes carrying out the real task of the citizen, that is active participation in the paid-labour market. While work is increasingly described in terms of development and emancipation, care is increasingly labelled as a necessary evil, duty, and dependency. This criticism does not imply a rejection of attempts to develop a broader labour-market structure, but instead advocates the creation of a structure that leaves space for a care system tailored to human needs. This means our welfare-state regime should not only generate a reasonable income for as many people as possible—either through paid work or through the social-security system—but it should also ensure that people have the time to provide for their own and each others' care needs.

Policy Initiatives

This search for a new social order, based on the importance of both paid and unpaid work, has led to much debate in the Netherlands, and is an important underlying theme in the present debate about restructuring the welfare state. There appears to be a certain consensus regarding the fact that society should change and indeed has changed. The traditional division of labour, with its obvious distinction between breadwinners and caretakers, has already been transformed into a diverse range of lifestyle and career options. There also appears to be a certain consensus on the fact that, if labour-market participation of both sexes is the objective, care can no longer be seen as a completely private affair, as this will place limitations on women's labour-market participation.

From a policy point of view this means that the sharp, gender-specific division of paid and unpaid labour is gradually disappearing. Government policy now, on the one hand, seeks to support the integration of unpaid labour into the world of paid labour, whereas, on the other hand, the support for (full-time) care diminishes. This is not to say, however, that central government intervention is relatively strong. In fact, there is a strong emphasis on the role of social partners in this area. Some recent measures in the field of social policy, working hours, and social security may illustrate this development.

Facilitating Childcare

An important condition for labour-market participation of women is the availability of childcare facilities. Until recently, institutionalized childcare was minimal in the Netherlands. Childcare centres have only appeared in state budgets since 1975, and an explicit relationship between childcare and labour-market considerations was first recognized officially at the end of the 1980s. At that time, the *Stimuleringsmaatregel Kinderopvang 1990–1993* (Stimulatory Measure Childcare 1990–1993) was introduced, by the then Minister of Welfare, Health, and Culture. The aim of this measure was to expand organized childcare and achieve a better spread of facilities throughout the Netherlands. The subsidy measure was extended for a number of years and was terminated on 1 January 1996, when policy responsibility for childcare was transferred to local authorities.

The measure has indeed resulted in a major growth in childcare, both state subsidized and funded by employers. However, even in 1995 the public-funded services only covered about 8 per cent of all children under 3 years of age (European Commission Network on Childcare, 1996, p. 148). At less than 1 per cent, the level of extra-school care—for four-to-thirteen-year-olds—is especially extremely low. In general it should be noted that government policy with regard to childcare provisions is in favour of decentralized arrangements between the social partners. This results in a rather 'austere' strategy whereby government tries to restrict itself to a pioneering role only.

Working Hours Act

The combination of paid and unpaid work may also be stimulated by expanding the possibilities of tailored working times. To support the growing demand for more non-standard working hours from both employers and employees, the 1919 *Arbeidstijdenwet* (Working Hours Act) has been totally revised. The new Act, which has come to force on 1 January 1996, has two main aims. In the so called *considerans* it is stated that the aim of the act is not only to focus on 'the safety, the health and the well-being of employees in relation to their work', but also 'to promote the combination of work and care tasks, as well as other responsibilities outside the workplace'. Within the scope of this chapter, the second aim is of course especially important. Here, the worlds of paid and unpaid labour are no longer separated. Instead, it is recognized explicitly that in most cases paid and unpaid labour have to be combined and that this fact should be taken into account when the actual working hours are determined (TK, 1994–5a, p. 1).

It should be noted, however, that the real impact of the broad protective aim of the new Working Hours Act remains unclear, as the Act is mainly concerned to deregulated working hours. It is also unclear which working time patterns have indeed too great an impact on the ability of employees to participate in social life and how, when the occasion arises, the interests of the employee will be weighed against the interests of the employer.

Promoting Part-Time Work

Another way to facilitate the combination of paid and unpaid work is to promote part-time work, both quantitatively and qualitatively. A number of Acts have already been adapted to improve the position of part-timers in the sense that hour thresholds have been removed in areas such as the minimum wage and minimum holiday pay regulations (TK, 1994–5b). The same applies for social-security hour thresholds that have been almost totally abolished. A recent example of the equalization of rights of full-

and part-timers is the revision of the *Pensioen- en Spaarfondsenwet* (Pension and Savings Act), which has become effective in July 1994. This revised Act has positive consequences for women's pension rights, as the application of a minimum ceiling on hours, or of a minimum-wage ceiling, is prohibited. As a next step, legislation has been prepared that prohibits employers from introducing distinctions in working conditions based on number of hours worked (TK, 1995–6). This Act, which has come into force on 1 November 1996, gives part-timers an explicit right to equal treatment in areas negotiated by the social partners, such as (above-minimum) wages, holiday pay and entitlements, overtime payments, bonuses, and training.

A legal right to part-time work, as proposed by *Groen Links* (Green Left) (TK, 1993–4), ultimately proved a bridge too far. The core concept of this bill was that every employee who had worked for longer than one year with a specific employer would be entitled to reduce working hours by a maximum of 20 per cent. The proposal was accepted by the Second Chamber, but failed to make it through the First Chamber in December 1997, because Christian Democrat senators voted it down for a combination of practical, principle, and party-political reasons.

Parental and Care Leave

Another option for simplifying combined care and paid work is to increase leave opportunities for parents. The Netherlands has only one formal arrangement in this area—*Wet op het ouderschapsverlof* (Parental Leave Act)—which came into force on 1 January 1991. This Act stipulates that employees (read parents) have a legal right to take temporary, unpaid, part-time leave. Both parents are entitled to work less hours with a minimum of 20 hours per week for a period of six months. This right is effective until the child is 4 years old and starts school. Because the specifications of the Act are considered rather rigid, the government, in a recent proposal, offered employer and employees more flexibility. In this perception, parental leave would no longer necessarily be a part-time leave option; full-time leave would also be possible. One attendant advantage is that part-timers working less than 20 hours per week would also be eligible. No amendments have been proposed, however, on the unpaid nature of parental leave (SZW, 1994, pp. 10–12).

One leave regulation that is not specifically aimed at parents is care leave. This type of leave offers employees the opportunity to care for a sick relative, usually immediate and close family members, at home. There is no legal entitlement to care leave in the Netherlands. However, there are regulations through which leave can be taken in exceptional circumstances. In a recent governmental publication, *Om de kwaliteit van arbeid en zorg: investeren in verlof* (The Quality of Labour and Care: Investing in Leave), a legal right to care leave is characterized as premature. However, government policy aims at enlarging the support for leave facilities at a company level and to stimulate some forms of career break (SZW, 1995a, p. 9).

Social Security: from ABW to nABW

Whereas in the world of paid labour care responsibilities become more and more integrated, at the same time it becomes more difficult to care on a full-time basis. Especially the recent changes in the *Algemene Bijstandswet* (ABW, Welfare Act) make clear that rights that can be derived from caring work are being curtailed. Before the reorganization, the Welfare Act provided benefits for different groups through the *Rijksgroepsregeling Werkloze Werknemers* (RWW, State Group Regulation for Unemployed Employees) and the *Algemene Bijstand* (ABW-sec, General Assistance Act). RWW was available for people with a labour history, young people, and school-leavers; all RWW claimants had a job-application obligation. The ABW-sec was intended for groups who had few ties with the labour market; ABW-sec claimants, therefore, were exempted from the job-application requirement. In practice, men were more likely to fall under RWW, while women (especially lone mothers) dominated the ABW-sec. One of the most important changes in the new Welfare Act (nABW), which has come into force on 1 January 1996, is the merging of the RWW and the ABW-sec. As a result, lone mothers too have to apply for a job. The only exemption is made for lone (or one of the married) parents who have to care for one or more children under 5 years of age (cf. Bussemaker et al., 1997).

Social Security: from AWW to ANW

Apart from the General Assistance Act, the *Algemene Weduwen- en Wezenwet* (AWW, General Widows and Orphans Act) has also undergone some major changes recently. From 1 July 1996 onwards, the General Widows and Orphans Act has been replaced by the *Algemene Nabestaandenwet* (ANW, General Next of Kin Act). Under the provisions of the AWW, a widow was entitled to (non-means-tested) benefit if she was 40 years or older, or cared for one or more unmarried children under 18, or was disabled.

The old Act was due for review for a number of reasons. One was that its point of departure was based fairly explicitly on outdated role patterns in which men provided the income and women were left 'unprovided for' following a husband's demise. In practice, it appeared that many widows had other income in addition to their AWW benefit. It also transpired (in 1988) that the Act contravened the non-discrimination principle laid down in the UN International Covenant on Civil and Political Rights (ICCPR). As a result, widowers were also eligible for a pension. Entitlements to— and thus the cost of—the AWW increased considerable as a consequence.

Under the new ANW, entitlement to benefit exist if the next of kin is responsible for caring for a child under 18, or if s/he is incapacitated for work, or if s/he was born before 1950. The introduction of a year threshold rather than an age threshold means that the entitlement of (older) widow(er)s with no care responsibilities will gradually disappear. Moreover, the ANW also stipulates income testing; the introduction of this income test has resulted in a considerable saving on public expenditure.

Towards a New Worker Profile?

From the overview given above, it can be concluded that the clear division between labour and care is gradually becoming faint. Care responsibilities become more and more integrated into the world of paid labour. This development has been described as the rise of a new worker profile (cf. Passchier, 1992; OECD, 1994). This new worker distinguishes himself from his former colleagues by the fact that he no longer has someone else to take care of hearth and home, but that he himself tries to combine paid and unpaid labour. The counterpart of this development is that the entitlements that can be derived from unpaid care labour are under pressure. In fact, devoting time exclusively to care is no longer supported by policy and income security should, in principle, be built through paid labour.

These policy initiatives seem an important step in the right direction, as they create incentives for a more equal division of labour and care. Labour and care is made more compatible within an individual life and is no longer organized along gendered lines. This could lead to the conclusion that the new employment order has already come to existence in the Netherlands, giving rise to a new worker. Such optimism, however, may be premature, as reality does not always reflect the ideal. In assessing the current state of affairs there seem to be at least three problems: the new worker is above all a woman; the new worker is above all advocated by flexibility requirements; and the new worker is above all stimulated by economic reasons.

The New Worker is Above All a Woman

We have introduced part-time work as a way of facilitating the combination of labour and care and as an important element of the new employment order. Until now, however, women especially work part time; in 1995, the figure was 57.8 per cent, compared to 10.1 per cent for men. In addition, it should be noted that part-time work plays a rather different role in the careers of men and women. For men, part-time work tends to remain an incidental and temporary phenomenon at the start or end of a professional career, while for women it is a common method of combining paid and unpaid work. This difference is illustrated by the fact that 66.9 per cent of the female population in the 30–45 age group works part-time, compared to 7.7 per cent of the men in the same age group (cf. Plantenga, 1996).

The fact that women, especially, work part time, and that they work part time during the critical time for career advancement, raises some doubts on the desirability of this development. Part-time work seems only an improvement of the quantitative position of women on the labour market, whereas little has changed in qualitative terms. As a result, part-time work does not actually affect the prevalent division of labour and care: in contrast to their full-time working male partners, part-time working women have little prospect of building a career and thus continue to combine household and caring tasks with a paid job. Therefore, the traditional division of labour is not reformed, but rather perpetuated.

The New Worker is Above All Advocated by Flexibility Requirements

Above, the need for a new employment order is advocated, because continuous and full-time working hours are hard to combine with extensive care responsibilities. Flexibility in working time is the keyword here. At this point in time, however, the flexibilization of working hours seems more stimulated by the demand side of the labour market, thus by employers seeking flexibilization, than by employees seeking to combine paid and unpaid work. The already extremely diverse reality of flexibilization not only refers to call-up work, short-term personnel, and 'temps', but also involves the flexible deployment of permanent staff. Relevant examples here are the buying and selling of so-called *arbeidsduurverkorting* (ADV, reduction of working hours) and/or holidays; the introduction of a four-day, thirty-six-hour working week; flexible working hours varying from a minimum of thirty-two to a maximum of forty-five hours a week; and the curtailing of additional payments for unsocial hours, like evenings and Saturdays and Sundays (SZW, 1995b, pp. 9–10).

What remains problematic is that the flexibilization debate is carried out primarily from the perspective of the employer and the 'classic' employee, and that little attention is given to the question of how this trend relates to other relevant developments on the labour market, such as the increasing supply of female labour, the rise of dual-income households, and the growing number of single-parent families. For the new employee, the employee with care responsibilities, flexibilization often becomes a problem, because irregular hours, shift rotas, and split shifts are hard to combine with the fixed routine of care responsibilities. Indeed, the new employee does not have much need for flexibility; what he or she needs most is differentiation, that is tailored, but fixed and/or predictable working times. This attunement problem between flexibilization and differentiation can only be solved somewhat satisfactory if the former occurs in a context of consultation and (social) security.

The New Worker is Above All Stimulated by Economic Reasons

As argued previously, the labour-market participation rate of women in the Netherlands has been low for a very long time. Although in recent decades there has been remarkable growth in the numbers of women in the work force, when placed in an international context, the number and the structure of women's employment remains rather exceptional. The striking aspect here is the high number of women working part time. When these part-time jobs are expressed in full-time equivalents, it appears that only in Spain do women have a lower participation level.

This low level of labour-market participation has increasingly become the subject of policy initiatives. The direct cause is a growing awareness of the importance of paid work. At a more abstract level is the question of the welfare state's tenability and whether or not we can afford to maintain it. The low participation rate of women (and/or other groups in society) is seen as a cost factor that undermines the competitive position of a specific country. Seen in this light, the integration of care into the world of labour becomes an instrument serving a 'higher' goal, i.e. increasing the participation rate of women. Therefore, the perspective is not on care as such, nor on the equal sharing of paid and unpaid work, but on competitiveness. The danger here is that the male-biased employment order remains unchanged. However, there is an attempt to make the combination of paid and unpaid work less difficult for women.

To summarize: the strict division of labour and care is to some extent abolished by the new policy initiatives. However, the changes in the socio-economic positions of men and women seem more gradual than structural. The biggest problem seems to be that women have indeed changed their labour-market participation behaviour, but men's participation behaviour has remained almost unchanged. Moreover, the way in which various flexibilization strategies are interwoven with the use of male and female employees seems to exploit and confirm the inequality between men and women, rather than to create possibilities for a more equitable distribution of paid and unpaid work.

Future Developments

The specific organization of the Dutch social and economic order is clearly in the throes of transition. The traditional male–female distinction between labour and care is no longer recognized and has made way for a more individualized approach. In practice this means that government policy in no way perceives women's labour-market participation as problematic. In fact, the opposite obtains: official policy underwrites general participation in paid work, evoking supportive socio-cultural and economic arguments. Moreover, policy also has some conception of the preconditions required for such general participation, i.e. childcare and leave options. However, wariness about centralized intervention means the role of government here has been rather restricted: responsibility for childcare has been placed increasingly within municipalities and private companies, while the social partners are expected to shape and develop policy on leave regulations. Government only plays a more guiding role in those areas where emancipation and employment policies mesh. This is apparent, for example, in policy relating to part-time work. Given the fact that part-time work is seen as serving various goals—increasing employment in terms of numbers of people in work, expanding flexibility within labour organizations, and simplifying the combination of paid and unpaid work— the collective importance is emphasized here and policy is aimed at improving the legal position of part-timers.

Given this state of affairs, at least three scenario's for the future can be discerned. The first meshes emphatically with an already existing trend in which the position of both sexes is merging in a quantitative sense, but where little is changing in qualitative terms. The insider–outsider problem thus acquires a new dimension. What is at issue here is no longer exclusively the contradistinction between people with or without a job, but between people with a good or a bad job. Good jobs are still occupied primarily by well-educated, full-time working, white males, aged between 25 and 45. Peripheral to these 'good' jobs is a whole outer shell of less paid, flexible jobs, usually performed by women, but also by minorities and people with poor or inadequate education or training; in other words, the underprivileged on the job market. This flexible outer shell allows, as it were, the core security and stability, or, seen from the opposite perspective: the essential flexibility is transferred to employees in the shell.

Obviously, this scenario has few attractions from a feminist perspective. At the same time, there is some cause for optimism as it can be assumed that society will not divide itself along such absolute gender demarcations. Rather, this first scenario will also provide the preconditions of a second, more integrated scenario in which women's increasing labour-market participation will result in an adjustment of traditional divisions of labour. In this scenario, men can be expected to take on some of the unpaid care tasks. Partly influenced by the improved legal position of part-timers, they could, for example, decide to work four days a week. Men's labour-market behaviour would thus begin to bear more resemblance to that of women. The opposite development is just as probable: women who, blessed with a good education and a good job, adapt their labour-market behaviour to that of men. This does not necessarily mean they refrain from having children, but rather purchase child- (and household) care on the market. As a consequence of this development differences between some men and some women will certainly decline, but differences between women will only become greater. Such a development is, of course, greatly stimulated by the emphasis on decentralized control. After all, a stronger role for social partners carries the danger that women with a well-paying job will be in a position to rid themselves of care responsibilities through facilities offered by employers, whereas such options will not be open to women in less well-paid jobs and with less comprehensive collective labour agreements. As a result, these women will continue to be confronted with the task of combining paid and unpaid labour. In other words, class distinction will become more prominent in this scenario.

A problematic aspect of this scenario is, moreover, that it appears to undermine preconditions for the most integrated, third scenario, most evocatively described in the OECD report *Shaping Structural Change* (1994). Important preconditions here are flexible hours without changing jobs, intermediate part-time work with the option of returning to full-time hours, flexitime, job sharing, and the ability to 'capitalize' time over the working week. Such a fundamental change in existing relations requires a powerful offensive that emphasizes the major importance of these changes. However, the precondition for such an offensive appear to be lacking, through, on the one hand, central government's limited 'centralized intervention', and, on the other hand, through the lack of a common denominator among the female labour force: when class differences become more central, it may become increasingly difficult to unite groups of women around a programme of common interest.

In short: the 'new employee' is not with us yet and neither is the society sketched in the OECD report. The current dynamic continues to bear more similarities to the second scenario—with all its inherent inequalities.

References

Bussemaker, J., Drenth, A. van, Knijn, T., and Plantenga, J. (1997), 'Lone Mothers in the Netherlands', in J. Lewis (ed.), *Lone Mothers in European Welfare Regimes. Shifting Policy Issues*, Jessica Kingsley Publishers, London, pp. 96–120.

European Commission Network on Childcare (1996), *A Review of Services for Young Children in the European Union 1990–1995*, European Commission, Brussels.

OECD [Organisation for Economic Co-operation and Development] (1994), 'Shaping Structural Change: The Role of Women', in OECD, *Women and Structural Change. New perspectives*, OECD, Geneva.

Passchier, C.E. (1992), 'Naar een nieuw "werker profile"', *Sociaal Maandblad Arbeid*, vol. 47, pp. 119–25.

Plantenga, J. (1996), 'For Women Only? The Rise of Part-time Work in the Netherlands', *Social Politics*, vol. 3, pp. 57–71.

Plantenga, J. and Doorne-Huiskes, A. van (1993), 'Verschillen in arbeidsmarktposities van vrouwen in Europa. De rol van verzorgingsstaten', *Tijdschrift voor Arbeidsvraagstukken*, vol. 9, pp. 51–62.

SZW [Ministerie van Sociale Zaken en Werkgelegenheid] (1994), *Voortgangsrapportage positie vrouwen in de arbeid*, Ministerie van Sociale Zaken en Werkgelegenheid, Den Haag.

SZW [Ministerie van Sociale Zaken en Werkgelegenheid] (1995a), *Om de kwaliteit van arbeid en zorg: investeren in verlof*, Ministerie van Sociale Zaken en Werkgelegenheid, Den Haag.

SZW [Ministerie van Sociale Zaken en Werkgelegenheid] (1995b), *CAO-afspraken 1995. Eerste interimrapportage*, 95/1, Ministerie van Sociale Zaken en Werkgelegenheid, Den Haag.

TK [Tweede Kamer der Staten-Generaal] (1993–4), 'Wettelijk recht op deeltijd', *Handelingen van de Tweede Kamer der Staten-Generaal*, 23 538.

TK [Tweede Kamer der Staten-Generaal] (1994–5a), 'Bepalingen inzake de arbeids- en rusttijden (Arbeidstijdenwet)', *Handelingen van de Tweede Kamer der Staten-Generaal*, 23 646, nr. 12.

TK [Tweede Kamer der Staten-Generaal] (1994–5b), 'Gelijke behandeling deeltijd-voltijd', *Handelingen van de Tweede Kamer der Staten-Generaal*, 24 020, nr. 1.

TK [Tweede Kamer der Staten-Generaal] (1995–6), 'Wijzigingen van het Burgerlijk Wetboek en de Ambtenarenwet in verband met het verbod tot het maken van onderscheid tussen werknemers naar arbeidsduur', *Handelingen van de Tweede Kamer der Staten-Generaal*, 24 498, nr. 1–2.

WRR [Wetenschappelijke Raad voor het Regeringsbeleid] (1990), *Een werkend perspectief. Arbeidsparticipatie in de jaren '90*, SDU Uitgeverij, 's-Gravenhage.

Zwinkels, M. (1990), 'Zorgen als ballast?', *Tijdschrift voor Vrouwenstudies*, vol. 11, pp. 247–59.

PART IV
HEALTH, REPRODUCTION, AND THE ENVIRONMENT

8 Gender Dimensions of Occupational Health and Safety in Canada: the Case of Fetal Protection from Toxins in the Workplace

THERESE JENNISSEN

Introduction

Reproductive-health protection[1] for women in the paid-labour force is a clear illustration of the interconnectedness of the public and private spheres of women's lives. It touches on the lives of women both as producers in the paid-work force and as reproducers of children and the family. By exploring the evolution of reproductive-health protection policy in Canada,[2] this paper highlights those factors that influenced policy change and shifted the boundaries between the public and the private, expanding the public sphere in an area that previously had been acutely private.

Focusing on one type of health hazard, toxins, the chapter seeks to understand how toxins have come to be defined largely in terms of their effects on the fetus. This has occurred even though we know that various toxins can adversely affect not only the fetus but many other parts of the reproductive system as well as the general health of both women and men. This chapter poses two questions: why has the fetus been singled out for special attention? and what are the implications of this for women and for men in the workplace? The answers to these questions are complex and lie in part in the early history of health-and-safety policy in Canada.

Reproduction, 'the bedrock of private life' (Pascall, 1986, p. 20)[3] became a public concern soon after women entered the wage-labour

175

market in Canada in the mid-nineteenth century.[4] Early protective legislation prohibited women from employment in some industries and put limits on their conditions of employment in others. The public debate over reproductive health protection eventually shifted as women began to challenge their exclusion from certain sectors of the economy and to call for equal treatment with men. The long and complex process of competing demands on the state for reproductive-health protection and equality ultimately resulted in fetal-protection policy. The tensions between protection and equality animated the public debates throughout the 1960s, 1970s, and 1980s and continue in the present day.[5]

Women's Health and Safety: the Shifting Policy Debates

Protecting Women in the Workplace

The Canadian state has played a role in regulating health and safety in the workplace since the 1880s. Although nineteenth-century wage earners were primarily male, many women and children worked in factories and shops in order to supplement the family wage. Early health-and-safety legislation was initially aimed largely at keeping women and children out of certain industries (e.g. mining) and/or limiting the hours and types of work that they could perform (e.g. in factories and shops).

There are a number of reasons for the development of protective legislation in the 1880s, but it is commonly accepted that the ideological base of protection lies in nineteenth-century, Victorian morality concerning the position of women in society. Women were regarded as physically and morally weaker than men and therefore in need of protection. Factory work, it was feared, would unleash a number of dangers for women. These perceived dangers included 'sexual weakness', insanity, and consumption. Victorian morality, however, had a material base; it served the interests of the newly-developing industrial-capitalist economy. The wage-labour system was thought to undermine the structure of the traditional family. The harsh industrial world was seen not only as conducive to moral corruption, but also detrimental to women's capacity to bear children and to keep the family structure intact (Jennissen, 1991). 'The introduction of women and children in the workshops', it was felt, would 'tend to modify seriously the family relations, if not annihilate them' (Jennissen, 1991, pp. 171–2). The traditionally very private issue of reproduction was thereby shifted onto the public agenda, not because women had asked for it, but because it served the interests of the private market economy. It served to ensure the continuation of procreation and family life in a nascent industrial-capitalist economy that depended on an available labour force.

Factory legislation was established in Ontario in 1884, and similar legislation followed in the other provinces. The Ontario Factory Act restricted the hours that women could work, and eventually women were excluded from night work altogether. The legislation also specified that separate lavatories for women be set up, and limits were established on how many women could be crowded together into one workspace. The Acts required proper ventilation of harmful gases, vapours, and other impurities generated in the course of the production process (Jennissen, 1991, p. 195). The Shops Act regulated conditions of work in shops and stipulated that women have suitable seating arrangements, limited hours of work, adequate meal breaks, and adequately ventilated places to work. In addition to being excluded from night-work, women in late nineteenth-century Canada were excluded from working in or around mines.

Occupational health-and-safety regulations for male workers have a different history. Generally, protection for the male worker was slower to develop and initially focused on protecting men from the physical dangers inherent in the railway and mining industries. Men's reproductive health was not considered in the early years of health-and-safety regulation, and even today, with information pointing clearly to the negative effects that some workplace hazards have on the male reproductive system, policy initiatives directed specifically at protecting their reproductive health are not forthcoming.[6]

Women's Equality in Conflict with Protection Policies

Although health-and-safety policies grew incrementally between the late nineteenth century and the 1950s, few fundamental changes were made during that period.[7] This was to alter dramatically in the late 1960s and early 1970s as Canada entered an era of reform. Amidst a wide range of other movements, the women's movement was revitalized, and occupational health and safety re-emerged in what Eric Tucker calls the 'second wave' of regulation (Tucker, 1990). Important changes occurred in the area of occupational health and safety as the result of pressure from trade unions, the New Democratic Party, environmentalists, researchers, and women's groups and as a result of changes that were occurring internationally, particularly those emanating from the International Labour Organisation.

By the 1960s the use of chemicals in the workplace had increased dramatically and the second wave of occupational health and safety concentrated on the health effects of these toxins. Health problems such as cancers, asthma, lung diseases, immune system disorders, and reproductive health problems are not immediately obvious. The emphasis on health represented an important breakthrough for workers whose health problems had previously been ignored because of the long latency periods and complex aetiologies of many diseases. With the exception of women's reproductive health, this trend was a departure from the late nineteenth century when the focus was primarily, although not exclusively, on safety. Occupational-safety policies tended to focus on obvious and immediate problems such as broken or severed limbs, scalds, burns, and other physical injuries. The focus on health exposed an entirely new range of work-related hazards, including the effects of chemicals.

Although our knowledge of the effects of chemicals on the human body is still very underdeveloped,[8] during this era there was an increased public awareness of the use of chemicals in the workplace as well as concern over their potential effects. Employers, moreover, were not unaffected by the studies showing the effects of toxins on the fetus. Offspring of workers are not covered by workers' compensation legislation in Canada. Lawsuits may be launched against a mother's employer on the basis that a child's anomalies were caused by hazards in the workplace. In order to protect themselves from liability cases involving adverse birth outcomes, some employers attempted to keep pregnant women out of their workplaces.

Public debates and debates in the trade unions centred around three important worker rights: the right to know about dangerous working conditions, the right to direct participation on health and safety committees, and the right to refuse dangerous or unhealthy work. Occupational health-and-safety acts were developed in various Canadian provinces, with the province of Quebec adopting an innovative protective-reassignment policy. During this same time, the Canadian Centre for Occupational Health and Safety was established to centralize and deliver information on a range of health-and-safety issues of interest to Canadians. Accompanying the second wave of government regulation was the promise that a healthy and safe working environment was one of the fundamental rights of all Canadians (Canadian Centre for Occupational Heath and Safety Act, 1978, c. 29, s. 2).

The rebirth of the women's movement was an important part of the dramatic changes in the 1960s. This was reflected in the growth of women's groups, an increase in women entering politics, growth in women's literature and art, and women's increased participation in the paid-labour market. Female labour-force participation was no longer marginal; women retained a continuous involvement in paid labour while marrying, giving birth, and raising young children. Paid labour had become an integral part of many Canadian women's lives. By 1971, 39.4 per cent of the Canadian workforce over the age of 15 were female, compared to 29.5 per cent in 1961, 20.7 per cent in 1941, and 17.6 per cent in 1921 (Vanier Institute of the Family, 1994, p. 65). During this period, women's equality had become an important social and political concern.

Grass-roots feminists and feminists working within more conventional structures brought forward a number of issues of importance for women's equality: birth control, access to abortion, affordable housing, pay equity, childcare, work, divorce, women's pensions, and women's health. In 1967, largely in response to pressures from the women's movement, the Canadian government established a Royal Commission on the Status of Women (RCSW). The 1970 Report of the RCSW contained 167 policy recommendations to promote equality for Canadian women. Institutional structures and mechanisms were established within government to develop and coordinate plans and policies that were to improve the situation of women in Canada. This 'national machinery for the advancement of women' took a number of forms (Canada, Status of Women, 1993). In 1971, a Cabinet Minister responsible for the advancement of women was appointed, and the office of the Co-ordinator for the Status of Women was established (it became the Status of Women Canada in 1976). In 1973, a government-funded independent Advisory Council on the Status of Women (which recently has been dismantled) came into being to 'bring before government and the public matters of interest and concern to women' (Canadian Advisory Council on the Status of Women, 1993). One of the matters it brought forward was the exclusion of women from certain jobs on the basis of their reproductive capacity. The government of Quebec and women from within the newly-developed government structures for dealing with women's issues were also beginning to take up this issue.

Varying perspectives about what constituted the appropriate boundaries between the public and private spheres came to the fore during this period and changed the course of the debates over occupational health and safety. Although women were now directly involved in the debate, not all women agreed on how these changes should occur. Women's equality issues came into conflict with many health-and-safety policies that promoted protection through the exclusion of women from the workplace. This conflict had an important impact on the direction that occupational health-and-safety policy was to take. On the one hand, there was the notion that women, because of their childbearing capacity, should be protected from hazards in the workplace, and a growing body of information stressed the seriousness of toxins in the work environment and their impact on human health. On the other hand, as women's groups pointed out, this differential treatment of women was effectively sex discrimination. As a result, in the 1970s, health-and-safety policy was revisited and revised from the perspective of women's equality.

Fetal Protection: a Compromise

A number of health-and-safety policies identified as discriminatory against women were revised during this time. The Canadian government, aware of the conflict that existed between protection and discrimination, was struggling for ways to resolve the dilemma, as the following letter to the International Labour Organisation illustrates (Miller Chenier, 1989, p. 14):

> The Government of Canada is aware that at the time of its adoption, Convention No. 45 was intended to prevent exploitation of women workers and was considered a step toward social progress. However, it is now considered within the various jurisdictions of Canada that the Convention limits the employment opportunities of women and that it is, therefore in contradiction to the principle of equality of treatment and opportunity between men and women workers to which the Government of Canada attaches a great deal of importance.

The case of atomic radiation is an important example of policy changes made to remove the discriminatory treatment of women. In 1946 the federal Atomic Energy Board of Canada (AECB) was established to control materials used in producing atomic energy, and in 1947 the Atomic Energy Control Regulations were developed. The regulations were revised in 1960 to include standards for the use of protective procedures and instruments, and to ensure that proper labelling and warnings about radiation were in place. At this time the revised regulations established permissible exposure levels for workers. The same levels were set for men and women, but persons under the age of 18, persons of vulnerable health for whom working with radiation was unsuitable, and pregnant women were excluded from employment in atomic energy (Miller Chenier, 1989).

In 1974, the regulations were changed to set differential, maximum permissible radiation exposure levels for men, women of childbearing capacity, and pregnant women (who were now permitted to work in this field). The various exposure levels created serious practical and administrative problems and had the effect of excluding women of childbearing capacity from work in the nuclear-energy industry (Miller Chenier, 1989). The result was that women were not being hired, because to hire them would cause the industry too many problems. This resulted in human-rights complaints in the early 1980s by women who were denied work in the industry because of their sex. Women pointed out that they were being excluded largely from traditionally male-dominated, higher-paying jobs, even though these same hazards existed in more traditional 'female job ghettos' such as hospital and health-care work (Langton, 1980).

Eventually, the regulations were amended again in 1985 to remove the differential exposure levels between men and fertile women. Women were now subject to the same exposure limits as men; pregnant women were required to inform their employers as soon as they found out they were pregnant. Lower maximum-exposure limits existed for pregnant women.

The tensions that existed between protection and equality for women in the Canadian workplace were played out in policy modifications in the 1960s and 1970s. As a result, women of childbearing capacity were no longer excluded from some places of work based solely on their sex.[9] Instead the 'protective' component of health-and-safety policy was limited to protection of the pregnant woman for the sake of the fetus, thereby shifting the boundaries between the public and the private so that effectively a smaller group of women was included.

Not all women agreed with the policy adjustments and the new directions of protective legislation. Fetal protection continued to be regarded by some women as discriminatory, and human-rights cases against employers continued (Labour Canada, Women's Bureau, 1988). Others saw the focus on the fetus as inadequate for protecting reproductive health, and the general health, of women and men. Miller Chenier argues this latter point in her 1982 study for the Canadian Advisory Council on the Status of Women. She concludes that (1982, pp. 44–5):

> Researchers, employers and legislators have focused on the incidence of birth defects, spontaneous abortions and stillbirths as prime measures of the effect of workplace hazards and have attributed such effects solely to transmission by the mother, ignoring the role of the father in reproductive outcome.

Meanwhile, 'men continue to work in environments that are dangerous to both their general health and their reproductive functioning' (ibid.). Although there is still a debate over protecting reproductive health in Canada, fetal protection remains a predominant theme. Currently, some of the trade unions in English-speaking Canada are expressing particular interest in policies of protective reassignment for pregnant or breastfeeding women, which shifts the narrow boundaries of fetal protection.

Protective Reassignment for Workers Who Are Pregnant or Breastfeeding Women: beyond Fetal Protection

Protective reassignment[10] for pregnant women or women who are breastfeeding refers to policies that give a woman in this situation the right to a modified work environment, a reassigned job, or in the event that neither of these can be achieved, a temporary leave of absence until her child is born and/or the woman has finished breastfeeding. A woman is eligible for reassignment if the job she is holding is deemed to be hazardous to the unborn child, the mother by reason of her pregnancy, or to the child she is breastfeeding. The woman is required to present her employer with a medical certificate attesting to the fact that the environment in which she is working may be dangerous. Quebec is the only province in Canada to have a protective-reassignment policy of this nature in place, although the federal government introduced a modified version for selected government employees in 1993.[11] In Quebec, the majority of the cases under this legislation are due to ergonomic risk factors. Other risk factors include chemical, biological, physical, and other (Lippel et al., 1996, p. 185, tableau 1).

The Quebec legislation was adopted in 1979 with the passage of the Occupational Health and Safety Act. According to the legislation the first consideration in protective reassignment is workplace modification. If this cannot be done, attempts are made to reassign the woman to a different job away from the hazard. Failing this, the woman is entitled to temporary leave of absence benefits and 90 per cent of her salary (Public Service Alliance of Canada, 1994).

In Quebec, when a woman cannot be reassigned or the workplace cannot be modified to accommodate her, she will be compensated 90 per cent of her salary as well as receive benefits. The money is provided directly by the employer at the regular rate of pay for the first five days after which she receives payments from the workers' compensation system, the *Commission de la santé et de la securité du travail* (CSST). This financial provision is a major advance for the status of women in Quebec and makes this policy unique in Canada. The policy has proven to be very popular with women in Quebec, where the number of requests was 20,642 in 1991 (Fudge and Tucker, 1993), with the vast majority of claims granted.

In theory, protective-reassignment policies require employers to clean up workplaces to accommodate pregnant or breastfeeding women, although it is not clear how effectively this works in practice and research remains to be done in this area.[12] One concern is that there is no compelling financial incentive for employers to reassign workers. In Quebec, compensation for women on temporary leave is paid out of the general compensation fund of the CSST and is not experience-rated. This means that assessment rates do not go up for individual employers who frequently use the temporary leave arrangement, creating a disincentive for employers to modify dangerous work environments.

However, while it is not clear that protective reassignment for workers who are pregnant or breastfeeding is cleaning up the workplace, it cannot be categorically opposed, because it provides an important measure of security for women. It provides women with some protection from hazards in the workplace as well as some economic security. In this sense protective reassignment for pregnant or breastfeeding women goes far beyond the very narrow limits of fetal-protection policies. Only a small group of Canadian workers, however, have the right to this policy.

Summary

The private sphere of reproduction became a public concern soon after women entered the wage-labour system in Canada. The nature of the public debate, however, shifted over time to a point where fetal protection became the main focus of reproductive-health protection. The argument made in this paper is that fetal-protection policies in Canada have developed as a political compromise between two very public and conflicting social trends. Canada's long history of excluding women from certain jobs, particularly in areas traditionally occupied by men, came into direct conflict with a strong women's movement in the 1960s and 1970s. Policy-makers were not able to simply remove barriers to women, because the resurgence in interest in health-and-safety issues, particularly toxic chemicals and their effects on the reproductive system and on the human body generally, had become important public issues. Fetal-protection policies, it is argued, served as an important political compromise for governments and policy-makers. For a number of groups (women, men, government, employers) fetal-protection policies appear to serve valuable functions.

For example, fetal-protection policies protect, to some extent, the fetus from hazards in the workplace and thus benefits society by producing healthy children with less demands on the health-care and social services. By selectively focusing on pregnant women, the policies do not discriminate, in theory, against non-pregnant women of childbearing capacity, thereby serving an equality function. These policies protect the employer from liability cases resulting from possible damages to a fetus that has been exposed to toxins in the work environment. Fetal-protection policies also serve important political functions, because governments provide some protection to those deemed to be the most vulnerable, while at the same time not increasing significantly the cost to employers.

Protective reassignment for pregnant or breastfeeding women provides women with a broader range of choices—a modified work environment, reassignment, or temporary leave from work with pay, benefits, and a guaranteed job upon return. The focus of the attention, in this case, goes beyond the fetus to consider the health of the pregnant or breastfeeding woman.

Implications of Fetal-Protection Policies for Women and Men

On the surface, fetal-protection policies appear to be beneficial to a number of interests in society. The following section outlines the implications of fetal-protection policies for Canadian workers by examining how well the objectives of protection and equality have been met. This paper does not question the need to protect the fetus from the harmful effects of the workplace, but it challenges the narrow perspective of fetal protection and the continued practice of removing women from their places of work.

How Protective Are Fetal-Protection Policies?

Fetal-protection policies deal with only one, albeit a very important, aspect of human reproduction. However, they ignore the importance of protecting the entire reproductive-health spectrum of both men and women for healthy reproductive outcomes. Toxins in the workplace can interfere with not only the developing fetus, but also with sexual functioning, the ability to conceive or cause conception, and carrying to term a healthy offspring free of diseases in childhood (see Figure 9.1). There is the continued belief that hazards are transmitted only through the woman's body, although there is evidence that they can also be transmitted through males (Olshan et al., 1990; Gold et al., 1994).

Fetal-protection policies, moreover, do not ensure protection of the embryo in the early stages of pregnancy. The embryo is most susceptible to chemical and biological damage during the first eight weeks of pregnancy when its major organs are developing. However, a woman may not be aware of her pregnancy until she has entered her second month or later. By this time considerable damage may have occurred to the embryo.

The term 'fetal protection' is problematic, because it implies that the fetus is somehow separate from the mother. Clearly the health and safety of the fetus cannot be separated completely from the health and safety of the mother at this stage in its development, because the fetus depends on the mother. Protective reassignment policies, on the other hand, are based on a clearer understanding of the relationship between a mother and her fetus/child. Not only is the fetus seen to be in need of protection but also the mother requires protection as long as she is carrying the fetus or breastfeeding her child.

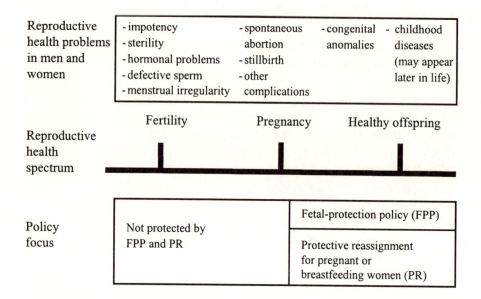

Figure 8.1   Female and male reproductive health

It has been established that 'all known reproductive toxins have other adverse effects on the health of adult workers' (Klitzman et al., 1990, p. 4). Toxins in the workplace are known to cause serious health problems, including asthma, cancer, heart disease, immune system disorders, and lung problems. The unknown effects of toxic chemicals far outnumber the known effects. In the United States, in 1984, comprehensive data were available for only 18 per cent of all drugs, 10 per cent of pesticides, and less than 10 per cent for all other classes of chemicals (Messing, 1991). The reproductive effects of only about 5 per cent of chemical and physical agents in the workplace in the United States are known (Gold et al., 1994). Clearly, there needs to be more research conducted on the chemicals that are used in places of work and in the environment generally. Cases of breast cancer are increasing rapidly in Canada, and yet a possible connection between breast cancer and the work environment/general environment has not been explored fully.

Fetal-protection policies have been more actively debated in male-dominated work environments while traditional 'women's work' continues to be seen as comparatively safe. This has occurred despite the fact that the same serious reproductive-health hazards (toxic chemicals and radiation) exist in female-dominated jobs such as hospitals, dry-cleaning institutions, laundries, and laboratories (Miller Chenier, 1982; Klitzman et al., 1990). Moreover, women are often exposed to hazardous toxins in the privacy of their homes. There is a need to acknowledge and study the female work environment not only from the perspective of reproductive health but also to understand the more general health-and-safety hazards characteristic of female-dominated jobs—hazards such as repetitive strain injuries, sick building syndrome, stress, and violence in the workplace. While fetal-protection policies are not designed to deal with these more general aspects of health, a preoccupation with fetal-protection policies has served to detract from this broader perspective.

Although fetal-protection policies appear to hold the fetus in higher esteem than they do the adult worker, in fact, they do not adequately protect either party. Protective reassignment for pregnant or breastfeeding women extends some protection to the breastfed child and the mother, although it may be that this is being accomplished through the traditional means of removing the woman from her place of work. By focusing on the removal of individual pregnant women, these policies divert attention away from any concrete changes that may need to occur in the production process and in the workplace.

Has Women's Equality Been Served through Fetal Protection?

Compared to earlier protective policies that excluded women from certain jobs, fetal protection represents, in a very limited sense, a slight shift towards equality for women (see Figure 9.2). Fetal-protection policies are directed toward excluding a smaller proportion of women (i.e. pregnant women as opposed to all women, or all women of childbearing capacity) from the workplace for a shorter period of time (i.e. during pregnancy rather than forever or as long as women have the capacity to reproduce). Theoretically, non-pregnant women (including those of childbearing capacity) are not to be affected by these policies. In practice, however, it is not clear that fetal protection is applied quite so rigorously, and evidence continues to suggest that women are still excluded from places of work by virtue of the fact that they are female (Fudge and Tucker, 1993).

The fact that fetal-protection policies seem to apply more often in male-dominated jobs brings into question how fairly fetal-protection policies are applied. Are they being used to keep women out of traditional 'male jobs'? The extent to which employers use these policies to exclude women from male-dominated jobs is not clear and is difficult to determine accurately.

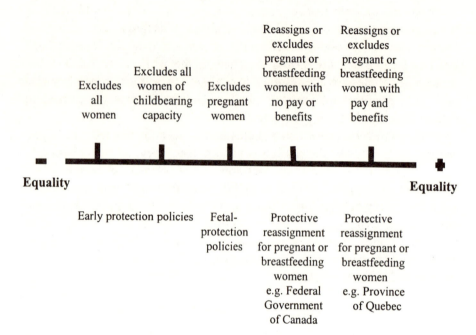

Figure 8.2   **Reproductive-health protection and equality in employment**

In terms of women's equality, protective reassignment represents a step forward from fetal protection. These policies are less discriminatory, because they provide a woman with an income, benefits, and a job to return to in the event that she had to be laid off.

Fetal-protection policies do not represent a significant shift from the traditional treatment of women throughout our history. These policies continue to take individual women out of their work environments rather than cleaning up the environments. They continue to focus on pregnant working women as mothers more than as workers. Women are still regarded as the only transmitters of harmful substances to offspring, despite evidence to the contrary. These policies ignore the fact that toxins can affect both male and female reproduction at many different points along the reproductive health spectrum, including childhood health. Moreover, they ignore the fact that all health, including reproductive health, needs protecting in the workplace.

What about Men?

Fetal-protection policies and protective reassignment deal exclusively with women and fetuses; men are not considered. This is problematic, because a number of agents, including chemicals, exist in the workplace that can render a man sterile, or impotent, or that can adversely effect sperm production. Current research also suggests that teratogens (i.e. hazardous substances that cause developmental abnormalities in an embryo or fetus) can be passed from a father to a child through seminal fluid (Olshan et al., 1990; Gold et al., 1994).

Although our knowledge base is growing, we still know very little about the toxic effects of chemicals on reproductive health; we know even less about the toxic effects on the male reproductive system. This is an area that requires serious attention, because policy-makers and governments are reluctant to make changes if the evidence is not conclusive.

Conclusion

The traditionally private issue of reproduction became an important public concern shortly after women entered the wage-labour market in Canada, and reproductive health protection continues to be an important focus in the field of occupational health-and-safety policy. Over the years, the public debates over what was appropriate state intervention in this matter shifted. Initially, women were regularly excluded from work that was considered dangerous to their reproductive health, morality, or ability to keep a family functioning. These policies eventually ran headlong into considerations of women's equality, and modifications to a number of occupational health-and-safety policies followed. The modifications to health and safety polices liberalized access to employment for women of childbearing capacity generally, but pregnant women were still given differential treatment in the name of protecting the fetus. Thus the focus of the public policy effectively narrowed.

Protective reassignment for pregnant or breastfeeding women provides important benefits to women and to the unborn fetus, but it may be that it continues the historic Canadian tradition of removing women from the dangerous work environment rather than cleaning up the environment and making it safe for everyone. It is simpler and less economical to employers to remove an individual, pregnant woman from a place of work for a limited period of time, even when paying most of her salary, than it is to clean up the workplace.

While protective reassignment is more beneficial for women in many ways, both protective-reassignment and fetal-protection policies suffer from a limited scope. They serve important political functions, because they appear to protect the vulnerable fetus, the potential baby, when in fact the entire reproductive system needs protecting; the entire human body needs protecting from hazardous work environments.

The future direction of health-and-safety policy in Canada is not clear at this point in our history. Although trade unions and governments have shown interest in adopting protective-reassignment policies for workers, it is questionable how much will change in the near future. Both federal and provincial governments in Canada are preoccupied with debt and deficit reduction and Canada's ability to compete in the global marketplace. Governments have been devolving themselves of responsibilities for social programs and services, including regulating the workplace, and the resulting cutbacks and lay-offs mean that the power base of trade unions is eroding. This rapidly changing political and economic climate will undoubtedly shift the tenor of the debates over the future of health-and-safety policy, and with trends toward globalization, the public debates may well be played out on the world stage.

Acknowledgement

I would like to thank Anthony Pizzino, Senior Officer of the Health and Safety Department of the Canadian Union of Public Employees, for his comments on this document and for providing important insight and valuable references. The views presented in this document, however, are those of the author.

Notes

1   The term 'protective' requires qualification. It implies that reproductive health was, in fact, protected, and it carries with it the implicit assumption that these policies were motivated entirely by a desire to protect reproductive health. As this paper will demonstrate, there is debate over how protective these policies were as well as why they were developed. The term 'reproductive-health protection' is used in this paper as a way of being consistent with its usage in the (mainly (English-language) Canadian and American) literature. Other words that are sometimes used and that convey a different message are 'exclusionary', or 'restrictive' policy.

2   Health-and-safety policy in Canada is the responsibility of various levels of government. At the provincial level the province of Quebec has embarked on a unique course of action that will be discussed briefly in this paper in the section on protective reassignment. For the main part, this paper deals with federal policy and the experiences of the province of Ontario.

3   Pascall refers to reproduction as 'the process of creating and sustaining human life. This includes conception, birth, and the care of children: it also includes daily maintenance (of labourers and others)' (Pascall, 1986, p. 24).

4   Reproductive-health protection is obviously only one public forum where issues of reproduction have been raised. Others include the debates over contraception, abortion, reproductive technologies, and the role of the state (to intervene on behalf of the unborn in cases where mothers are using drugs).

5   For a discussion of a similar debate in the British context, see Lewis and Davies (1991).

6   Some chemical (e.g. anaesthetic gases, DBCP, lead, mercury, PCBs) are known to contribute to adverse reproductive-health outcomes in men, but more research is required in this very underdeveloped area. Evidence is increasingly suggesting that some childhood cancers could be related to parental occupational (paternal and maternal) exposure to chemical and physical agents and that childhood cancers should be considered part of the array of occupational reproductive-health hazards. See Olshan et al. (1990); Gold et al. (1994).

7   The exception to this is the development of workers' compensation legislation, which focused on compensating accident victims not on protecting the health of workers (Jennissen, 1981).

8   It has been estimated that in the United States there are approximately 20,000 workers exposed to toxic materials (though not necessarily all reproductive toxicants). Of the 104,000 chemical and physical agents in the workplace as determined by the National Institute for Occupational Safety and Health Registry of Toxic Effects of Chemical Substances, the reproductive effects of at least 95 % of them have not been assessed. See Gold et al. (1994, p. 363).

9   In Ontario, lead is an important exception to this trend. The blood-action lead level has been set at a lower level for women than men. A pregnant woman is

required to notify her employer, who will send her to a physician, who then decides whether or not she should be removed from the workplace.

10   Protective reassignment is sometimes referred to as preventive reassignment or precautionary leave. In Quebec, it is referred to as *le retrait préventif de la travailleuse enciente ou qui allaite*.

11   In June 1993, Bill C-101 was proclaimed. It modified the Canada Labour Code and the Public Service Staff Relations Act. These amendments included provisions for protective reassignment of pregnant and breastfeeding women covered by the two Acts, but a woman can only take leave *without pay*. Moreover, only selected workers are covered by this arrangement. See Public Service Alliance of Canada (1994).

12   One study of the use of protective reassignment in Quebec concluded that in the vast majority of cases women were removed from the workplace rather than modifying workplaces to make them safer (see Public Service Alliance of Canada, 1994, p. 20). A note of caution about this information is in order, however, because it only includes cases where an intervention has occurred and does not include those cases that may have been settled immediately by a woman and her employer. That is those cases where the legislation may not have been resorted to, are not included in the data collection. This can present an inaccurate picture of what is occuring. It did not include cases that were dealt with informally, although studies have been done on the use of protective reassignment for pregnant or breastfeeding women in Quebec.

References

Canada, Status of Women (1993), *Canada's National Machinery for the Advancement of Women: a Case Study*, Status of Women, Ottawa.

Canadian Advisory Council on the Status of Women (1993), *Expanding Our Horizons: the Work of the Canadian Advisory Council on the Status of Women and Its Context*, Canadian Advisory Council on the Status of Women, Ottawa.

Fudge, J. and Tucker, E. (1993), 'Reproductive Hazards in the Workplace: Legal Issues of Regulation, Enforcement, and Redress', *Legal and Ethical Issues in New Reproductive Technologies: Pregnancy and Parenthood. Research Studies of the Royal Commission on New Reproductive Technologies*, vol. 4, Supply & Services, Ottawa, pp. 161–338.

Gold, E.B., Lasley, B.L., and Schenker, M.B. (1994), 'Introduction: Rationale for an Update', *Occupational Medicine: State of the Art Reviews*, vol. 9, pp. 363–72.

Jennissen, T. (1981), 'The Development of the Workmen's Compensation Act of Ontario, 1914', *Canadian Journal of Social Work Education*, vol. 7, pp. 55–71.

Jennissen, T. (1991), 'Regulating the Workplace in Industrial Ontario: the Origins of Occupational Health and Safety Policy in Canada, 1880–1914', unpublished Ph.D. thesis, McGill University.

Klitzman, S., Silverstein, B., Punnett, L., and Mock, A. (1990), 'A Women's Occupational Health Agenda for the 1990s', *New Solutions*, vol. 1, pp. 1–11.

Labour Canada, Women's Bureau (1988), *Annotated Bibliography on Reproductive Health Hazards in the Workplace in Canada*, Labour Canada, Ottawa.

Langton, M. (1980), 'Double Exposure: the Fight Against Reproductive Hazards in the Workplace, *Healthsharing*, vol. 4, no. Fall, pp. 13–17.

Lewis, J. and Davies, C. (1991), 'Protective Legislation in Britain, 1870–1990: Equality, Difference and their Implications for Women, *Policy and Politics*, vol. 19, pp. 13–25.

Lippel, K., Bernstein, S., and Bergeron, M-C. (1996), *Le retrait préventif de la travailleuse enciente ou qui allaite: réflexions sur le droit et la médecine*, Les Editions Yvon Blais, Cowansville.

Messing, K. (1991), *Occupational Safety and Health Concerns of Canadian Women: a Background Paper*, Women's Bureau of Labour Canada, Ottawa.

Miller Chenier, N. (1982), *Reproductive Hazards at Work: Men, Women and the Fertility Gamble*, Canadian Advisory Council on the Status of Women, Ottawa.

Miller Chenier, N. (1989), *The Selective Protection of Canadian Working Women*, Women's Bureau, Labour Canada, Ottawa.

Olshan, A.F., Teschke K., and Baird, P.A. (1990), 'Birth Defects among Offspring of Firemen', *American Journal of Epidemiology*, vol. 131, pp. 312–21.

Pascall, G. (1986), *Social Policy. A Feminist Analysis*, Routledge, London.

Public Service Alliance of Canada (1994), *Protective Reassignment of Pregnant or Breast-feeding Workers*, Public Service Alliance of Canada, Ottawa.

Tucker, E. (1990), *Administering Danger in the Workplace: the Law and Politics of Occupational Health and Safety Regulation in Ontario, 1850–1914*, The University of Toronto, Toronto.

Vanier Institute of the Family (1994), *Profiling Canada's Families*, The Vanier Institute, Ottawa.

9 Power, Policy, and Health: European Women's Perspectives on the Human Genome Analysis

JALNA HANMER and INEKE KLINGE

Introduction

This chapter describes European Union funded research into women's perspectives on the ethical, social, and legal applications and implications of the human genome analysis. It draws attention to the gendering of policy-making and the differential impact on women of applied science in genetics. Women's views on the human genome analysis demonstrate factors that shape the construction of the boundaries between the public and private spheres and their significance in the context of gender. Women identify dilemmas and contradictions clustering around social or public versus individual or private interests. The legitimacy of the division into the public and the private are contested when considering individual choice, autonomy, and control as against state involvement. Values expressed as responsibility, plurality, and tolerance promote the importance of the acceptability to society of new developments. The relationship between genetic therapy and health care raises the issue of appropriate arenas for public policy.

The human genome analysis is being publicly promoted as a health programme in the science media, such as the UK television programme *Horizon*. As is customary in science developments, there has been little public debate on the massive expenditure involved and the social desirability of the human genome analysis. Traditionally, the funding of science proceeds without direct public accountability for major expenditure or for the impact on human life of the associated technological innovations. Only in Germany, with the national sensitivity of some of its population to eugenics, has there been sustained criticism, with demands for a moratorium and outright cessation of the programme. Decision-makers have not discussed the potential military, commercial, and social implications and applications of the human genome project with the general population or those groups most likely to be affected by the technological applications arising from it.[1] While this may be seen as standard practice, the extent of scientific and social disquiet before a major programme begins is unusual. This implies both a challenge to the view of science as a process of discovery unencumbered by social objectives and to the view of science as a purely positive activity.[2] However, it fits well within the paradigm of science as an unstoppable, inevitable activity.[3]

This chapter draws on a study commissioned by the European Commission, DG XII, Biomedicine Programme.[4] This study examined the issues that would need to be included if a full public debate on women's perspectives on the human genome project were to occur. It is likely that the funder did not begin to appreciate the depth of the critique women would present and hence was open to a proposal they might otherwise have rejected. As one of the responsible officials explained, the proposal was interesting because 'we do not know anything about women's views'. This illustrates both the lack of mainstream interest in women's views and the marginality of feminist literature on the new reproductive technologies and developments in human genetics.[5]

As women's views had not been previously assessed separately, it could not be assumed that women think themselves to be affected in the same way as men by these developments. It seemed important to examine the ethical basis from which women in the European Union make judgements about scientific, medical, and legal developments in this field, as women's gendered experience may lead to a differently focused ethical discussion. A final aim was to present women's concerns and ethical thinking in the hope that these will be useful in future public-policy decision-making on the human genome analysis and its applications.

The research involved a pilot study in an area where women were known to have limited knowledge. Therefore, in constructing the samples for the interviews and the questionnaires in the then twelve Member States, account was taken of the differing positions women occupy in relation to the human genome project. The samples were drawn from women who were most likely to have sufficient knowledge to have an informed opinion—that is women who see the programme as directly relevant to themselves through current and future medical interventions, women in the community with responsibilities for promoting and improving health care for women, women who work in this scientific field, and women whose work includes making the views of women known to a wider public. Women in these four categories are both actual and potential opinion-makers, and could be located through relevant organizations in each of the twelve countries then constituting the European Union. Thus each sample country contained a range of women: some of whom are in occupations or who are personally in the forefront of the scientific developments under discussion and some of whom have very limited knowledge, although located in the type of organization where more extensive knowledge is appropriate.

Stratified samples were developed for a second reason: it was not possible to randomly sample sufficient women to make statistical comparisons. Twenty-six specific professional and organizational types were identified within the four major categories, and each national researcher was asked to obtain one interview within each type. As not all countries had women in every group, 277 interviews were conducted in total. Each researcher also was asked to obtain 100 completed questionnaires based on the four categories. As this was not always possible in every country the total received was 977. Interview questions and questionnaires were translated into the nine languages of the European Union and distributed to the researchers. The twelve research teams collected data, submit the questionnaires for centralized analysis, and provided national research reports on the interviews.

The questions explored with women covered their knowledge of and views on the human genome project, the applications of genetic screening and gene therapy, and personal and demographic data.

Views on the Human Genome Analysis

Views on the desirability of the human genome analysis varied from very positive to very negative. Only a few women had no doubts about its value and they cite a number of factors: the improvement of humankind through the prevention and therapy of disease by 'improving the ability to predict, diagnose and treat genetic disease' (P);[6] the increase in knowledge and the further progress of science is described as the progress of humanity; 'Identifying and mapping the genes on the human chromosomes and sequencing the pairs of nucleotide bases of which genes are composed' is seen as a fascinating enterprise, the creation of an enormous database (UK, P); the knowledge is described as: 'It is like breaking the code and looking into the crystal ball' (DK). Others, however, compare the sequencing of DNA with 'deciphering the *Encyclopaedia Britannica* letter by letter, without understanding what you read' (B), or with 'it is as if we are about to open a letter which was never addressed to us' (DK).

Other advantages are described as providing answers to questions on the understanding of the way organisms work, of evolution, of the origin of humankind, of the self—questions that represent the interests of philosophers (G). Future improvements in the applications of screening and therapy are said to have the following advantages: people will 'know their limits and be able to take more informed choices in questions about having or not having children' (NL), or in adjusting their lifestyle; individual decisions based on genetic information will decrease costs of health care, provide a better basis for the administration of drugs (UK), and improve the quality of life. A few women believe that genetic defects will become eradicated in the future, in comparable ways to tuberculosis (IRL). Some women, who doubt whether there will be useful therapeutic advantages, stress the importance of the expected spin-off, comparable to space projects. These responses mirror those of current public policies that do not recognize a conflict of interests between the public and the private.

Women have views on the origins of the human genome project. They see it as a response to human curiosity to explain and understand life, the progress of molecular biology, the needs of researchers for discoveries, and the 'loneliness of science'. This is a traditional view of science and the scientific quest. When women explore who is responsible for the human genome project it becomes clear that the majority doubt the traditional view of science and the scientific quest as being value-free and just for scientific curiosity or to have more control. Women see responsibility lying with many different actors: science, financiers of science, science policy, society, including themselves. If women think the responsibility lies with scientists and geneticists it usually makes them suspicious; they think of 'the scientists who flourished in the hotbed of Hitler' (G), and the financial exploitation of scientific knowledge becomes a concern.

Information Issues

The information that women possess about the human genome analysis, in this study, is almost certainly unusually high in relation to the general population of women in the EU Member States. Even so, between one quarter and three-quarters of the women who responded to questionnaires or by interview regard themselves as completely uninformed. There are national differences, but throughout Europe women with adequate or sufficient knowledge work in scientific and medical fields in laboratories, hospitals, or universities. The specific understanding women have varies greatly. Some of the women interviewed are able to explain in detail the human genome analysis project, but generally the term, human genome analysis, is unfamiliar to women not working in scientific areas. Genetics as a term is more familiar, but its meaning is not clear to many women, including those with higher education outside science disciplines.

Women have less information on gene therapy and genetic alteration than on genetic screening. Most women from all countries, however, do not think they have sufficient information and would like more, including women from disability groups and organizations concerned with infertility, who stress the difficulty of obtaining relevant knowledge. In all countries women are substantially more dissatisfied than satisfied with the level of information on all interventions. Across the European Union, even women who regard their information as adequate do not always think it is sufficient. This is a substantial finding as it applies generally and the lack of information raises profound issues about women's ability to make ethical decisions and to influence public policy.

A perceived lack of information also calls into question the reliability of sources and the knowledge they provide. Women are much more likely to receive information from the media than any other source, but very few women think that this information is adequate. The media can be the only source, even for some professional health-care providers such as physicians. Medical specialists are the second source of information for women, and the adequacy rating, while not high, is better than for the media. Counsellors, advisory services, educational institutions, family, and friends are sources of information for even fewer women. This is a reflection of the general lack of discussion on the human genome project, screening, alterations, and therapies. These findings apply across the European Union.

Confidence in the information received is affected by women's views about the sources of the information given. The media are not always trusted. For example (IRL):

> Full information was not given in the report I read on Down's syndrome. Only a small percentage are severely disabled. I know that 80 per cent are mild to moderately disabled, which means they can lead independent lives. I don't think the (media) information is true, basically.

Women question the validity of media reports, seeing them as inadequate due to lack of expertise or because of the interests the media represent. Some women note a tendency for the media to be biased towards science and fascinated by technology.

Specialist media sources are deemed more reputable. These include material from family-planning clinics and professional journals. Here the information is seen as 'minimal and factual' (I). However, the belief that there are sources without a point of view is challenged: 'all sources have their own particular bias and it would be necessary to get information from every available source in order to get a balanced view' (UK). Or a lack of confidence may reside, not in the media itself, but in science: 'science is not neutral, because it is connected with political power or personal beliefs' (I, B). Thus any dissemination, however faithful to its sources, contains a point of view. Direct contact with medical professionals or genetic counselling when pregnant is another major source of information.

In six countries—the UK, Portugal, Basque Country/Spain, Netherlands, Italy, and Belgium—women are more confident than not that the information they have received is correct; but in Denmark, Germany, Ireland, and Greece the reverse is true. As the samples are small and nonrandom, these national differences may be of no consequence, but given that the sample is stratified and draws on the most informed layer of women, any doubt about the correctness of the information received raises important ethical and social issues.

The same sources that women gain information from are given as desirable sources, that is medical and scientific personnel, medical and scientific media, the media generally, educational institutions, women's organizations and disability groups, family and friends. Not all these sources are providing as much information as women would like, particularly for women's organizations. Danish women express a wish for more factual information and some would like it to be digested by women's organizations for them. One informant raised a common issue: 'No women's organization has ever dealt with genetic issues other than conception outside a woman's body' (I). Women who point out that the preparation and distribution of information tend to be governed by certain interests, in particular the interweaving of the commercial and politico-ideological, want more information from sources they trust politically. Multiple sources appears to be a way of dealing with the issue of trustworthiness and relevance.

Questions on the applications of genetics, because of their greater familiarity, enabled women to comment more fully on ethical issues.

Genetic Screening: Dilemmas and Contradictions

Overall, women are more likely than not to think screening should take place in the general population, except for women in Germany. Women in all countries consider that screening provides benefits, particularly for the health system and society generally but also to the economy, with the exception of women in Germany; few of whom think screening offers benefits in any way or to anyone. Women who do not think there should be screening of embryos or adults are particularly concerned about social issues. These issues include the relation of the individual to the state, to science and technology, to commerce and industry, to religion and spiritual life.

Women's ethical thinking attempts to mediate between apparently irreconcilable social possibilities opened up by technology. The dilemmas and contradictions that women identify cluster around social versus individual interests. These issues are at the boundary between the public and private domains. Resolving dilemmas and contradictions that pit individual or private interests against those of the state and society is at the heart of women's ethical thinking in four areas: identifying and reducing hereditary conditions versus eliminating or discriminating against individuals; choice, autonomy, and control: individual versus social interests; scientific developments versus natural life/religious/spiritual values; the state and its social institutions/formations versus individual rights.

Hereditary Genetic Conditions

The reasons why women support screening may focus on one or the other side of the public–private division: 'Any prevention is better than any therapy' (I, B); 'Prevention of a sufferer's birth will have only positive social consequences' (I, B). Women with disabilities express both opinions: 'nobody has the right to bring into life a person who will be troubled throughout life' (G); and 'personally, I prefer that five invalid children are born than a whole population be subjected to genetic screening' (D).

Women in some countries are very sensitive to the racism, the fascism, and the possibility of social exploitation that may arise with genetic screening (D, G, B, P). The women interviewed in Germany reject screening for religious reasons, estimates of the technological effects, historically based fear or anxiety, personal threats in the case of women suffering from hereditary conditions, and the extension of state power. For example, under hospital conditions women can give up their opposition to screening, feeling that '[t]his kind of knowledge contains something creative, which makes it difficult to resist', or women can feel that they have a general difficulty in saying no, or feel they have no option but to submit, 'I am always asked things that I know will happen in any case' (D).

Women point out that some conditions are routinely screened for already by prenatal screening. Those who favour screening could place stringent conditions on their answers in an effort to mediate a perceived contradiction between social benefit and individual harm, such as 'screening should only be for the benefit of the individual and the information should never be used against them or lead to personal or social discrimination' (B, I, P). Dilemmas and anxieties include fear that in the future people with health problems will be further marginalized and stigmatized and face social discriminations.

Choice, Autonomy, and Control

The issues of choice, autonomy, and control are raised through consideration of who is to be screened: whole populations or specific groups. Most women regard the issue of genetic screening of whole populations as against specific groups to be different, although women have advanced reasons for why both are undesirable socially. Certain conditions are more likely to be seen as acceptable for screening—such as heart disease and age-related conditions—while other women express concern over what conditions should be on the list.

Mediation of the contradiction between social 'good' and individual harm is a major focus of women's views. Women want limits on screening of adults and embryos that exceed those currently in effect in most European countries. The type of limits women would like are remarkably similar across the European Community. Focusing on the individual, one basic principle is that not only should individuals not be forcibly screened but individuals should be completely free to decide if they want to take part in genetic screening. The view that government bodies should decide who to screen is far more likely to be rejected than accepted, as is the suitability of doctors as decision-makers.

Scientific Developments

As well as a concern for individuals and the groups to which they may belong, there is the question of genetic inheritance. Women scientists can be critical of the human genome analysis, questioning the wisdom of placing so much emphasis on genes (NL, P):

> Genes are not autonomous structures. Their function depends on the interaction with the rest of the organism. With personal attributes, there is a considerable degree of uncertainty about the extent to which a certain predicted trait will be expressed or whether it will be expressed at all.

The same questioning of scientific values is made of the applications that flow from the identification of particular genes: 'Early diagnosis is of questionable value in the absence of therapies. Those diseases that are not treatable should not be screened for' (B, P). The opposite view, that there are no reasons to obstruct the progress of science or screening for embryonic conditions, is held by a very small minority.

Whether inspired by religious or other spiritual sources, human genome analysis can be seen as a manifestation of human overestimation, of scientists playing God, and of falling prey to the dogma of practicability, that is, what can be done must be done. This may sacrifice the self-determination of the individual, the sense of responsibility for the weaker or underprivileged, and the principles of plurality and tolerance (B).

The State and its Social Institutions

There is disbelief that screening can be successfully regulated and that it will not be used against people. Views expressed by German women are particularly negative on these two factors. Women may focus on who makes the decisions to explain their reluctance. Another concern is access to knowledge; genetic screening can lead to personal and social discrimination in relation to schooling, employment, insurance, interpersonal and psycho-social life, and forensic science (I, D, B, P). Privacy, confidentiality, and civil rights can be threatened through the danger of disclosing and misusing genetic information (B, P). The social issues concerning control of these techniques have no easy answers: 'Is there any guarantee that no exploitation will happen? Who will give this guarantee and how will he keep it?' (I, B).

Concern is expressed about tailoring people to jobs on the basis of their genetic constitutions, as this approach ignores humanizing the work environment. The example of Silicon Valley hiring practices in the US is cited as and example of selection of those able to physically withstand the work processes (D). For insurance companies, screening of potential applicants extends their ability to insure without running the risks implied by illness. Women think an extension of economic interests will lead to a denial of a justification for 'deviant life' and will increase discrimination against those who are ill and sick (I, B). The commercialization of human genome research through patenting also raises ethical concerns (D).

Health Care and Screening

The limiting of screening to an individual health issue that is capable of being controlled by medicine can be seen as crucial to the maintenance of individual rights. However, women who are specialists in the field are concerned that there should be a legal framework that progresses in parallel with scientific developments to avoid possible exploitation and abuse. Screening of adults is rarely thought to be against religious beliefs and practices or to be dangerous to their health, but women overwhelmingly think strict limits must be set on the application of genetic screening in terms of who can be screened, for which conditions, and who can undertake genetic screening. Specialists in the field suggest additional limits: screening should take place in established centres that will take responsibility for the information they give to individuals, and these institutions should not be under the control of the medical and scientific staff directly involved.

Widespread support is given for ensuring respect for confidentiality, rejection of obligatory pre-implantation or prenatal screening followed by abortion, setting up of advisory and counselling services, and offering health education. The state is seen to have a role to play: it can pursue social policies advantageous to people who have adverse genetic conditions and make society sensitive and accepting of them. Resolving the social implications of genetics requires interdisciplinary groups of academics and professionals to work together.

While genetic screening raises questions concerning the legitimacy of current boundaries between public policy and private concerns, these are amplified by gene therapy and genetic alteration.

Gene Therapy and Genetic Alteration: Shifting Boundaries

Gene therapy raises many of the same issues, but because it is more experimental and contains the possibility of germ-line therapy women identified additional issues. As with screening, intervention for any reason other than therapeutic is rejected. Many women take the view that genetic intervention should be guided by necessity and the possibility of success, without giving rise to negative effects in the patient's future. Success should be certain before treatment is allowed. Adults need correct information and must make the decision. These are the basic principles that women cling to for safety, but a few women do not accept that gene technology is part of medical science, even though it is increasingly penetrating medicine (D).

Gene therapy and genetic alteration is connected to the field of embryo research and embryo experimentation. Implanting an altered embryo will require large-scale experimentation to be able to offer this as a therapy. While there is an identifiable resistance against this instrumental use of embryos, and possibly a lack of knowledge about the experimental phase, many interviewed women have no problem accepting embryo research and experimentation, as they do not convey the status of personhood to early *in vitro* cell stages.

In general, women think that treatable conditions should be considered for gene therapy, but many women expressed fears for the future. Women are sceptical about the possibilities and consider genetic therapy and alteration to be very dangerous. Specific fears include that genetic knowledge will be used to change the characteristics of people and to create profit. Their experimental status may lead to unanticipated illnesses. Fear does not lessen with knowledge. A very fundamental concern is that potential 'benefits' of genetic interventions are being assumed without reference to a wider public discussion or argument about what is acceptable to society (I).

Law and Social Control

As with screening, a large historical shadow from eugenics informs women's responses. In some countries scepticism towards genetic interventions prevails (G), and in others there is fear for the future of humanity as a whole (D). Effective social control requires a legal framework and also an informed public in order to exercise actual control over medical practice. Many women think that existing frameworks are inadequate. Women are very explicit about demanding that legal-ethical frameworks should not be left to the medical professional bodies, but instead should be developed in heterogeneous interest groups and should be submitted to thorough public debate (B, Basq/E).

The enforcement of law involves questions such as: will individuals be able to hold anyone responsible? Will civil or criminal damage suits be allowed for iatrogenic damage or for negligence in offering gene therapy? May alteration of embryos affect kinship? To whom will the baby belong? Will law suits be permitted by children against their parents for having, or not having, them submitted to gene therapy? Will there be legal protection of genetic information and disclosure to third parties? Will legal protection of social obligations towards the diseased and the disabled continue? Will commercial interests in genetic research adversely affect the maintenance of the distinction between disease prevention and enhancement of physical characteristics? Women want effective regulation of the institutions that carry out these interventions.

Scientific Developments

Only a few women scientists and medical personnel express an unqualified 'that's progress', or a belief that geneticists themselves have set adequate limits to the applications of genetics. A more frequently expressed view by women specialists and women more generally is that nature always has limits and excessive intervention can endanger the natural flow and order. Gene therapy involving germ-line cells is described as endangering human inheritance and the future of the human species, and a call is made for science to find its humanistic dimension.

Women fear that genetic interventions bring about major changes in our view of humankind: 'Today we face an impasse on all levels, because of beliefs and activities leading to the emergence of another social ethic, one that rejects so called abnormality or difference'. The view is that the urge for perfection will become a motive for blurring the present distinctions between treating disease and enhancement of characteristics. Social influence will define the medical assessment of a condition as serious.

Women foresee unequal access, violation of self-determination of persons, and social discrimination of disabled people. Gene therapy and genetic alteration will change concepts of family, parenting, motherhood, and caring (UK). There is fear of exploitation of the poor and comparisons

are drawn with use of organs and blood of the poor. Will sex selection
become accepted?[7] (IRL). Women say that the social implications of
routine genetic therapy and alteration will led to tragic, multidimensional,
and international consequences unless there is limitation. Both some
women scientists and women more generally conclude that this time
racism and fascism will be worse than in the past.

Health Care, Gene Therapy, and Genetic Alteration

Genetic therapy or alteration can relate to health care in the view of most
women, but how is not so readily apparent given economic considerations,
priorities in resource allocation, the necessity of complementary services,
equal access, and the impact on public perception of health care. Women
want positive therapies without experimentation: 'Therapy should only
take place when it will not adversely affect patients', 'Genetic
interventions should never be permitted for experimentation'. Women who
recognize that experimentation is basic to the development of therapy seek
controls that are clearly defined, multiple, and multilateral ('who will
guard the guardians?'), and the elimination of profit: 'Private profit centres
should not be permitted'. But even with these provisons, not all are
reassured. As one medical specialist says: 'No limit can reassure me. I trust
neither the state nor social institutions'.

Ethical Considerations Constructing and Deconstructing the Boundary between the Public and Private

Therapy results in two views on ethics: the first is that ethics are basic to
any intervention, and the second is that considerations of ethics disappear
once an intervention becomes widespread. Women note the phenomenon
of 'subsiding ethical concern' once a new therapy has reached a certain
stage of diffusion and thereby has become accepted (D):

> As I accept plastic surgery today, tomorrow I will accept any intervention,
> even if I personally will not use it. Will the widespread view that personal
> attributes and psychological traits should not be modified be affected in the
> same way?

There is an awareness that the notion of therapy is not objective and women expect shifts and changes in its meaning. Of crucial importance, then, is who will define new conceptualizations of therapy or the quality of life? Women express a similar concern with respect to the distinction between somatic gene therapy (allowed) and germ-line gene therapy (forbidden).

Only a few women express the view that there are no new ethical issues involved in gene therapy and genetic alteration. Existing ethical concepts governing treatments used in medical practice—i.e. acceptability, safety, consent, privacy, and disclosure—are considered adequate by a few women who have confidence in the self-regulation of ethics by medical professionals. This trust extends to the law and the state through the view that gene therapy should be governed by the same legal system that applies to all medical activity and all difficult medical cases.

The majority, however, contest this understanding of science and ethics. They stress that it is an illusion to think that dividing lines exist between scientific research, the development of innovative treatments, and clinical practice. They do not agree that ethical issues should only be discussed in the context of the assessment of applications. This perspective requires accountability to the polity prior to developments of science and its applications, and is foreign to Western modes of scientific and commerical production. To implement it would require a radical reassessment of the boundaries of public policy.

These are gender-neutral concerns, but women also have gender-sensitive understandings of the applications and implications of the human genome analysis which further affect the boundaries between the private and public.

Women, Men, and Gendered Responses

Women interweave gender-neutral and gender-sensitive responses, and these arise where women perceive differences with regard to genetics between women, children, and men. Gender sensitivity begins with the individual woman and moves from the private towards the boundaries with the public. Concerns include effects on carriers, and the experiences of parenting, reproduction, pre-implantation screening, and embryo research.

Carrier Status

Screening and its impact on women and men can be seen as similar, except for screening during pregnancy, as genetic problems affect everyone and both mothers and fathers can be genetic carriers of disabling conditions. 'It's a power issue and not confined to gender' (P). Both women and men face social problems as a result of screening. Women may refer to differences while recognizing that at some level the issue may be the same for women and men: 'Although women and men have different ways of expressing their feelings, both will have to develop psychological skills to deal with potential diseases' (F, P). But women are said to accept carrier status more easily than men, and are more hurt by it because of their greater acceptance of their contribution to the child's future: 'We have always looked to women in relation to abnormalities and women have always accepted the responsibility and the blame' (IRL). One woman gave an example: 'My own mother felt guilty when I was born, she took it more personally than my father' (G).

Parenting

Medical specialists spoke of the difference between the responses of men and women to the suggestion that a parent be screened in order to give information about a child. Men can be very resistant, as they find it hard to accept that there may be something wrong with them or their babies. The parallel example is men's relative unwillingness to be involved in infertility treatment. 'Society considers only women are responsible for everything related to childbirth' (IRL). Responsibility for disabled children may be shifted onto women and the husband may leave: 'Women suffer marginalisation and rejection from society and by husbands' (IRL). A related phenomenon is the increasing tendency to ask for DNA fingerprinting by men seeking to verify paternity (B).

Women draw attention to the social reality of women's lives, mentioning the greater responsibility of mothers for the embryo, childbirth, and of the different ways women have of relating to maternity and their children. A minority drew attention to the possible benefits of gene therapy especially for women; it would relieve their tasks as primary caregivers (IRL).

Reproductive Processes

Women give various reasons for welcoming the screening of fetuses. Screening may help a woman decide if she wants to terminate a pregnancy, but 'Women ultimately have to decide whether to have an abortion and women have to deal psychologically with this situation' (F, P). Screening of fetuses is approved in order to detect conditions that result in babies who cannot survive or will be stillborn or who will be 'vegetables' (B). As reproduction results in women being subjected to more complicated and painful examinations than men, less invasive types of prenatal screening receive positive mention, such as screening through ultrasound examination and chemical indicators in the blood of pregnant women.

Agreement to termination of pregnancy because of a genetic condition in the fetus is influenced by the belief that the fetus and child will suffer. While many women are opposed, it seems that the presentation of termination as a psychological (not ethical) issue for the individual mother-to-be, by activating her sense of responsibility for the well-being of the child, is decisive in the agreement to terminate (G). If a woman feels she will let her future child down by allowing it to be born, then she has reached a psychological state receptive to suggestions of termination.

Pre-implantation Screening

Pre-implantation screening raises the most intractable ethical, social, and legal problems and issues for women. Gender-related issues become overtly paramount for most women in relation to mothering, and also in relation to more generalized masculine and feminine behaviour around reproduction. The view is that if pre-implantation screening and/or intervention become routine, women and men will be differently affected physically, socially, and psychologically. The paramount physical difference arises from the procedure of *in vitro* fertilization itself, necessary for screening of embryos (UK, P):

> Women are the bearers of children and that is why they have a more central involvement in the process of pre-implantation screening and it is ultimately their bodies which will become the focus of medical decisions and interventions.

Their own health can be placed at risk. If women feel themselves more responsible for the future child, they will also be more sensitive to social pressure. Psychological differences concern expectations about pregnancy and childbirth and the burden of the decision-making process, which bears more heavily on women (P). Women are said to have a different relationship to their egg cells than men to their sperm. Women consider their cells as more precious (DK).

Pre-implantation screening raises issues of conception, pregnancy, and childbirth. Women's views on conception outside a woman's body affects their views on pre-implantation screening. Not all women approve (IRL):

> I find the actual production of the embryo in the first place to be the difficulty, not the screening. Conception outside the womb raises moral and ethical issues for me personally. The extent to which it happens and how embryos are used is very distasteful.

Women make a connection between pronatalism and pre-implantation screening and think there is too much pressure on women to conceive at all costs. Women's replies can focus on the social rejection or marginalization of women who are childless, and the need to set up advisory services for women before they begin to pursue any route available to achieve pregnancy.

Embryo Research

Embryo research is controlled by legislation in some, but not all, European countries. Women's views on acceptable research varied between total protection for embryos at every stage, to views of an embryo as nothing without the woman who wants to carry it. This latter perspective is at variance with the right-to-life position, which conceives of the embryo as a person without consideration of the mother who can give it life. Women who recognize the mother's subjective position as involving choice, autonomy, and control are hesitant to open a discussion on legislation on embryo research as it can revive public debate on abortion, and many women fear future restrictions.[8] Past experience with legislation on abortion can create despair that appropriate bioethics can be developed (B).

Reproductive Control and Autonomy

While women's positions are compex and diverse, their views on appropriate ethical responses seek to establish a balance between public intervention and privately made choices. The contradictions involved in this balancing act surface yet again when considering the potential impact of the human gemone analysis on their personal reproductive control and autonomy. While the interviewed women are more likely than not to think they have total, or considerable, control over their reproductive life, just over a simple majority in Greece, Ireland, Basque Country/Spain, and the UK would like more control. Even so, most women do not think genetic manipulation will increase their reproductive control or autonomy, but rather fear that these developments will be personally restrictive.

Some women explain that they have successfully gained autonomy by rigorously distancing themselves from the institutions in charge of medical care, which they see as curtailing their self-determination through the screening of pregnant women by the examination of amniotic fluid, ultrasound, and determination of their child's sex (D). Women think other women should be given the choice, but fear that soon they will feel they have to agree to screening of embryos, 'otherwise they will be seen as bad mothers' (G). A few express the view that women need more protection, because science represents the supremacy of men (I), and because history shows that women have been prevented from formulating and realizing their own interests for years (D). The public-policy issues of how and who is to provide protection or 'choice' intensifies when the problem is perceived as gendered.

Moving Forward on Public-Policy Debates

Future directions for ethical, legal, and social considerations of the implications and applications of human genome analysis are based on a view of developments as equivalent to the major events of the twentieth century: 'It will be the atomic bomb of the next century'. Women, especially the scientists, see human genome analysis as the new paradigm for biomedicine and consequently for society and public policy. The issues of most concern are the development of science, the role of regulation and legislation, control of science and scientists, information and education, and democracy and decision-making.

Access to sufficient and reliable information is described by many women in all countries as a precondition for decision-making about the value of human genome analysis and the potential use of technologies that arise from it. Feminist approaches to (bio)ethics start from the assumption that 'ethics' is a collection of concepts that are not unambiguous and universal but, instead, are continuously being subjected to redefinition. Women in this study define ethics as personal morality, maturity of citizens, as well as of societies and education. Women question public policy-making that separates scientific developments from their applications, both in general and specifically, as has happened with the human genome analysis project.

This study demonstrates that women want to be involved in public policy debates on human genome analysis, but there is no basis for this to occur without information circulating within society and through women's organizations on gendered psycho-social implications as well as technical aspects. Women scientists are amongst the most critical; they have the greatest knowledge, but no safe outlets, for disseminating their concerns. Women are both in the private domain and, from a gendered perspective, become the private domain for human genome science; they become the matter for experimental applications.

The boundaries in the public-policy debates on science can be shifted and some European nations have more science-policy consultation processes with the public than others, e.g. Denmark. But progress is very slow, as coordinated attempts by women to influence public-policy debates may not necessarily succeed, e.g. in the Netherlands.[9] While these are bleak conclusions, their continuance depends on an insecure stability in the present state of public knowledge, scientific developments, governmental and business decisions.

Notes

1   Biotechnology is one of three major areas for the future economic growth identified in the European Union White Paper, *Growth, Competitiveness, Employment* (Commission of the European Communities, 1993). Genome analysis, human and more generally, provides the necessary scientific basis for

technological developments, and has been an area of public-policy development for some time. There is growing financial investment in and profit from biotechnology. The military uses are less well documented as would be expected.

2   Women, too, can be part of a scientific establishment that brooks no interference. During the research two well-connected, senior women scientists objected to the study, one in the UK and one in France. This necessitated personal interviews with the national senior researchers where they were told what to think, what to say, and how to do it. Further, complaints were made to the relevant committee and personnel in DG XII. It should come as no surprise that contrary to the original intention, this study has not been given wider circulation by its funder, the Commission of the European Union, as this example illustrates the power and confidence of the scientific public-policy elite to define the agenda.

3   The human genome analysis was hotly debated amongst scientists and its origins include professional fights for dominance between biologists and physicists for control of the programme. In the US, human genome analysis is located in two major defence establishments; one the developmental home of the hydrogen bomb and the other of the atom bomb. Human genome analysis requires computational facilities of the Department of Energy (DOE), and the computational knowledge of physicists. In Europe, there are major sites in England and Germany; the third big player is Japan.

4   J. Hanmer and I. van Wingerden (1992), 'Women's Perspectives on the Ethical, Social and Legal Applications and Implications of the Human Genome Project', No. GENO-0036-GB (EASE).

5   The Report to DG XII contains bibliographies in German, Dutch, and English. There is an extensive feminist literature on the new reproductive technologies.

6   The twelve EU Member States in the study are abbreviated as follows: Basque Country/Spain (Basq/E), Belgium (B), Denmark (DK), France (F), Germany (D), Greece (G), Ireland (IRL), Italy (I), Luxembourg (L), Netherlands (NL), Portugal (P), United Kingdom (UK).

7   Over time the answer could be yes. For example, in the Netherlands in 1995, when a gender clinic was opened, the government moved from an initial critical reaction to the view that there was no reason to close the clinic, adopting the response of 'it necessitates reflection'.

8   Attitudes to abortion, and by extension to embryo selection and experimentation, also are basic to women's views of human genome analysis, its implications and applications. This is not a straightforward association, as attitudes to and social practices concerning abortion are mediated by other social values and experiences, for example arising out of religion, politics, or national history, and especially gender identity, behaviour, and relations. At the time of the research, abortion dominated political events in Ireland, but in all other countries of the European Union abortion is an important issue that from time to time may become a national preoccupation.

9   A promising effort was undertaken by the Dutch Platform for Science and Ethics of the Rathenau Institute. Adopting the Danish model of a consensus conference on 'Predictive Genetics. Where Are We Heading?', however, did not lead to the inclusion of sex- and gender-specific implications.

Reference

Commission of the European Communities (1993), *Growth, Competitiveness, Employment. The Challenges and Ways Forward into the 21st Century. White Paper*, COM(93) 700 final (4.12.93), Office for Official Publications of the European Communities, Luxembourg.

10 Women and the Planning Process in the Man-Made Environment in the Netherlands—Linkages and Policy Imperatives

MARIJKE VAN SCHENDELEN and LIESBETH OTTES

Introduction

The built environment determines the framework within which people shape their lives, be it in relation to the home, the neighbourhood, the infrastructure required to go to work or shopping, or to make use of social, cultural, and recreational facilities. Social developments are influenced by the built environment, which, in turn, may lead to friction between the social structure and the physical environment. The friction may be alleviated or removed by restructuring the built environment; for example by building new towns, renovating existing urban areas, changing the facilities provided, or constructing new infrastructure.

In this article the emphasis will be on the administrative, legal, and sociological shifts in the perception of the public and the private spheres, and their relation to physical planning. It is important to relate these shifts and changes to the changing position of women in society. This is done by using three planning targets that are characteristic of planning policy as it is applied in the social welfare state, viz. the care for social health, the care for social order, and the division of the limited space that is available. An effort is made to determine how far women have played a role in this, either as a subject or an object, and to what degree these positions are connected.

In practice this means that we will have to ask ourselves to what degree women are associated with the public or with the private domain by the government, the market, the users, and those attempting to influence policy. A second question refers to the way in which women themselves have begun to act as private or public agents in planning the built environment. A final question concerns the object of physical planning and to what degree the influence of women is considered in terms of property, management, use, and significance of the built environment.

The Public and the Private Spheres: Aspects and Agents

In a planning context there are a number of distinctly different dimensions in the division between what is considered private and what is understood to be public. In a legal sense there is a notable difference between the private and the public spheres, although these differences do not necessarily coincide with the sociological meaning. The privacy within one's home is protected by law, but what about the privacy of the inhabitants among themselves? The difference between the bedroom, the entrance, and the garden? How private is private space, and how public is public space? (Stokkers and Tummers, 1987; Spain, 1992).

Property protected by private law, such as a shopping centre, can in a way be a public environment because of its public function. On the other hand, a public building, such as a school and its play area, will only be accessible to specific target groups. The same applies to the street or the square: very much public spaces but considered by one or more user groups to be 'their' private area. Legal status, use, control, significance, and considerations of 'ownership' of the physical space do not provide a unanimous answer to the question to what degree a given space is in the private or the public domain.

The planning of public space has an administrative dimension, involving the provision of decent housing and good infrastructure. For almost a century this task has been considered to be a responsibility of government, including in the Netherlands and in other West-European countries, particularly with the rise of the welfare state. As Wilson (1977, p. 2) has stated:

> The Welfare State has always been closely connected with the development of the family and has acted to reinforce and support it in significant ways.

This it has done by offering various forms of service, both in money and in kind, and also by means of forms of social control and ideology.

Many sociologists and political theorists stress the importance of the welfare state in Dutch society (Van Doorn and Schuyt, 1978; De Swaan, 1988; Esping-Andersen, 1990; Schuyt, 1991; Van Kersbergen, 1995). The planning and design of the built environment has always been considered an essential element of the Dutch welfare state. From the start two objectives have been of primary importance: care for social hygiene and health, and the establishment of a social order by means of physical planning. Over the years a third objective has been added: the careful planning of the use of space, necessitated by increasing limitations on availability and conflicts over its use. Realizing these three goals continues to be in the care of the government. In the Netherlands, as in West Europe, during the period after the Second World War, the welfare state was considered to be capable of rendering a society 'organizable'. In other words, the system of public administration could order and organize society according to political and social targets. The last decade, however, has been marked by increased emphasis on privatization and on the importance of market agents. As a consequence, not only government but also private agents, such as project developers, building firms, and transport companies, have begun to increasingly make their mark on physical planning. Public–private partnership increasingly determines the preconditions within which government, the market, and the users are functioning.

The loss of the capacity to 'organize society' is also the result of a different development. The awareness and maturity of the citizen, a result of education and greater prosperity, has led many citizens to become strongly involved with the management of their immediate living and working environments. In the last few decades, physical planning has evolved a planning process in which government in many cases no longer disposes but negotiates with those directly involved, so as to arrive at a solution that is acceptable to most parties (Cockburn, 1977; Verloo, 1992).

The former dominance of government within physical planning has been replaced by a negotiation space, in which roughly three players can be distinguished: government, the market agents (i.e. the developers), and the users (men and women). Shifts in power and influence between government and market, and between government and users, now determine relations between public and private agents.

Social Hygienists and Female Behaviour

It hardly needs pointing out that in our society women are considered to be representatives of the private domain. A large number of feminist studies have been published that trace the roots of this phenomenon and chart its consequences. The process whereby society became more 'gendered' may have its origins in the rise of bourgeois society in the nineteenth century. Male citizens enjoyed public esteem in their role as 'public man'; women who became publicly known ran the risk of being labelled a 'public woman' or prostitute (Davidoff et al., 1976; Wilson, 1977; Landes, 1988).

The development of a bourgeois culture, industrialization, and urbanization were part of the common process that brought about the development of the welfare state. Living and housing conditions in the crowded cities and the related epidemics were a serious cause for concern. Self-interest and altruism among the upper classes led to a number of drastic socio-hygienic measures, first in France and England, next in Germany, Belgium, and the Netherlands. Noteworthy urban measures and operations were realized because of the need to provide light and air in the cities, water mains and a sewer system, parks and leafy thoroughfares, and a proper transportation system. Poor housing conditions for the proletariat prompted serious concern among the upper classes, leading, on the one hand, to urban renewal and forcing the removal of the inhabitants to the urban periphery or to different shanty towns; and on the other hand, leading to reformist experiments by captains of industry, such as Fourier, Owen, and later Krupp and Van Marken, who wanted to ensure proper housing for their workers and their families.

It is striking how hygiene and moralistic principles were linked together in the nineteenth century. The fear of the *classes laborieuses et classes dangereuses* that prevailed among the bourgeoisie, together with the mixture of images of cholera, crime, prostitution, social unrest, and social misery in their perception of the big city, led to a great deal of attention been given to the social and physical environment (Chevalier, 1958). The English reformer Sir Edward Chadwick considered overpopulation in the period between 1830 and 1840 to be 'one of the causes of ill health . . . but the overcrowding is also noticed as a cause of extreme demoralisation and recklessness and recklessness again as a cause of disease' (Wilson, 1991, p. 34). Reform, to Chadwick and his followers, always contained elements of control, curtailing excesses among the rabble and keep them on the straight and narrow. Women were often blamed for the demoralization of the populace and for men seeking distraction in the tavern. Homeliness was considered an important condition for a moral and healthy life. It followed that the wife was expected to devote herself entirely to the family and the home, and to ensure domestic hygiene and health for the members of the family. At the end of the nineteenth century, women from the upper classes, such as Octavia Hill in England and Hélène Mercier in the Netherlands, supported by public benefactors such as Ruskin, provided schooling and education for their proletarian sisters. They organized domestic-science education, training for social work, and introduced the phenomenon of the (female) 'housing supervisor' (Bervoets, 1994).

In fact, nineteenth-century social hygienists implicitly formed a pact with the female section of the urban populace. Engineers were charged with the construction and maintenance of public facilities and provisions in the area of social hygiene, in cooperation with the municipal government; it was the woman's task to see to it that these were properly used by all the family within the privacy of the home.

There were other elements of the urban domain that were introduced for the sake of social hygiene. One example was the concept of the 'English park'; an innovation that was copied all over Europe. Although the public gardens were a place for recreation and enjoyment, they were also intended to be a healthy alternative for the 'temptations of the inn and the tavern with their frequent accompaniment of immorality and vice' (Ponte, 1991, p. 380). Design and organization were not merely based on hygienic arguments, involving, for example, proper ventilation and sluicing of ponds, but also on the concept of educating—'civilizing'—the public. This was done partly through the creation of botanical gardens, aviaries, and other elements intended for education and 'elevation', and partly by setting up a 'natural' environment in which seeing and being seen by the public, it was hoped, would be conducive to bring about socially acceptable behaviour (Elias, 1977). In these surroundings, too, the wife was expected to be the guardian of decency and decorum. Because of the protection it provided, the English park was also the area where women, if suitably behaved and accompanied, could move around freely in the public domain, the illusion of shelter and privacy being created by its specific layout.

From the Social Question to the New Town Policy

In nineteenth-century Europe the 'social question' very much occupied the minds of the bourgeois. The philanthropic urge of the industrialists, social reformers, and other private persons wishing to provide decent housing for the working class resulted in mounting pressure on the government to declare this area to be the responsibility of the state. For the benefit of the new citizens, usually coming in from the provinces, large new blocks of flats were built at great speed. At first simple urban regulations, for example the Nuisance Act, served to regulate building activities. It soon became clear, however, especially in social and liberal circles, that the quality of construction should also be put under state control. By the end of the nineteenth century this had led to new laws in most European countries. It is striking how closely linked this was to state control in the field of health care. Not surprisingly, in the Netherlands the Housing Act and the Health Act were decreed on the same day in 1901.

Under the influence of Geddes and others the scope of the discussion broadened. The theme of 'the ideal city' developed as a reaction to unchecked growth and rampant urbanization. At first in Britain, but soon on the continent as well, many were attracted to the 'Garden City Movement' led by Ebenezer Howard, which resulted in the construction of rustic housing estates surrounded by green areas that were intended to offer genuine protection to the family (Howard, 1898; Geddes, 1949; Meller, 1990). It is true that the breadwinner was obliged to cover great distances to go to work in the city, but the wife and children were able to lead their life undisturbed, in an atmosphere of seclusion and privacy. Private initiatives were imitated by the state and by semi-official bodies, such as housing corporations. Precisely as a result of the connection between social hygiene, morals, and care for the deprived, the garden city enjoyed great popularity among the government and the citizens (Creese, 1966; Hall, 1988). The bourgeois ideal of the closed family was used as a means of controlling the working classes, who tended to live in an extended family culture within the close-knit community located in the popular quarter (Bott, 1957; Young and Willmott, 1962). The result was increased privacy within the family in all walks of life, with the side effect of diminished cohesion at the level of the neighbourhood.

It was in fact the 'Garden City Movement' in urban planning that laid the base for the division in urban functions that in the 1930s were further developed by le Corbusier, Van Eesteren, and others and set down in the *Charte d'Athènes*. Until quite recently their precepts provided the starting point for European urban planning. The city centre represented the public sphere of trade, industry, manufacture, services, and recreational facilities. The outlying areas of the city and the suburbs in their green settings emphasized the private world of the family (Bahrdt, 1961). The urban district or neighbourhood was introduced as the socio-territorial unit that was meant to replace the village, with the church serving as the central meeting place—a role that was taken on by the library rooms in socialist neighbourhoods. Selection of the residents by housing corporations and mutual social control made possible by the open environment ensured socially undisturbed and homogeneous surroundings in which the state tried to create a close social cohesion within the neighbourhood and the district. These efforts were, however, not really successful because of the family increasingly wanting its privacy.

The post-war New Towns were laid out on a larger scale, but may also be considered to be complementary to the city. Here too, the emphasis was on the anti-urban, closed character, creating the kind of ambience in which wife and children are allowed to thrive free from worry (Osborn and Whittick, 1963; Van der Cammen and De Klerk, 1986).

Even today, city centres and residential neighbourhoods are considered to be complementary, although this is starting to change. In the 1960s criticism of the division in function and in people's worlds was beginning to make itself heard. Jane Jacobs was one of the first to sound a critical note in the professional world of city planners, planning engineers, and urban sociologists (Jacobs, 1961). But then the inhabitants of urban neighbourhoods who either did not have the opportunity or did not wish to live in the green areas started to raise their voices. By the end of the 1960s they began their crusade for a liveable city. As a result of the pressure they generated, the process of urban renewal finally took off, which in recent years has led to a renewed appreciation of the city. In fact, the women's movement, urban squatters, and urban environmentalists, in particular, made no secret of their urban living requirements. Feminist women demanded urban public space on behalf of both men and women. They did not wish to move to the New Towns, because they could not accept their monofunctional character, both in a cultural and in a functional sense. Their dominant family culture, with the emphasis on the private world, made it difficult for women to participate in public life. In addition, work and culture were functionally inaccessible when one lived so far away. The process of gentrification and the growing number of single households and two-income families that now live in urban centres are in many ways a result of the changed attitude toward the dichotomy between the public and private domains (Little et al., 1988; Bondi, 1991; Droogleever Fortuyn, 1993; Little, 1994). The motives of the women's movement and their arguments in favour of cohesion between the public and private worlds, both in the planning and cultural senses, have resulted in a lively interest in urban living. In the Netherlands and in Germany, this interest is further strengthened by the increased awareness among citizens and government of environmental problems and the related importance of public transportation. Planning policy nowadays not only aims at making the city function but also at directing the process of suburbanization (Ottes et al., 1995).

Gentrification and Privatization of the City

The rediscovery of the city as a place to live has led to a considerable increase in the urban population in the Netherlands. The city, and more particularly its urban centre, is no longer *the* exclusive public domain where all public functions are located and where the public character dominates as a matter of course. Many new urban dwellers prefer to live in the city rather than in a suburban residential neighbourhood. Because they often have a double income they are in a position to realize their preference for urban housing. They are attracted by the public character of the city, but also make every effort to provide space in the urban setting for their private lives. The rise in prices that is a consequence of the process of gentrification, in which urban areas are transformed into expensive locations, may eventually cause some of the original urban functions to disappear, such as commerce, industrial activities, and recreation for the less affluent inhabitants that are still living there. In addition, it is not unusual to find that the new urban dwellers successfully demonstrate against traffic pollution, caused by the provision of supplies to shops, customer traffic, and parking, or that they agitate against existing cafes and bars because of the noise they generate. Many new residents consider not just their own living space but also the immediate surroundings to belong to their private domain—not in the legal sense of the word but in their use and enjoyment of them—and with the help of environmental laws they actively defend their position (Zukin, 1991, pp. 179–216).

At the same time, many urban facilities are being relocated to the urban periphery, where ground prices are lower and where it is possible for them to function without interfering with the comfort of other users. Now that private interference in the public domain of the city is becoming ever more frequent, the need for a properly regulated relationship between the two worlds is increasingly important. Good physical planning and organization of the limited urban space, solving problems of traffic and transportation, but also a degree of tolerance, are important conditions in the quest for solutions.

Not only do the new urbanites with high incomes lay claim to the urban public domain; in the older districts of the city a process of privatization has started as well. Here it was the process of urban renewal, supported by the local authorities, that resulted in the reorganization of public space, thus making it possible to provide areas where children can play and older people can walk. Playgrounds, small parks, and public gardens have been built in places that formerly were used commercially or where cars used to be parked. As a result of urban renewal and environmental legislation, many industries that were creating a public nuisance were removed to industrial parks. In the early urban renewal projects the government even attempted to create a living environment that was not unlike the monofunctional suburban neighbourhoods. This meant concentrating shops in monofunctional centres, moving them away from the old neighbourhoods. The resistance of the shopkeepers and of the residents resulted in more attention being given to multifunctionality. As a consequence of residents' participation in the planning process and their opportunity to influence decisions, many renovated neighbourhoods have retained their urban character in which additional space for private interests has been created, while at the same time keeping their appeal as a multifunctional area.

Notwithstanding the success of urban renewal, the Dutch government continues to be concerned that the old popular neighbourhoods are threatening to become pauperized, especially in a social sense. A campaign of so-called 'neighbourhood control' has been instigated so as to stop ghettos from developing. The inhabitants are supposed to maintain and supervise their immediate living environment as well as possible, both by their own efforts and with the guidance of community workers. The purpose of neighbourhood control is twofold: facilitating residents, who are from many different ethnic and cultural backgrounds, to work together on a project in the hope that it will lead to social cohesion; and allowing the immediate living environment to be regarded as an area of collective care for which the residents themselves are responsible. The Department of Public Works is no longer the only agency that looks after the public domain. The government is consciously aiming for 'public–private partnership' in the control and management of public space. The pavement, the street, and the park should be seen as areas of collective responsibility by the residents, as an extension of household tasks and private care for the home, the garden, and the stairwell. The official policy of neighbourhood control is an effort to generate a sense of collective responsibility at the neighbourhood level, and it appears to be based on the traditional concept of the neighbourhood as a socio-territorial framework for integration, as was the case in the period just before and after the Second World War. However, the present reintroduction of the concept of the neighbourhood totally lacks a sociological basis. Patterns of activity have changed and mobility has increased. Women's availability for caring tasks can no longer be taken for granted. In addition, the inhabitants of these neighbourhoods are nowadays part of social networks consisting of relatives, friends, and colleagues that are spread over the entire city or even outside of it. Sometimes neighbours or people living nearby are accepted into these networks, but they are only a small part of the whole. Given these trends, current efforts to make the local inhabitants not only take an interest in their living environment but also to make them responsible for the public domain, either personally or collectively, are doomed to failure (Anderiesen and Reijndorp, 1990).

A further development is also contributing to the increasingly privatized character of the urban domain, bringing with it the danger of the development of so-called 'gated communities'. The government's physical-planning policy is aimed at situating new building locations in the city or adjoining locations. As a result of the 'compact city' policy, based in part on environmental considerations but also on the strong intermingling of people's public and private activities, old port areas and other industrial terrains are now being converted into large residential areas with a considerable density. The efforts that are sometimes made to turn these into multifunctional areas have mostly failed and the general result is a monofunctional residential neighbourhood, not the mix of private housing and offices that would have been preferred. The office market has its own housing requirements, which do not always accord with the desire for multifunctionality cherished by politicians and planners. This applies even more to the residential locations on the edges of the city. The plans that are developed by the government in collaboration with project developers in public–private partnership lead to the creation of suburban living environments on urban territory. The higher income groups that are targeted for these developments are solicited with large advertisements showing semi-detached villas in a green setting, and are built in an 'environmentally friendly residential neighbourhood'. Once again the garden city is the frame of reference, with its emphasis on green spaces and privacy. At present, the outcome of many building projects is a living environment with a gross density of thirty dwellings per 1,000 square metre; which means that there is no supporting base for any but neighbourhood provisions and that no cost-effective system of public transport can exist. The amount of residential space that is taken up and the impossibility of efficient public transportation in these neighbourhoods leads one to wonder what is supposed to make them environmentally friendly, let alone whether living here could still be considered urban living because of the lack of public functions in the area (de Vreeze, 1994).

The Suburbs as a Public Domain?

In the New Towns and other suburbanized areas a reverse tendency may be noted. The monocentric character of many cities is changing into a polycentric structure at the level of the urban region. By now, public centres have been constructed in the outlying districts of the New Towns for the benefit of the direct surroundings. In a number of cases there have developed into centres with an urban regional significance; for instance, the establishment of a megacinema, or specialization in an unusual assortment of a specific product, such as a whole series of furniture stores (a so-called 'furniture mall'). The strongly private character of the monofunctional residential quarters is to a certain degree opened up by strengthening these public centres and zones. Other developments, too, will break open the original monofunctionality. The newest shopping centres are planned to include a multitude of functions. Residential buildings, shops and offices, and occasionally a sports complex are being integrated into the centre. The call for social safety is an important incentive in this, as are the increased acceptance of multifunctionality and the intermingling of public and private domains in a sociocultural sense. Problems of a management and organizational nature prove to be solvable by public–private cooperation, and covenants are agreed upon from the first initiative up to and including subsequent control and maintenance.

Finally, a third development contributes to the increasingly intermingling of the public and private domains at the suburban level. There is a growing interest in working from the home. A few experiments to establish neighbourhood locations for those working from the home have so far not been successful. However, not everybody is happy about the development of homework. The women's movement as well as the trade unions are critical, particularly about the intermingling of private life and public activities in the world of paid employment. The decisive factor is the amount of influence and space given to the home workers.

Politicizing Mobility?

Government policy in relation to the compact city and the increased ways in which the public and private domains are interwoven in city and suburb may lead to greater multifunctionality in the different areas, but this does not solve the problems of traffic and transportation, although this is one of the goals of the compact-city policy. Reducing mobility has after all been the primary aim of environmental policy in the Netherlands since the 1980s. To attain this goal, measures pertaining to planning and mobility need to be established.

The development of mixed functions in urban and suburban areas in the Netherlands is linked with the politicization of issues around mobility at the levels of neighbourhood, city, and region. In the cities, increased attention has been given to pedestrians and cyclists, who not only reside there but also need routes to benefit from other functions and facilities. It has been recognized that urban dwellers have activity patterns that lead to a great number of intersecting connections right across the city. Of late, this also holds valid for people who until recently hardly participated in such traffic generation: women and the elderly. Even more so, it is the great variety in functions and the differentiated job market in the urban area that provide many households with the incentives to choose to live there. Here, not only the breadwinner but also the wife and the children have greater choice in relation to work, schooling, and recreation and in this way share in the public life.

The compact-city policy is totally dependent on a sound public transport structure. Everyone involved in environmental planning agrees that this is so, but subsequent policy decisions have so far not materialized. Decisions taken on paper a few years ago and declared official policy in practice come up against any number of organizational, administrative, and financial problems, with the result that private transport, and in particular automotive traffic, grows by leaps and bounds. This holds true for commuter traffic, which is not just a matter of longer distances between the job and the home but also of more cars on the road. The increased participation of women in the job market has not so much led to increases in travelling back and forth at neighbourhood level but makes itself felt in the number of displacements in the entire urban area, or even outside this area. It should be added that commuter traffic only accounts for 30 per cent of total personal automotive displacements. In addition to 30 per cent of business traffic in the Netherlands, 40 per cent of automotive traffic is registered as 'leisure-time' displacements. Further research has shown that only half of this may be considered to be truly leisure-time driving, visits to recreational facilities, or going on vacation; but that the other half should be termed 'socially necessitated' traffic: driving to do the shopping, to take care of relatives or good friends (volunteer aid), to visit the hospital, etc. Official redefinition of categories of mobility is required; one that recognizes the different private motives involved, especially as here it is often a question of shifting boundaries between public and private goals. If people needing care are receiving such care from official agencies it would be a matter of commuter traffic; if it is done by the family it suddenly becomes 'leisure' traffic.

Automotive mobility also continues to grow because of the complex patterns of activities many people increasingly have to contend with. The straightforward division between the private world and public life in traditional households is becoming less prominent. Traditionally, the wife would take care of the private life in the home and the neighbourhood, and was able to do this on her bicycle or on foot, while the husband took the car into the city to earn the family income; instead, both man and woman participate in public life, the home front being cared for by both, and if not, almost always by the wife. Next, the combination of public and private activities has become a fact of life for the growing army of single people. Considering the state of affairs in public transportation, only the car provides succour for most of those having to combine several tasks (Van Schendelen, 1995a).

Conclusions

Answering the questions stated in the introduction, one may conclude that the exclusive relationship of women with the private domain is by now disappearing in the Netherlands. This is not least a result of the change in the position and attitude of women themselves, who have detached themselves from the private domain and who increasingly participate in public life in all its facets. As a result, the way the concepts of private and public find environmental expression in a sociological sense is also changing fast. The intermingling of worlds and functions has now become part of Dutch planning policy, which is stressing the need for the compact city and for a considerable interweaving of functions. This is the opposite of the former approach, which held that a division of functions was best and any intermingling of functions was either banned or ignored.

The development of a multifunctional built environment has numerous administrative consequences. In a legal sense, property relations may be laid down in the city's land register; but in an administrative sense, covenants and contracts between public and private parties are necessary to develop a multifunctional area and to manage and maintain it, since buildings, public spaces, but also the traffic infrastructure are used both for public purposes as well as for private ends.

The introduction also asked about the way in which women themselves have begun to act as private or public agents in the field of physical planning. The conclusion is that increasing account has to be taken of women acting as agents. Many female architects, urban planners, planning engineers, and urban sociologists in their positions of researcher, policy-making official, or politician have contributed to the implementation of policies that result in the intermingling of the public and private spheres in environmental planning (Van Schendelen, 1995b).

Shifting the boundaries between what is private and what is public is but one step. Thinking in dichotomies must also be overcome; in a sociological sense private and public spaces are a continuous and interwoven phenomenon. Women demand privacy, both in the home and in the street, and at the same time (more) access to public space. In the home work is carried out, and in the public spaces private lives are led. Private activities such as living, caring, and recreation merit attention in public spaces in equal measure with activities that have traditionally been part of public life, such as paid employment, administrative/managerial activities, and sports.

The third conclusion is that the integration of the public and the private domains, in a legal, sociological, and administrative sense, are best served in an urban environment. Here the conditions exist for the realization of differentiated individual patterns of activity. Monofunctional areas such as residential neighbourhoods, industrial terrains, shopping centres, and office districts have no future validity, in any case not for the users and consequently probably neither for investors and developers.

Nevertheless, efforts to develop further the mixing of functions run into difficulties. The former urge to separate functions was not only dictated by notions of 'private' and 'public', but came very much as a result of the need to develop residential areas that would not be polluted by stench, noise, and dirt. The present compact-city policy that aims for a strong intermingling of functions within the limited urban space available, confronts policy-makers all the more with conflicting claims on space by the traffic infrastructure, industry, housing, recreational facilities, etc. Pollution of the soil and the air by industry and traffic pressures cannot be dealt with in a totally effective way as yet. It is true that the Dutch environmental policy aims at tackling environmental problems as much as possible at source, and that enormous sums are reserved by the government for the purification of polluted soil, but even so a certain degree of environmental zoning cannot be avoided in compact-city policies.

Noise nuisance and air pollution caused by greater mobility are also at odds with an urban living and housing environment. On the one hand, the compact-city policy was instigated to keep mobility in check, and, on the other hand, the traffic arteries and rail connections are seen to be environmental hazards so that conflicts arise from the tendency towards ever greater density in the built environment, especially near railroad stations and along major thoroughfares. This impasse can only be broken by huge investments in low-noise, electrified public-transport systems and a network of bicycle paths, and by keeping automotive traffic out of the built-up areas as much as possible. However, this requires big public investments at a time when the government increasingly turns to private parties and has actually privatized public transport.

Finally, we may conclude that the intermingling of public and private worlds, in both the sociological and physical sense, is happening at a time when the government, as keeper of public values and domains, is withdrawing more and more from urban and regional planning in all its facets. As a result the market—i.e. project developers and private transport companies, on the one hand, and buyers, tenants, and users on the other— are the ones increasingly deciding the outcome of environmental planning. It is unclear which party here is strongest. A government restricting its influence and consequently a shift in power to the market, also requires a different relation between the parties in the market and an increased in their sense of responsibility as far as public interests are concerned. One may wonder if this can realistically be expected from them. After all, is maintaining a system of checks and balances not the traditional task of the government? Or will the market follow social developments and recognize the changed position of women as independent human beings in both the private and public worlds?

References

Anderiesen, G. and Reijndorp, G. (1990), *Eigenlijk een geniale wijk. Dagelijks leven in de Indische Buurt*, Uitgeverij Het Spinhuis & Centrum voor Grootstedelijk Onderzoek, Amsterdam.

Bahrdt, H.P. (1961), *Die moderne Grossstadt. Soziologische Überlegungen zum Städtebau*, Rowohlt Taschenbuch Verlag, Reinbeck bei Hamburg.

Bervoets, L. (1994), *Opvoeden tot sociale verantwoordelijkheid. De verzoening van wetenschap, ethiek en sekse in het sociale werk in Nederland rond de eeuwwisseling*, Stichting Beheer IISG, Amsterdam.

Bondi, L. (1991), 'Gender Divisions and Gentrification: a Critique', *Transactions of the Institute of British Geographers*, NS vol. 16, pp. 190–8.

Bott, E. (1957), *Family and Social Network. Roles, Norms, and External Relationships in Ordinary Urban Families*, Tavistock Publications, London.

Cammen, H. van der and Klerk, L. de (1986), *Ruimtelijke ordening. Van plannen komen plannen*, Het Spectrum, Utrecht.

Chevalier, L. (1958), *Classes laborieuses et classes dangereuses à Paris pendant la première moitié du XIX siècle*, Librairie Plon, Paris.

Cockburn, C. (1977), *The Local State. Management of Cities and People*, Pluto Press, London.

Creese, W.L. (1966), *The Search for Environment. The Garden City: Before and After*, Yale University Press, New Haven, Conn.

Davidoff, L., L'Esperance, J. and Newby, H. (1976), 'Landscape with Figures: Home and Community in English Society', in J. Mitchell and A. Oakley (eds.), *The Rights and Wrongs of Women*, Penguin Books, Harmondsworth, pp. 139–75.

Doorn, J.A.A. van and Schuyt, C.J.M. (eds.) (1978), *De stagnerende verzorgingsstaat.* Boom, Meppel.

Droogleever Fortuyn, J. (1993), *Een druk bestaan. Tijdsbesteding en ruimtegebruik van tweeverdieners met kinderen*, Amsterdam University Press, Amsterdam.

Elias, N. (1977), *Über den Prozess der Zivilization. Soziogenetische und psychogenetische Untersuchungen*, 2 Bde., 4. Aufl., Suhrkamp, Frankfurt am Main.

Esping-Andersen, G. (1990), *The Three Worlds of Welfare Capitalism*, Polity Press, Cambridge.

Geddes, P. (1949), *Cities in Evolution*, Williams & Norgate, London.

Hall, P. (1988), *Cities of Tomorrow. An Intellectual History of Urban Planning and Design in the Twentieth Century*, Basil Blackwell, Oxford.

Howard, E. (1898), *To-morrow: A Peaceful Path to Real Reform*, Swan Sonnenschein, London.

Jacobs, J. (1961), *The Death and Life of Great American Cities*, Vintage Books, New York.

Kersbergen, K. van (1995), *Social Capitalism. A Study of Christian Democracy and the Welfare State*, Routledge, London.

Landes, J.B. (1988), *Women and the Public Sphere in the Age of the French Revolution*, Cornell University Press, Ithaca, NY.

Little, J. (1994), *Gender, Planning and the Policy Process*, Pergamon, Oxford.

Little, J., Peake, L., and Richardson, P. (eds.) (1988), *Women in Cities. Gender and the Urban Environment*, MacMillan Education, Basingstoke.

Meller, H. (1990), *Patrick Geddes. Social Evolutionist and City Planner*, Routledge, London.

Osborn, F.J. and Whittick, A. (1963), *The New Towns. The Answer to Megalopolis*, Leonard Hill, London.

Ottes, L., Poventud, E., Schendelen, M.C. van, and Segond von Banchet, G. (eds.) (1995), *Gender and the Built Environment. Emancipation in Planning, Housing and Mobility in Europe*, Van Gorcum, Assen.

Ponte, A. (1991), 'Public Parks in Great Britain and the United States: from a "Spirit of the Place" to a "Spirit of Civilization"', in M. Mosser and G. Teyssot (eds.), *The Architecture of Western Gardens. A Design History from the Renaissance to the Present Day*, The MIT Press, Cambridge, Mass., pp. 373–86.

Schendelen, M.C. van (1995a), 'Emancipatory Policy for Mobility in the Netherlands', in L. Ottes, E. Poventud, M.C. van Schendelen, and G. Segond von Banchet (eds.), *Gender and the Built Environment. Emancipation in Planning, Housing and Mobility in Europe*, Van Gorcum, Assen, pp. 135–42.

Schendelen, M.C. van (1995b), 'The Influence of Women's Studies on the Environmental Sciences of Physical Planning, Housing and Mobility in the Netherlands', in L. Ottes, E. Poventud, M.C. van Schendelen, and G. Segond von

Banchet (eds.), *Gender and the Built Environment. Emancipation in Planning, Housing and Mobility in Europe*, Van Gorcum, Assen, pp. 185–99.

Schuyt, C.J.M. (1991), *Op zoek naar het hart van de verzorgingsstaat*, Stenfert Kroese Uitgevers, Leiden.

Spain, D. (1992), *Gendered Spaces*, The University of North Carolina Press, Chapel Hill, NC.

Stokkers, A. and Tummers, L. (1987), 'Een aanzet tot de problematisering van de begrippen privé en openbaar binnen de bouwkunde', in *Inrichten*, Zomeruniversiteit Vrouwenstudies Groningen.

Swaan, A. de (1988), *In Care of the State, Health Care, Education and Welfare in Europe and the USA in the Modern Era*, Polity Press, Cambridge.

Verloo, M. (1992), *Macht en gender in sociale bewegingen. Over de participatie van vrouwen in bewonersorganisaties*, SUA, Amsterdam.

Vreeze, N. de (ed.) (1994), *De periferie centraal. Inspiratie en ambities bij de ontwikkeling van perifere VINEX-lokaties*, Stimuleringsfonds voor Architectuur, Rotterdam.

Wilson, E. (1977), *Women and the Welfare State*, Tavistock Publications, London.

Wilson, E. (1991), *The Sphinx in the City. Urban Life, the Control of Disorder, and Women*, Virago Press, London.

Young, M. and Willmott, P. (1962), *Family and Kinship in East London*, Penguin Books, Harmondsworth.

Zukin, S. (1991), *Landscapes of Power: from Detroit to Disney World*, Univerity of California Press, Berkeley, Calif.